Twentieth Century Actor Training

Actor training is arguably the most unique phenomenon of twentieth-century theatre making. Here, for the first time, the theories, training exercises, and productions of fourteen of the century's key theatre practitioners are analysed in a single volume.

The practitioners included are:

- Stella Adler
- Eugenio Barba
- Bertolt Brecht
- Peter Brook
- Joseph Chaikin
- Michael Chekhov
- Jacques Copeau
- Jerzy Grotowski
- Joan Littlewood
- Sanford Meisner
- Vsevolod Meyerhold
- Włodzimierz Staniewski
- Konstantin Stanislavsky
- Lee Strasberg

Each chapter provides a unique account of specific training exercises and an analysis of their relationship to the practitioners' theoretical and aesthetic concerns. The collection examines the relationship between actor training and production and considers how directly the actor training relates to performance.

With detailed accounts of the principles, exercises and their application to many of the landmark productions of the past hundred years, this book will be invaluable to students, teachers, practitioners and academics alike.

Alison Hodge is a lecturer in Drama at Royal Holloway College, University of London. She was a founder and co-artistic director of Theatre Alibi before working as Assistant Director to Włodzimierz Staniewski at Gardzienice's Centre for Theatre Practices, Poland. She has directed a wide range of theatre projects from Stephen King's *Misery* at the Criterion Theatre, London, to a six-month actor training project in association with London's Institute of Contemporary Arts.

Twentieth Century Actor Training

Edited by Alison Hodge

London and New York

First published 2000
by Routledge
11 New Fetter Lane, London EC4P 4EE

Simultaneously published in the USA and Canada
by Routledge
29 West 35th Street, New York, NY 10001

Routledge is an imprint of the Taylor & Francis Group

Typeset in Garamond by Taylor & Francis Group
Printed and bound in Great Britain by Biddles Ltd, Guildford and
King's Lynn

British Library Cataloguing in Publication Data
A catalogue record for this book is available from the British Library

Library of Congress Cataloging in Publication Data
A catalog record for this book has been requested

ISBN 0–415–19451–2 (hbk)
ISBN 0–415–19452–0 (pbk)

For

Chris, Hannah and Sophie

Contents

Illustrations

Contributors

Clive Barker began his career in the early 1950s as an actor with Joan Littlewood's Theatre Workshop company, appearing in, amongst others, Brendan Behan's *The Hostage* and the company's devised show, *Oh What A Lovely War!* He has directed productions, written plays and recorded documentaries for radio and television. From the mid 1960s he combined professional work with lecturing in the universities of Birmingham and Warwick. His actor training methods and ideas are set out in *Theatre Games* (Methuen, 1977) and he is joint editor of *New Theatre Quarterly* (Cambridge University Press).

Sharon Marie Carnicke is Associate Professor and Associate Dean of the School of Theatre, University of Southern California. She has written a study of the avant-garde director and playwright Nikolai Evreinov, *The Theatrical Instinct* (Peter Lang, 1989). She has published numerous articles on Stanislavsky in *Theatre Journal*, *The Drama Review* and *Theatre Three*. She has also been anthologised in *Wandering Stars* (Iowa University Press, 1992) and *Film Acting* (Routledge, 1999). She has directed plays in America and Moscow, and her translations of Chekhov's plays have been produced throughout the United States. Her latest book is *Stanislavsky in Focus* (Harwood Academic Press, 1998, Gordon and Breach International).

Franc Chamberlain is Senior Lecturer in Performance Studies, University College, Northampton and Course leader of the BA in Performance Studies. Since 1991 he has been the Editor of *Contemporary Theatre Studies* (Harwood Academic Press).

Alison Hodge has worked as professional director since 1982. She was co-founder and Artistic Director of Theatre Alibi (1982–9), and Assistant Director with Gardzienice Theatre Association (1990–91). She is currently a freelance director and Lecturer in Drama, Royal Holloway College, University of London.

Dorinda Hulton lectures in drama at the University of Exeter. She has worked extensively as an artistic consultant for new work with different companies including Theatre Alibi and Foursight. She co-edited the series *Theatre Papers* (Dartington College of Art, Devon) and is currently an editor for the documentation project Arts Archives.

David Krasner is Director of Undergraduate Theater Studies at Yale University. His publications include: *Resistance, Parody, and Double Consciousness in African American Theatre, 1895–1910* (St Martin's Press, 1997) and is the editor of *Method Acting Reconsidered: Theory, Practice, Future* (St Martin's, forthcoming) and co-editor of *African American Theatre History and Performance Studies: A Critical Reader* (Oxford University Press, forthcoming). He is also co-editing *African American Theatre History* with Harry J. Elam, Jr (forthcoming). He was a professional actor for thirteen years and studied Method Acting principally with Paul Mann, Kim Stanley and Barbara Loden.

Robert Leach is Reader in Drama, University of Birmingham. His publications include *The Punch and Judy Show: History, Tradition and Meaning* (Batsford, 1985), *Vsevolod Meyerhold* (Cambridge University Press, 1989) and *Revolutionary Theatre* (Routledge, 1994). He has contributed to several anthologies, including *Eisenstein Rediscovered* (Routledge, 1993) and *The Cambridge Companion to Brecht* (Cambridge University Press, 1995). He has directed several plays in Britain and Russia, and is the Artistic Director of Heartlands Theatre.

Lorna Marshall is a freelance teacher and director based in London. She has worked with companies such as the Royal National Theatre, Shared Experience and Théâtre de Complicité, and currently teaches at RADA. She has written two books with Yoshi Oida: *An Actor Adrift* (Methuen, 1992) and *The Invisible Actor* (Methuen, 1997). Her own book on physical acting is due to be published by Methuen in 1999.

John Rudlin was formerly Senior Lecturer in Drama, University of Exeter. His publications include: *Jacques Copeau* (Cambridge University Press, 1986) and *Commedia dell'Arte: an actors handbook* (Routledge, 1994). He edited and translated *Copeau, Texts on Theatre* (Routledge, 1990) with Norman Paul. He is director of Centre Sélavy in France.

Peter Thomson has been Professor of Drama at Exeter since 1974. He was Advisory Editor to the *Cambridge Guide to World Theatre*, is General Editor of the forthcoming *Cambridge History of British Theatre* and an Associate Editor of the *New Dictionary of National Biography*. His work on Brecht includes (with Jan Needle) *Brecht* (Blackwell, 1981) and *Mother Courage and Her Children* (Cambridge University Press, 1997). With Glendyr Sacks he edited *The Cambridge Companion to Brecht* (1994).

Ian Watson teaches on the Theatre Programme at the University of Pennsylvania and is on the Editorial Committee of *New Theatre Quarterly*. His book on Eugenio Barba and the Odin Teatret, *Towards a Third Theatre*, was published by Routledge in 1993.

David Williams is currently Professor of Theatre at Dartington College. He has taught and made performance in Australia and England, in theatre, dance, and spaces in between. Publications include books on Peter Brook's Centre, the Théâtre du Soleil and contemporary directors; and he has been a contributing editor to *Performance Research* (Routledge) and *Writings on Dance* (Melbourne, Australia).

Lisa Wolford is Assistant Professor of Theatre at Bowling Green State University. She is author of *Grotowski's Objective Drama Research* (University Press of Mississippi, 1996), and co-editor (with Richard Schechner) of *The Grotowski Source Book* (Routledge, 1998). Her writings have appeared in *TDR*, *Slavic and Eastern European Performance*, *New Theatre Quarterly* and *Text and Performance Quarterly*.

Acknowledgements

I should like to thank the following individuals and institutions for permission to reproduce the various photographs enclosed: Ute Eichel and The Berliner Ensemble, The Marie Hélène Dasté Collection; Michel Dieuzaide, Nina Soufy and CICT; The Dartington Trust; The Billy Rose Theatre Collection, New York Public Library at Lincoln Center; the Theatre Workshop Archive; Andreas Lüdtke; the Gardzienice Archive; Odin Teatret; Open Theatre Archive, Kent State University Libraries, Department of Special Collections and Archives.

For permission to publish extracts, we gratefully acknowledge the following: The Samuel Beckett Estate; The Calder Educational Trust and Grove/Atlantic, Inc; Zbigniew Taranienko; Leszek Kolankiewicz; Arts Archives, Arts Documentation Unit, Exeter. Every effort has been made to contact copyright holders. Where this has not been possible, we would be pleased to hear from the parties concerned.

I want to thank Talia Rodgers for commissioning this book for Routledge and for her tremendous support throughout its development. I wish to express my personal gratitude to Włodzimierz Staniewski and Mariusz Gołaj for discussing their work at length. I would also like to thank the following individuals for their invaluable assistance in the development of this book: Nancy Birk, Grzegorz Bral, Richard Allen Cave, Bill Coco, Lizzie Heathecote, Sally Holloway, Peter Hulton, Daniel Jamieson, Błajez Kowalewski, Graham Ley, Patrick Morris, Katie Normington, Rosemary Quinn, Donald Soule, David Wiles and Anna Zubrzycka. On behalf of Dorinda Hulton, I would also like to express deep gratitude to Joseph Chaikin.

Finally, I wish to thank my husband, Chris Hurford, and dedicate this book to him and my children.

Introduction

Twentieth Century Actor Training is a collection of introductory essays on what is arguably the most important development in modern Western theatre making. Actor training in Europe and North America is a phenomenon of the twentieth century, and has come to inform both the concept and construction of the actor's role, and consequently the entire dramatic process. The centrality of actor training is evidenced by the fact that many of the innovators in this field have been responsible for both unique training techniques and for some of the landmark theatre productions of the twentieth century. This book considers some, but inevitably not all, of the key practitioners.

The early pioneers in the development of Western training methods are represented by the work of four Europeans: Konstantin Stanislavsky, Vsevolod Meyerhold, Michael Chekhov and Jacques Copeau. From the mid century the central aspects of Bertolt Brecht's epic acting and the ensemble work of Joan Littlewood are considered together with the key North American exponents of the Method: Lee Strasberg, Stella Adler and Sanford Meisner. Finally, innovative practices in the latter half of the century are explored through directors from both sides of the Atlantic: Joseph Chaikin, Jerzy Grotowski, Peter Brook, Eugenio Barba and Włodzimierz Staniewski.

Whilst much has been written about these figures individually, this book considers the breadth and lineage of actor training's development since Stanislavsky's first explorations. In addition, key elements in each practitioner's work are summarised: from basic principles of performance to their exploration through specific exercises, and finally to their manifestation in theatre production.

Origins

Western culture has enjoyed a long history of actor apprenticeship, but not the systematic traditions of actor training that are integral to Eastern performance cultures such as the Noh theatre – which dates from fifteenth-century Japan – and Kathakali, the ancient dance-theatre form from southern India. It was not until the beginning of this century that an explosion of interest in the power and potential of actor training took hold in the West. This was partly through a growing awareness of the rigorous training in Eastern traditions but also through the widening influence at the turn of the century of objective scientific research. Western European practitioners began to search for absolute, objective languages of acting that could offer models, systems and tested techniques to further the craft. In this context, Stanislavsky was the first actor/director to fully investigate the process of acting and to publish his findings. His seminal texts (*An Actor Prepares*, *Building a Character* and *Creating a Role*) came to be essential reading for many European and North American actors.

Once this attempt at rationalising the acting process was under way, its increasing pedagogical aims led to the opening of a number of new studios, schools, academies, laboratories and theatres throughout Europe and the United States. These centres intended not only to investigate the nature of acting, but also to disseminate their research findings and ultimately prepare the actor for work. Each system or approach to actor training had quite different assumptions and ideas about the nature and purpose of theatre, and what the responsibility of the actor was within the process of making it.

The director and the actor

Most of these new 'systems' were initiated by a relatively new breed in theatre: the director. The rise of the modern theatre director brought about a seismic shift in theatre structures; the dual functions of the nineteenth-century actor/manager had given way to the more specialist position of the modern director as the process of theatre making became further refined. This figure was engaged with all aspects of theatre production. No longer necessarily a performer, the director was to become the central figure of twentieth-century theatre making. Undoubtedly, the emergence of the director has furthered the opportunity for a more objective examination of the nature of the actor's work. But despite encouraging the development of actor training, the rise in status of the director has competed with the tradi-tionally powerful role of the leading actor. Whether this new, potentially dictatorial auteur has ultimately facilitated or disempowered the actor is a complex issue – but it is striking that all of the practitioners discussed here have valued the implicitly collaborative nature of the director–actor dynamic.

Increasingly, twentieth-century directors have sought to incorporate the actor in a new or revitalised role as a theatre maker. Some performers, involved in highly intensive collaborative relationships with directors, have been central to the realisation of a new aesthetic – Ryszard Cieslak in Grotowski's Poor Theatre, for example. During intimate, preparatory work with Cieslak whilst developing his role in *The Constant Prince*, Grotowski acknowledges that 'for months and months Cieslak worked alone with me'

(Richards 1995: 122). The significant contribution by the actor is particularly noticeable in devised work, where the performance text is often drawn from the actor's personal material. Joseph Chaikin's Open Theater is a paradigm of this collaborative and personal process: 'it has sometimes been possible to join with others in a common effort so intense that at the end of a project I have been unable to say which part was my work and which part belonged to someone else' (Chaikin 1972: xi).

In training, the emphasis on the actor's creativity beyond the interpretation of the text was often achieved through processes which implemented new skills and re-contextualised old ones. The exploration of the actor's improvisatory skills in the work of Copeau, for example, refer both to traditional techniques of the commedia dell'arte as well as to educational work with children's creativity and game-play encountered by Suzanne Bing in The Children's School, New York, from 1917 to 1919.

Innovation and reform

Whilst the key factors of the early twentieth-century interest in actor training are partly a knowledge of Eastern traditions, partly the influence of objective scientific research and partly the rise of the theatre director, further momentum came from the widespread desire to develop new theatre forms.[1]

Indeed, despite the seemingly radical moments of theatre's history which many of the practitioners included in this volume have come to symbolise, the nature of these innovations point more towards theatre reform than revolution. John Rudlin describes how Jacques Copeau sought 'dramatic renovation' at the beginning of the century, considering theatre to be a 'renewable entity'. Stanislavsky's co-founder of the Moscow Art Theatre, Nemirovich-Danchenko, declares his desire 'to reconstruct [theatre's] whole life...to change at the root the whole order of rehearsals and the preparation of plays' (Nemirovitch-Dantchenko [*sic*] 1937: 68), whilst Grotowski begins by asking what is indispensable to theatre, rather than whether we need theatre at all. Even Brecht's development of a theatre of efficacy was one that sought not to revolutionise theatre but rather, through its epic form, to revolutionise its audiences. These practitioners are concerned to work within theatre rather than to reject or abandon its notional limitations, which is arguably the project of more hybrid forms of performance.

Early theoretical influences

The theoretical roots of early-twentieth-century training can in part be traced to eighteenth- and early-nineteenth-century France. Denis Diderot's *Le Paradoxe sur le comédien*, first published in 1830 (*The Paradox of Acting*, 1883), initiated a sustained debate in Western Europe over the nature of the actor's process. It was Diderot's materialist analysis of the acting of his time which laid bare an essential paradox: that, whilst the actor appeared to be experiencing 'real' feelings, the opposite was more probably true. The good actor, in his view, was capable of mechanically reproducing these emotions in performance. Diderot suggested a dualistic model of the actor, the inner mind controlling the outer expression of feeling, thereby achieving 'penetration and no sensibility' (Cole and Chinoy 1970: 162).

But, as Joseph Roach reveals in *The Player's Passion*, the deeper ramifications of *Le Paradoxe* can only be fully understood when interpreted in the light of Diderot's wider body of writing.[2] Roach demonstrates that Diderot not only proposed the dualistic model of the actor but, through further investigations of the psychophysical aspects of the human body, also anticipated 'emotion memory, imagination, creative unconsciousness, public solitude, character body, the score of the role and spontaneity' (Roach 1985: 117). These were ideas which Stanislavsky also came to engage with during his own experience of acting and training at the beginning of the twentieth century.

Born in 1863, Stanislavsky's practical understanding of acting was informed by his own theoretical research – which was likely to have included Diderot's writings, already available in Russia. The growing scientific belief of the inseparability of the mind and body interested Stanislavsky greatly, as did the proposition of the French psychologist Théodule Ribot, who claimed that emotion cannot exist without a physical consequence. As Carnicke points out in her chapter, Stanislavsky echoed Ribot's belief with his assertion that: 'In every action there is something psychological, and in the psychological, something physical' (Stanislavskii 1989: 258).

The emphasis on both is important because, as with all the practitioners included here, theories concerning the mind and/or body dynamic remain a continuous source of investigation and interpretation within actor training. The conclusions drawn from their practical explorations were redefined by others as their work progressed and this has given rise to some misinterpretation of their findings. Stanislavsky's work is a case in point, where the chequered history of the publication and translation of his books led to a partial and erratic presentation of his system. For example, in America his exploration of an actor's psychological processes was initially more familiar than his later work on the Method of Physical Action, which examines the external, physicalised construction of character. This has inevitably given rise to multiple interpretations of his work, and has obscured his belief in the symbiosis of the mind and body.

This last phase of Stanislavsky's work, especially his belief in beginning with scoring the physical actions, greatly interested Jerzy Grotowski who, in the development of his psychophysical techniques, was concerned with establishing the actor's expressive and imaginative freedom through the discipline of physical structure. It was essential for Grotowski that the actor justified, through real or imaginary means, every specific detail of their personal training. Lisa Wolford considers this connection between Stanislavsky and Grotowski, recognising that both directors sought to help the actor 'live truthfully on stage', although that 'truth' was expressed through different aesthetic frameworks. She also considers Meyerhold's codified physical training methods as being influential in Grotowski's work. In turn, Meyerhold's ideas are echoed in the work of Eugenio Barba, who actively sought his own form of biomechanics in his early training sessions: 'We defined biomechanics as a very dynamic reaction to an external stimulus. ... We attempted to re-invent it, to rediscover it in our bodies according to our own justifications' (Barba 1979: 74).

Cross fertilisation

The nature of cross fertilisation amongst twentieth-century practitioners is complex. This book does not attempt to deal directly with these issues, but as each chapter is introduced chronologically, it is possible to recognise both the similar interests and the outright rejection of previous ideas which have helped to clarify new trajectories. In some cases practitioners have been trained within each other's systems and then moved away from them. Both Meyerhold and Chekhov were former actors with Stanislavsky at the Moscow Art Theatre. Both went on to develop their own, distinct working methods. Robert Leach points out that Meyerhold rejected the Moscow Art Theatre's naturalism as 'something of an irrelevance' as he searched for a system that would reach beyond imitation. Although he sought this through extensive training of the body, he retained two key ideas from Stanislavsky: justified actions and clear objectives for characters. Chekhov retained more of his former director's ideas, although he re-interpreted or transformed many of them in the light of his desire to nurture the personal creativity of the actor. Copeau evolved his school as the single alternative to the dominance of the Comédie Française training available in early-twentieth-century France. John Rudlin maps out his immense legacy through those that trained with him, from Michel St Denis to Etienne Decroux and those who were influenced by him, such as Jacques Le Coq.

Some practitioners have, of course, re-interpreted elements of former approaches. Perhaps the clearest example of this is the Method, both in terms of its connections to the Stanislavskian system and through its re-interpretation and refinement of it by three of its foremost exponents. Joan Littlewood also draws on Stanislavskian approaches, but combines them with the movement training of Rudolf Laban. Thus, rather than re-interpreting Stanislavsky, she finds the interface with a completely different system of movement training. Other practitioners reject their own training: Chaikin worked as a method actor before wholeheartedly abandoning its tenets to formulate his own – partially out of an exasperation with what he saw as its dogmatic assumptions.

Finally, and unsurprisingly given this extraordinary fluidity of influences, collaboration is a prevalent characteristic amongst later practitioners. For example, Brook, Barba, Staniewski and Chaikin have all worked with

Grotowski in various contexts. Barba and Staniewski both actively partici-pated in Grotowski's Laboratory Theatre. Chaikin and Brook invited Grotowski to introduce his training techniques to their actors but, as Chaikin points out, whilst his 'inspiration and urgent sincerity have affected me and many others…still, we are on different journeys' (Chaikin 1972: xi).

Antonin Artaud

The writings of the French actor, director and poet Antonin Artaud (1896–1948) have provided a significant reference point for many in the second half of the twentieth century. His seminal collection of essays *The Theatre and its Double* (1970) were first published in English in 1958. Artaud's ideas challenged accepted ways of perceiving, and he rejected what he regarded as the rationalist and reductive tendencies of Western theatre. He called for a theatre which celebrated the non-verbal elements of consciousness that could ultimately arouse therapeutic emotions within his spectators. It was Artaud's passionate belief that 'theatre will never recover its own specific powers of action until it has also recovered its own language' (Artaud 1970: 68). As a result, Artaud felt it was necessary to 'create word, gesture and expressive metaphysics, in order to rescue theatre from its human, psychological prostration' (Artaud 1970: 69). As Grotowski points out: 'Artaud left no concrete technique behind him, indicated no method. He left visions and metaphors' (Grotowski 1969: 86). However, these visions and metaphors have offered inspiration to many, notably to Peter Brook and actors from the Royal Shakespeare Company in the Theatre of Cruelty season of 1964.

Interculturalism

Artaud's encounter with Balinese theatre at the Colonial Exposition of 1931 deeply influenced his ideas and led him to call for a more sensuous, physical actor. Artaud envisaged an 'athlete of the heart' who had to make use of his emotions 'as a boxer uses his muscles' (Artaud 1970: 89). Throughout the twentieth century, Occidental theatre's deepening awareness of Oriental traditions has played a large part in both the development of actor training and performance aesthetics. Some practitioners – Stanislavsky, Chaikin, Grotowski and Barba, for example – have drawn on the martial arts and/or holistic practices such as yoga in the preparation of the actor's 'body/mind'.[3] Peter Brook and Eugenio Barba have travelled widely in the East to under-stand at first hand the richness of the traditions performed in their proper cultural context, whilst Meyerhold, Brecht and Littlewood have all been influenced by Asian theatre techniques in their anti-illusionist theatres.

This particular avenue has led Western theatre to re-enter a political and social debate. The intercultural issues arising from the research into, and in some cases appropriation of, Eastern theatre practices have been passionately discussed over the last twenty years, and some of these practitioners (particularly Brook and Barba) have been at the centre of this discourse.

The actor's presence

Ian Watson defines Barba's intention in his development of a theatre anthropology as 'a systematic study of Oriental Theatre' in order to understand the source of the actor's 'presence'. The control of the actor's 'presence', Barba concluded, was a common performance principle in many Oriental traditions; two fundamental elements contribute to this phenomenon: 'the use of learned body techniques designed to break the performer's daily responses, and the codification of principles which dictate the use of energy during performance'. These elements Barba describes as essential components in the actor's arsenal of 'extra daily' techniques.

'Presence' is a rather abstract term often referred to within this book in different contexts of actor training. It is important to recognise that the understanding and interpretation of the actor's presence is wide ranging in training; Barba's analysis is that of being fully in the immediate moment which owes something to concentration and the control of the actor's energy. Within Gardzienice's performances, I argue that the actors operate beyond the dualistic performance paradigm as identified by Diderot, to achieve a heightened state of presence that enables the actor to operate on several levels of consciousness simultaneously.

Dorinda Hulton's definition of presence relates to Chaikin's sound and movement exercise. Within this context she suggests the actor is not uniquely concerned with the presence of 'self' but is more concerned with being 'in operation with imagery'. The actor's attention is completely absorbed in this interactive task. When the full engagement of the actor with an immediate process

> allows a particular kind of shifting balance, or dialogue, between body and mind, in listening to and watching for the emerging form, the emerging image, and is able, moment to moment, to come into alignment with it...[Then] there is a perceptible quality of 'presence'.
>
> (p. 161)

Systems or principles

The search for methodologies of Western actor training in the twentieth century precipitated debate around two key questions. First, could a single, universal system be achieved which would contain a complete method of actor training? This was Stanislavsky's initial project but, as Carnicke emphasises, the notional system ultimately suggests various pathways for the actor: 'In choosing a path, each actor reinvents and personalises the

System.' Stanislavsky's hope was for 'a guide...a handbook, not a philosophy' (p. 33–4).

Second, could the fundamental techniques of one acting system be applicable in the creation of any form of theatre? This again was Stanislavsky's belief. But some practitioners have found limitations within his system, particularly when attempting to move away from psychological realism and the interpretation of existing texts. Meyerhold was one of the first to feel it as restrictive. He reacted against the psychological assumptions of naturalistic theatre, maintaining that performers were capable of more than mere imitation. Through a sustained and intensive training of the body within his biomechanical exercises he too sought a methodology that would cope with all styles of theatre but through a greater articulation of the performer's physical, spatial and rhythmical vocabulary. Later practitioners resisted the notion of anything as absolute as a universally applied method. It was, for example, Chaikin's belief that systems were

> recorded as ground plans, not to be followed any more than rules of courtship. We can get clues from others, but our own culture and sensibility and aesthetic will lead us to a totally new kind of expression, unless we imitate both the process and findings of another. The aesthetic remakes the system.
>
> (Chaikin 1972: 21)

Ultimately, many twentieth-century practitioners have eschewed the notion of a comprehensive system in favour of identifying first *principles* within the context in which their training operates. These principles are made manifest through specific actor training techniques and amplify distinctive ethical positions, but do not in themselves constitute a 'system'. Copeau speaks of understanding the 'dramatic principle in oneself' in his quest for sincerity on stage. Brecht's actor cannot simply observe without at the same time interrogating the social forces at play. Strasberg describes an actor as the individual who can 'create out of himself' but in order to achieve this the actor must be prepared to 'appeal to the unconscious and the subconscious' (Strasberg 1965: 82).

But whilst the context in which these training principles evolved remain an essential part of their identification, many have endured and influenced the work of those who followed. This suggests that some principles are fundamental, capable of transcending their origins and therefore justifiably can be recognised as part of a matrix of key concepts in twentieth-century Western actor training. Collectively, the essays included here begin to uncover these key ideas.

Within the social, political or aesthetic context in which each theatre practitioner was working, exercises which could be regarded as paradigmatic of the overall practice are introduced. The exercises documented are not intended to be offered in the spirit of a handbook. They are concrete examples of the kind of territory that each practitioner has covered, and aim to demonstrate the physical realisation of core principles. Finally, each chapter connects these training practices to some of the remarkable productions that arose from them.

Notes

1 At the turn of the century Chekhov's major works were yet to be written. Realism in the theatre was still in its infancy and yet to be fully explored. However, in parallel with the other arts, some practitioners had already begun to reject its 'lifelike' ambitions. The early symbolists were already encouraging a view of theatre as a place in which poetry, dance, music and painting could be brought together and combined to depict ideas through another more subjective language. These early innovations would also lead theatre in quite different directions.
2 Roach points out that *Le Paradoxe sur le comédien* was conceived by Diderot very closely with his other works of that period, the *Eléments* and *Le rêve de d'Alembert*, and that the three works which each take the human body as a central theme 'may usefully be interpreted as a triptych...' (Roach 1985: 129).
3 I am referring to this term as used by Zarrilli in his discussion of what he describes as the 'body/mind problem in acting' (see Phillip Zarrilli's *Acting (Re)Considered, Theories and Practices*, pp. 10–16).

Bibliography

Artaud, A. (1970) *The Theatre and its Double*, trans. V. Corti, London: Calder and Boyars.

Barba, E. (1979) *The Floating Islands: Reflections with Odin Teatret*, trans. J. Barba, F. Perdheilhan, J.C. Rodesch, S. Shapiro, J. Varley, Denmark: Thomsens Boytrykheri.

Chaikin, J. (1972) *The Presence of the Actor*, New York: Atheneum.

Cole, T. and Chinoy, H. Krich (1970) *Actors on Acting, The Theories, Techniques, and Practices of the World's Great Actors, Told in Their Own Words*, New York: Three Rivers Press.

Diderot, D. (1883) *The Paradox of Acting*, trans. Walter Herries Pollock, London: Chatto Windus.

Grotowski, J. (1969) *Towards a Poor Theatre*, trans. M. Buszewicz and J. Barba, ed. E. Barba, London: Methuen.

Nemirovitch-Dantchenko [*sic*], V. (1937) *My Life in the Russian Theatre*, trans. John Cournos, London: Geoffrey Bles.

Ribot, T. (1897) *The Psychology of Emotions*, London: Walter Scott Ltd.

Richards, T. (1995) *At Work with Grotowski on Physical Action*, London: Routledge.

Roach, J. (1985) *The Player's Passion, Studies in the Science of Acting*, Newark: University of Delaware Press, London: Associated University Presses.

Stanislavski [*sic*], C. (1980) *An Actor Prepares*, trans. E. Hapgood, London: Methuen.

—— (1983) *Building a Character*, trans. E. Hapgood, London: Methuen.

—— (1983) *Creating a Role*, trans. E. Hapgood, London: Methuen.

Stanislavskii, K.S. (1989) *Sobranie sochinenii*, vol. 2 [*An Actor's Work on Himself, Part 1*], Moscow: Iskusstvo.

Strasberg, L. (1965) *Strasberg at the Actor's Studio: Tape-Recorded Sessions*, ed. R. Hethmon, New York: Theatre Communications Group.

Zarrilli, P. (1995) *Acting (Re)Considered, Theories and Practices*, London and New York: Routledge.

1 Stanislavsky's System
Pathways for the actor

Sharon Marie Carnicke

Life and career

Born in 1863, Stanislavsky's life saw profound scientific and social changes take place as the nineteenth century became the twentieth century. Living in Russia, he experienced artistic traditions from both Europe and Asia. Before his death in 1938, he witnessed three great revolutions: realism's overturn of nineteenth-century histrionics, modernism's rejection of realism, and Russia's political move from monarchy to communism. The first two shaped his career and made him world famous; the last turned him from a wealthy man into a poor one, from an artist who shaped modern theatre into one who was shaped by political forces. 'I have lived a variegated life', he wrote, 'during the course of which I have been forced more than once to change my most fundamental ideas' (Stanislavski [*sic*] 1952: 3).

Born Konstantin Sergeevich Alekseev into one of Russia's wealthiest manufacturing families, he lived a privileged youth. He regularly visited plays, circuses, ballets and the opera. He expressed adolescent theatrical impulses in a fully equipped theatre, built by his father in 1877 at the family estate, and as he grew, he often used his wealth to further his talents as actor and director. Until the communist revolution, he personally financed many of his most productive artistic experiments: in 1888 he founded the critically acclaimed theatrical enterprise, the Society of Art and Literature; in 1912 he started the First Studio to develop his System for actor training.

Until the age of thirty-three, Stanislavsky performed and directed only as an amateur. In early nineteenth-century Russia, many actors had been serfs, appearing at the behest of their owners; even after the abolishment of serfdom, actors continued to be regarded as lower-class citizens. Hence, whilst the Alekseev family loved theatre, they discouraged their children from professional aspirations which threatened social embarrassment. The critics, too, respected decorum when they tactfully praised an anonymous 'K. A_____v' for outstanding performances in productions by the Society of Art and Literature. In 1884, Konstantin Alekseev began to act without his family's knowledge under the stage name Stanislavsky.[1]

With the founding of the Moscow Art Theatre in 1897, Stanislavsky turned professional. The playwright and theatre educator Vladimir Nemirovich-Danchenko had chosen the impressive amateur as his co-director in an idealistic effort 'to reconstruct [theatre's] whole life...to change at the root the whole order of rehearsals and the preparation of plays' (Nemirovitch-Dantchenko [*sic*] 1937: 68). Their first meeting at a Moscow restaurant lasted a legendary eighteen hours. Their conversation set into motion the company that would bring the latest European ideas in stage realism to Russia and new standards in acting to the world.

In order to understand the revolutionary impact of their endeavour one need only compare the 1896 production of Chekhov's *The Seagull* at the Imperial Aleksandrinsky Theatre with the Moscow Art Theatre's staging two years later. The first relied on nineteenth-century conventions. It served as a benefit for a popular comic actress and featured a star. The cast met for a few rehearsals, learning their parts on their own, and supplying their own costumes. The theatre used sets from the existing stock. Despite its mythic failure on opening night, *The Seagull* attained, in Danchenko's word, 'routine' success (Nemirovitch-Dantchenko [*sic*] 1937: 63). By this, he meant that the Aleksandrinsky production entertained its audiences in typically nineteenth-century fashion, without any concessions in staging or acting to Chekhov's twentieth-century innovations in drama. In contrast, the Moscow Art Theatre put eighty hours of work into thirty-three rehearsals in order to cultivate an ensemble of actors without stars. Sets, costumes, properties and sound (including humming crickets and barking dogs) were all carefully designed to support a unified vision of the play. The directors held three dress rehearsals. Even so, Stanislavsky considered the 1898 *Seagull* under-rehearsed (Benedetti 1990: 82).

With this production, Stanislavsky became known as Chekhov's definitive director, and the Moscow Art Theatre took its place in the history of twentieth-century theatre.[2] Moreover, from this point forward, Stanislavsky's name and that of the Art Theatre became inextricably linked. His work on Chekhov's major plays (1898–1904), Gorky's *The Lower Depths* (1902), Ibsen's *An Enemy of the People* (1900), and his playing of such roles as the fussy old Famusov in Griboedov's *Woe From Wit* (1906) created his reputation as a leading realistic director and a gifted character actor.

No sooner had the Moscow Art Theatre established itself as the leader in realism, when symbolist playwrights and theatricalist directors revolted against representational theatre. Symbolists wanted to get beyond the illusions of reality by creating poetic expressions of the transcendental and spiritual. Theatricalists enjoyed making spectators aware of the conventions of performance, sets and costumes, much like abstract artists bring viewers' attention to canvas and paint. Both groups fostered non-realistic theatrical forms. Whilst Stanislavsky tackled the new styles with productions of symbolist plays in 1907 and 1908,[3] these efforts left little imprint on the character of the Art Theatre, which remained a bastion of realism.

Stanislavsky, however, wished to explore more widely. At various times during his career he experimented with symbolism, verse, opera, Western behaviourist psychology, Eastern ideas on the mind/body continuum, and trends in criticism of art and literature. In short, he willingly embraced anything that could illuminate acting and drama. Paradoxically, whilst the Moscow Art Theatre fostered his fame as a master of psychological realism, it also clipped his wings in other directions. Whilst the actors saw his experimentation as eccentric, Danchenko considered 'Stanislavskyitis' dangerous to the stability of the theatre (Benedetti 1990: 204). As a sharp businessman, he insisted that the Theatre build firmly upon its initial success with realistic styles. As a consequence, Stanislavsky moved his experiments to a series of studios, adjunct to the main stage and independently financed.

Take the System as a case in point. Stanislavsky became the first practitioner in the twentieth century to articulate systematic actor training, but he did so largely outside the confines of the Moscow Art Theatre. He began to develop what he called a 'grammar' of acting in 1906, when his performances as Dr Stockmann (*An Enemy of the People*) had begun to falter. He used new techniques for the first time in 1909 whilst rehearsing Turgenev's *A Month in the Country*. Although he had banned Danchenko from attending these rehearsals to alleviate tension, he still met with resistance from the actors who had succeeded in Chekhov's plays without 'eccentric' exercises. In 1911, a frustrated Stanislavsky threatened to resign if the company did not adopt his System as their official working method. Danchenko relented, but reluctantly. After one year, the seasoned actors still remained sceptical and Stanislavsky stepped outside of the Art Theatre and created the First Studio in order to work with more willing actors.

The Bolshevik revolution of 1917 left Russia in chaos. Civil war raged until 1921, food and necessities became scarce, and inflation made the ruble all but worthless (Vernadsky 1969: 316). In the upheaval, Stanislavsky lost the wealth and privileges of his youth. The Soviets confiscated his family home and factory. He began to sell his remaining possessions to survive. 'My life has completely changed', he wrote. 'I have become proletarian' (*O Stanislavskom*, Nemirovitch-Dantchenko [*sic*] 1948: 158–9). When his son fell ill with tuberculosis, he could not afford treatment (Stanislavskii 1961: 60). Facing eviction in 1920, Stanislavsky turned for help to Lenin's newly appointed Commissar of Enlightenment, Anatoly Lunacharsky, who was himself a playwright. Lunacharsky pleaded with Lenin on Stanislavsky's behalf, stressing that he was 'about to see his last pair of trousers' (Hecht 1989: 2). The state relented by allocating Stanislavsky a modest house with two rooms for rehearsals.[4]

The Moscow Art Theatre also struggled in post-revolutionary Moscow. At the time of the Revolution, the theatre required 1.5 billion rubles to operate, whilst its box office receipts totalled only 600 million (Benedetti 1990: 250). Without more profit or governmental subsidy the theatre could not survive. Both sources of income proved impossible in the wake of the revolution. The theatre mounted only one new production between 1917 and 1922 – Byron's *Cain*. Its set could not be built as designed due to the lack of funds. Therefore, Stanislavsky decided to use a simple black backdrop for the production. Even so, enough velvet to enclose the full stage could not be found in Moscow (Benedetti 1990: 244).

Stanislavsky and the Moscow Art Theatre looked to the West, and more specifically to America, for financial survival. As Stanislavsky soberly wrote to Danchenko in 1924: 'America is the sole audience, the sole source of money for subsidy, on which we can count' (Stanislavskii 1961: 84). Thus, the company split into two. Stanislavsky led the most famous actors on tour throughout Europe and the United States; Danchenko kept the theatre open in Moscow. The tours lasted two years (1922–4) and were unabashedly intended to make money for the floundering theatre. Only fame, however, resulted.

Many of the Moscow Art Theatre's talented actors traded their fame for employment in the West as actors, directors and teachers, rather than return to difficult lives in the new Soviet Union. These émigrés (Richard Boleslavsky, Maria Ouspenskaya and Michael Chekhov amongst them) promoted Stanislavsky's ideas on actor training. They helped move the System beyond the bounds of Russia.

Whilst on tour, Stanislavsky turned to writing for personal income. He published *My Life in Art* and *An Actor Prepares* in the United States in English (a language which he could neither speak nor read) so that he could gain control over international royalties. The Soviet Union had not yet signed the International Copyright Agreement, and therefore Russian publication would not protect his rights (Carnicke 1998: 71–7). His decision to publish abroad undeniably helped promote the System throughout the world.

Upon returning to Moscow, Stanislavsky and his theatre faced growing Soviet control over the arts. The state deemed realism superior to any type of formal or abstract art, and the physical, material world superior to anything spiritual or transcendental. Danchenko had read the writing on the wall. In recognising the importance of realism to the Soviet regime, the Moscow Art Theatre had sent their oldest most realistic productions to the West (Carnicke 1998: 29–33). By 1934, when Socialist Realism became the only lawful artistic style, governmental control turned into a stranglehold. The Soviets co-opted Stanislavsky, too, for the political cause. The press of the 1930s hailed Stanislavsky as the precursor of theatrical Socialist Realism, whilst a Soviet commission censored and edited his books to bring them into agreement with Marxist materialism (Carnicke 1998: 78–82).

Sadly, the private man did not exactly match the public image. Despite his early, much publicised work on psychological realism, Stanislavsky had continued with his politically incorrect interests in Yoga, symbolism and the formal structures of drama and action. As Stanislavsky explains, 'Human life is so subtle, so complex and multifaceted, that it needs an incomparably

Figure 1.1   Konstantin Stanislavsky, 1922

large number of new, still undiscovered "isms" to express it fully'
(Stanislavskii 1989: 458). He supported his former student, the theatricalist
director Meyerhold, at the very time that Stalin sentenced such artists to
hard labour and execution. Stanislavsky even dared to criticise the mediocre
repertory at the Art Theatre, now chosen by communist Mikhail Geits,
appointed by Stalin as the theatre's so-called 'Red Manager'. Correspondence
with Stalin (brought to light after the fall of the Soviet Union) suggests that
Stanislavsky lived the last four years of his life in internal exile, according to
Stalin's policy of 'isolation and preservation', reserved for internationally
known Soviet citizens. The ageing Stanislavsky, now frail with a heart condition, made such confinement relatively easy to explain in the press. From
1934 to 1938, he left his home only for brief visits to doctors, whilst his
nurses and close associates – his 'wardens' – monitored what information

reached him from the outside world (Smeliansky 1991: 9). But for his international fame, Stanislavsky may have suffered more than the internal exile which Stalin imposed upon him in 1934.

Ironically, Stanislavsky conducted his most non-realist work during these last years. In the privacy of his home, he worked on opera, Shakespeare's plays, and his last planned production, Molière's *Tartuffe*. However partial Stanislavsky's public image, his System embodies a holistic and multivariant approach to acting that escapes the bounds of politics.

The System

Stanislavsky's name has become omnipresent in Western theatrical discourse because of his lifelong, obsessive passion to turn the practice of acting into a system. 'I believe that all masters of the arts need to write', he said, 'to try and systematise their art' (Filippov 1977: 58). He had begun to do so at the age of fourteen, keeping detailed notebooks on every performance he gave or saw. His project culminated in an autobiography, piles of drafts for three acting manuals, a myriad of unpublished notes, lesson plans and jottings. However, he never deemed his System or his books complete; they remain dynamic, experimental explorations of the unique communicative power of theatre. At his death, he had approved final drafts for only two volumes: *My Life in Art* and the first volume of *An Actor's Work on Himself*, or what we in the West know as *An Actor Prepares*.[5]

Stanislavsky's effort to 'systematise' his art in writing was far from easy. Acting, like riding a bicycle, is easier to do than to explain. No wonder acting is more effectively taught in classrooms than through textbooks. In order to surmount this difficulty, Stanislavsky chose to write his manuals as if they were 'the System in a novel' (Stanislavskii 1961: 52). He thus creates a fictional classroom to portray, rather than explain, the process of acting. He introduces characters who struggle to act well and their teacher who struggles to help them. Stanislavsky puts his characters into changing contexts which continually challenge their ideas about what it means to act. In endless Socratic dialogue, they explore the mysteries of acting, they argue their various points of view, and they sometimes break through to clear understandings of their intractable art.

Taken together, Stanislavsky's books and manuscripts encode a coherent and remarkably consistent set of assumptions about acting. All his exercises, techniques and interests partake of these essential ideas.

The first, most pervasive of these is Stanislavsky's holistic belief that mind and body represent a psychophysical continuum. He rejects the Western conception that divides mind from body, taking his cue from French psychologist Théodule Ribot, who believed that emotion never exists without physical consequence. Echoing Ribot's assertion that 'a disembodied emotion is a non-existent one' (Ribot 1897: 95), Stanislavsky insists that: 'In every physical action there is something psychological, and in the psychological, something physical' (Stanislavskii 1989: 258).

Many critics and teachers privilege one element in this continuum over the other. In the United States, Stanislavsky's work with emotion answered the American fascination with Freudian psychology. In the Soviet Union, Stanislavsky's work with physical aspects of acting made his System better conform to the tenets of Marxist materialism. This bifurcation of the System is mistaken (Carnicke 1998: 149–51). For Stanislavsky, the mental is always imbued with the physical and vice versa. Only three months before his death, he cautioned his directing students that: 'One must give actors various paths. One of these is the path of [physical] action. But there is also another path: you can move from feeling to action, arousing feeling first' (Stanislavskii 1987: 565).

Following from this first assumption, Stanislavsky posits that physical tension is creativity's greatest enemy, not only paralysing and distorting the beauty of the body, but also interfering with the mind's ability to concentrate and fantasise. Performance demands a state of physical relaxation, in which the actor uses only enough muscular tension to accomplish what is necessary. Stanislavsky suggests that actors practise the breathing and poses of Hatha Yoga to build habits of relaxation. He also teaches progressive relaxation, contracting and releasing each muscle of the body in turn, in order to learn the experiential difference between the two.

A second major assumption behind the System involves Stanislavsky's belief that successful acting places the creative act itself in the laps of the audience. By insisting on the immediacy of performance and the presence of the actor, Stanislavsky argues against nineteenth-century traditions, which taught actors to represent characters from the stage through carefully crafted intonations and gestures. However well rehearsed, Stanislavskian actors remain essentially dynamic and improvisatory during performance. Stanislavsky calls such acting (which 'is cultivated in our theatre and mastered here in our school') 'experiencing' (Stanislavskii 1989: 59). He adopts this idiosyncratic term from novelist Leo Tolstoy, who had argued that art communicates felt experience, not knowledge (Tolstoi 1964: 85–6; Carnicke 1998: 107–20).

Stanislavsky relates 'experiencing' to states of mind that seem more familiar: 'inspiration', 'creative moods', the activation of the 'subconscious'. He compares it to the sensation of existing fully within the immediate moment – what he calls 'I am' and what Western actors generally call 'moment-to-moment' work. He describes this state as 'happy', but 'rare', when the actor is 'seized' by the role (Stanislavskii 1993: 363). The Russian word carries many different nuances, amongst them 'to experience', 'to feel', 'to become aware', 'to go through', 'to live through'. Unfortunately, English has never found a suitable translation for this term, often playing upon the last option and mistranslating Stanislavsky's ideal as 'living the role' (Carnicke 1998: 109).

Following from this second assumption, Stanislavsky designs the whole System to foster 'experiencing'. From a theoretical point of view, the System merely collects and codifies the principles of human creativity necessary to the actor. Stanislavsky assumes that the ideal creative state occurs of itself when the actor works through the various elements that comprise the 'natural laws' of the actor's 'organic creativeness' (Stanislavski [*sic*] 1952: 566). From a practical point of view, the System suggests specific techniques that help actors develop a state of mind and body that encourages 'experiencing'. Stanislavsky believes that this 'sense of self' (as he calls it) provides the 'soil' (Stanislavskii 1989: 95, 265) from which the role can grow. It combines two alternating, nearly simultaneous perspectives: being on stage and being within the role (Carnicke 1998: 118–19). It is 'proper to the stage', 'inner' in its concentration, 'outer' in the actor's physical presence and 'creative'.

The following exercises from the System[6] reveal the wide spectrum of Stanislavsky's interests. They fall into two broad groups: techniques that foster a proper 'sense of self' and hence induce in the actor a creative state of 'experiencing', and methods that offer pathways into dramatic texts for the successful creation of characters.

Group I

The actor develops a theatrical *sense of self* by learning to control the skills of *concentration*, *imagination* and *communication*. Many exercises in this group derive from Stanislavsky's fascination with Yoga.

Concentration

Stanislavsky expects total mental and physical concentration on stage. He calls this psychophysical state *public solitude*. In it, actors tune out anything external to the world of the play. They behave in public as if in private. Stanislavsky teaches the importance of such a state of absorption by relating the Hindu story of a maharaja, who offers the position of governmental minister to the person able to carry a pitcher of milk around the walls of the bustling city without spilling a drop (Stanislavski [*sic*] 1948: 81; Stanislavskii 1989: 164).

1   Psychophysical concentration begins with sharpening the senses through observation (Stanislavskii 1990: 400).

Sight

• Look at an object or person for thirty seconds, look away, and give an accurate description.

- The classic mirror exercise: two partners face each other; one reflects the other as an image in a mirror. The leader moves and the image follows so exactly, that an observer should not be able to tell who leads and who follows.

Hearing

- Close your eyes, relax, and listen only for sounds in the surrounding room; broaden your focus to sounds within the building; broaden your focus once more to sounds from the street. Open your eyes, and describe what you have heard as precisely as possible.

Touch

- Close your eyes; someone will hand you an object. Examine it thoroughly through touch alone. Return the object, open your eyes, and describe it as exactly as possible.

Smell

- Close your eyes, relax, and focus on what you can smell within the surrounding room. Open your eyes and recall precisely what you sensed.
- Imaginatively recreate familiar smells: the sea, hot chocolate, roses.

Taste

- Describe the present taste in your mouth to another person.
- Imaginatively recreate familiar tastes: lemon, vinegar, sugar.

Affect

In addition to the five physical senses, Stanislavsky adds a sixth, emotion. Indeed, in Russian the word for 'feelings' applies equally to emotional and physical sensations. To illustrate the link between emotion and other senses, Stanislavsky relates two anecdotes. The first involves two travellers, who stop at a precipice overlooking the sea. As they look down at the raging water, one recalls all the details of a near-drowning, 'how, where, why'. The other recalls the same incident but with details that have lost clarity over time. Only the first exhibits the heightened affective sensibility (*emotional memory*) helpful to actors. The second story tells of two men, who hear a familiar polka. As they try to remember where they have heard it before, one recalls sitting near a column with the other at his side. 'We were eating fish', he reminds his friend, as the smell of perfume wafted by. Suddenly the memories of the polka, fish and perfume bring back to them their bitter, drunken quarrel that night (Stanislavski [*sic*] 1948: 157; Stanislavskii 1989:

284–5).[7] Stanislavsky advocates that actors sharpen their emotional memories, just as they do other senses, through exercise.

- Read voraciously (newspapers, novels, anything in print), visit museums, concerts and art exhibits. In short, develop your experience of the world and your ability to empathise with others through a broad liberal education (Stanislavskii 1989: 316).
- Recall your mood when you last sat on the beach at daybreak (Stanislavskii 1990: 502).
- Recall a moment of joy, sadness, ecstasy, or any other emotion or mood (Stanislavskii 1990: 502).

2   Stanislavsky further trains concentration through *circles of attention* that can be *small*, *medium*, or *large*. He calls points of focus on stage (whether animate or inanimate, visible or imagined) *objects of attention*. Actors learn to limit their focus to only those objects within defined circles. In his fictional classroom, Stanislavsky uses pools of light to help his students understand such focus. He first trains a spotlight on a table, illuminating only the small number of objects lying upon it – a small circle of attention; light then pools over the table, its chairs and a sofa nearby – a medium circle; then finally light floods the entire stage – a large circle (Stanislavski [*sic*] 1948: 71–3; Stanislavskii 1989: 158–63).[8]

- Walk in a small circle and notice what objects fall within it; broaden your walk to a circle of medium size, adding more objects of attention; finally walk in as big a circle as the room allows taking in all objects as you walk.
- Sitting still, mentally establish a small circle around you and notice what falls within it; broaden your attention to a medium circle; take in the whole room as the largest circle of attention available to you.
- When performing, define your circles of attention carefully to include all objects necessary to the scene. However, if your attention starts to wander, create a small circle in order to re-focus your concentration.

Imagination

The System values an actor's capacity to treat fictional circumstances as if real, to visualise the details of a character's world specifically, and to daydream or fantasise about the events of the play. Stanislavsky taught that an actor should not speak without an image in the mind's eye and suggests developing a 'filmstrip' of images to accompany the performance of every role (Stanislavskii 1989: 130). Such *visualisation* energises the imagination.

1   Training the imagination begins by strengthening inner vision.

Visualisation

- Close your eyes and imagine that you are a tree. Define your species (see the shape and colour of the leaves), how old you are (see how thick your trunk, how high your branches), and conjure a vision of where you grow. Then, pick a particular moment from your life and create it imaginatively. What was the weather? The time of day? What could you feel? See? Hear? What event (perhaps historical like a battle, or romantic like a lovers' tryst) occurred beneath your boughs that day? Specify all details as precisely as possible (Stanislavski [*sic*] 1948: 61–3; Stanislavskii 1989: 133–6).
- Choose several words at random; using them all, imagine a single, harmonious picture (Stanislavskii 1990: 400).
- Take a familiar event (your acting class, a ball game, a concert). Progressively change the circumstances under which it occurs: time of day, weather, number of participants. Find an explanation to justify each change, and fantasise how the event would unfold differently (Stanislavskii 1990: 400).

2 Stanislavsky further trains imagination by invoking the *magic if*. He borrowed this technique from his six-year-old niece, with whom he loved to play 'what if' games (Stanislavskii 1989: 119).

The magic if

- Pass around different objects using 'what if' to change your relationship to them. What if this glass of water were poison? What if this glass ashtray were a frog? What if this book were a bomb? (Stanislavskii 1989: 99–100).
- Take an object and change your relationship to it in successive moments: my book, the library's book, my mother's book (Stanislavskii 1990: 401).

Communication

For Stanislavsky, there can be no drama without interaction amongst scene partners and between actors and audience. Words are one vehicle for such interaction, but dialogue represents only a part of the play's total communicative power. Hidden beneath the words is *subtext*, a term that describes anything a character thinks or feels but does not, or cannot, put into words. Actors infer the content of subtext by noticing inconsistencies between what is said and done, or by apparently nonsensical shifts in conversation. Actors communicate subtext through non-verbal means (body language, the cast of the eyes, intonations and pauses). Influenced by Yoga, Stanislavsky imagines communication as the transmitting and receiving of *rays of energy*, much like psychic radio waves. Our breathing puts us in touch with these rays. With every exhalation, we send rays out into the environment, and with every inhalation we receive energy back into our bodies (Stanislavskii 1986: 220–1).

1 To control non-verbal expression, Stanislavsky teaches actors to recognise and manipulate the rays of energy that carry communication.[9]

Rays of energy

- Close your eyes, relax, and feel your breath moving through your body. Visualise the breath as warm, yellow sunlight, energising you. As you inhale, see the light travelling from the top of your head down to your toes; as you exhale, reverse the direction of the breath.
- Close your eyes, relax, and feel your breath moving through your body. As you inhale, breathe the energy in from the surrounding room; as you exhale, send the energy back out into the furthest corner.
- Stand apart from the group, hands held with palms outward. Radiate energy from your hands to someone else in the room. Does anyone in the room feel a transmission?
- One actor stands behind another in single file. The person behind concentrates on a simple command (open the door, sit down, shake my hand), then radiates it to the person in front, who carries out the command.

2 Stanislavsky teaches actors to refine non-verbal communication by improvising situations that involve naturally silent moments.

Improvisations on silent moments

- In a library, A wishes to greet B, who resembles a famous actor; B does not wish to be disturbed.
- After a serious argument, A and B have fallen silent; A wants to make up, but doesn't wish to say so.
- A blind person is at home, when a thief breaks in.
- A sits on a park bench, wanting to meet B, but C has just sat down on the same bench to read a paper. A wants C to leave.
- Recreate a dentist's waiting room.
- Recreate the platform at a rail-road station (Stanislavskii 1990: 404).

3 The actors incorporate words as elements of communication only after a firm grounding in non-verbal means. Stanislavsky asks actors to improvise familiar situations using their own words.

Improvisations using words

- An art exhibit. Several visitors and one art dealer.
- A thrift store. Several customers and one salesperson.
- A is waiting for B, but C arrives instead.
- A visits B to ask for money; B refuses.
- A day at work: the boss, the secretary, the janitor (Stanislavskii 1990: 405–7).

Group II

The System offers actors a variety of ways to *work on roles*. Some begin with imagination and intellect: *affective cognition* and *the scoring of actions*. Others rely on physicalisation: *the method of physical actions* and *active analysis*. All assume that careful reading of the play precedes rehearsal. When his fictional students admit that they have 'read' *Othello* on trolleys and buses, from books with pages missing, by studying only their own parts, or by recalling productions they once saw, Stanislavsky reprimands them. 'The first acquaintance with a role is the first stage of creative work' (Stanislavski [*sic*] 1961: 112; Stanislavskii 1991: 279). In an extended metaphor, he compares this acquaintance to the first meeting of lovers, in which the author seduces the actor. Rehearsals bring them ever closer, resulting in their marriage. The relationship eventually leads to the birth of a new human being, the character (Stanislavskii 1989: 456–66).

Affective cognition (also called cognitive analysis)

This technique for analysing a play consists of two parts. First, the cast comes together to discuss each element in the play and all the historical details of its world in extended *sessions at the table*. (This work relies on intellect, hence 'cognition'.) Second, actors work individually by visualising distinct moments from their characters' lives, thus imaginatively empathising with them. (Visualisations trigger emotional, hence 'affective', responses.) Such fantasy incorporates the elements and details discovered by the cast as a whole. Stanislavsky's work on the role of Famusov (Griboedov's *Woe from Wit*) utilises this technique. He mentally sees himself in Famusov's house, walking through its many rooms, visualising himself sitting in the study, sleeping in the feather bed, ascending the staircases. Thus, Stanislavsky creates a personal vision, a 'filmstrip', of himself in the role (Stanislavskii 1991: 69–74).

The process of affective cognition

- Analyse all details in a play to illuminate the lives of the characters.
- Research the history and social world of the play.

- Visualise your character going through a typical day, walking through the house, eating, working, sleeping, socialising. Incorporate all the details discovered in your analysis of the play and your research.

The scoring of actions

Stanislavsky believes that *action* distinguishes drama from all other arts, citing as proof Aristotle's definition of tragedy as the 'imitation of action'. Stanislavsky also invokes the etymology of *drama* from the Greek root, *dran*, 'to do' (Stanislavskii 1989: 88). 'People on stage act', he wrote, 'and these actions – better than anything else – uncover their inner sorrows, joys, relationships, and everything about the life of the human spirit on stage' (Stanislavskii 1923: 165).

In the System, *action* denotes what the actor does to solve the *problem*, set before the character by the *given circumstances* of the play and production. Thus, action seeks to accomplish something: to persuade an opponent, to climb the ladder of success, to revenge one's father's death. Expressed as an active verb, action is both 'mental'/'inner' and 'physical'/'outer'; it must be 'apt' in relationship to the circumstances. Moreover, Stanislavsky distinguishes between *actions*, through which the events of the play unfold, and *activities* (such as eating, cleaning the house, dressing), that create contexts for scenes. For example, in Shakespeare's *Macbeth*,[10] Act III scene 4, Lady Macbeth 'hosts' her husband's banquet (her activity), and simultaneously 'covers up' for her husband's crazed reaction at seeing Banquo's ghost (her action) (Shakespeare 1974: 1326–7).

Taken together, the actions of all the scenes tell the story of the play much as a score of music organises sound. As actors rehearse, they write down the sequence of their actions, creating personal *scores of actions*, which guide them during performances. Each action follows 'logically' and 'consecutively' from what precedes it. Moreover, each actor searches for a uniting thread that links together all the characters' actions to produce an overall sense of what the play conveys to the audience. Stanislavsky calls this unifying force *through-action*. Lady Macbeth might strive to control the uncontrollable, a through-action that might explain her trust in the witches, her ambition to be queen, her ability to overlook the immorality of Duncan's murder. Simultaneously, because one can never succeed in controlling the uncontrollable, this overarching action also logically leads to her breakdown and suicide. Stanislavsky warns his students not to be too hasty in defining what unites a role. Often, an actor finds a through-action in the last stages of rehearsal or even during performance.

1 Begin with distinguishing between actions and activities and learning to execute them.

Exercises on actions

- Strike a pose; observers select an active verb expressed by your pose. Now, improvise a scene using the verb.
- Choose active verbs and execute them, changing the circumstances under which they are performed. *Sit down* in order to relax, in order to hide, in order to better hear what's happening in the next room, in order to read a book; *enter the room* in order to visit close friends, in order to meet your lover, in order to interview for a job; *shake your partner's hand* in order to apologise, in order to be hospitable, in order to meet a famous casting agent.
- Change the object of attention for various actions. *Wait for* your spouse, your friend, your child; *write a letter by hand* defining who you are (spouse, lover, spy, lawyer) and to whom you are writing (lover, client, opponent, boss, parents) (Stanislavskii 1990: 402, 408–9, 411).

2   The process of identifying actions begins with breaking the play into segments, what Stanislavsky calls *bits* and what has come to be called colloquially 'beats'.[11] Each bit embodies a single action and begins whenever the action of the scene shifts, not with the playwright's divisions of the play. For each *bit*, the actor first examines the given circumstances and describes the character's situation in an adjective. For example, in *Macbeth*'s banquet scene, Lady Macbeth is 'embarrassed' by her husband's crazed behaviour in public (Shakespeare 1974: 1326–7). Note that Stanislavsky includes in the given circumstances not only all details in the play, but also historical and social research as well as whatever the director and designers of the production have decided. The character's situation, thus described, poses a *problem*, which must be solved by means of action.[12] The actor next decides what the character needs to do to solve the defined problem, thus leading naturally to the specific *action* for that segment of the play. In an effort to deal with her embarrassment, Lady Macbeth 'covers up' for her husband's behaviour. Stanislavsky also advocates using the *magic if* to help identify action. 'What would I do *if* I found myself in the circumstances of the scene?' The answer, expressed as a verb, suggests the action (Stanislavskii 1989: 96–7).[13]

During performance, the actor places full attention on carrying out the required action, with the character's emotions arising as a natural result. By focusing solely on action, the actor experiences something akin to the role's emotional life as a subsidiary effect. As Stanislavsky explains, 'If our preparatory work is right, the results will take care of themselves.' He concludes by warning that actors make a common mistake when they worry about the result, rather than the action (Stanislavskii 1989: 212–14).

The process of identifying an action

- Isolate a single bit within any scene on which you are working. Be sure that you identify a single segment.
- Define your character's circumstances as an adjective.
- Then ask yourself, 'What would I do if I were in this situation?' Be sure to answer with an active verb that can be employed during the performance of the scene.

The method of physical actions

This rehearsal technique assumes that emotional life may sometimes be more easily aroused and fixed for performance through work on the physical life of the role, rather than through inner work. In this method, the actor discovers and then performs the logical sequence of physical actions necessary to carry out the inner, purposeful actions of scene (as identified above). Stanislavsky gives an example of such a sequence. An actor who plays the character of Salieri in Pushkin's *Mozart and Salieri* murders Mozart (the action) by means of a series of physical actions: first by choosing a wine glass, next by pouring the wine, next by dropping in the poison, and only then by handing the glass to his rival (Stanislavskii 1989: 217). Such physical actions are best suggested to actors by the text. In the banquet scene, Lady Macbeth carries out her overall action, 'to cover up' for her husband's mad address to a ghost, through a number of strategic physical moves. First she seats her startled guests, thereby reassuring them that her husband is well ('Sit, worthy friends. My lord is often thus'). She then takes her husband aside in order to shame him into better behaviour by upbraiding him like a child ('O, proper stuff!/This is the very painting of your fear'). Next she returns him to the table ('My worthy lord, your noble friends do lack you'). Finally she turns her attention back to the guests, reiterating her first reassurance ('Think of this, good peers/But as a thing of custom'). This series of physical and strategic actions helps her accomplish her 'cover up' (Shakespeare 1974: 1326–7).

Stanislavsky refers to the sequence of physical actions as a score. Notice that he uses the same word here as he does for the sequence of actions throughout the play (see above). Do not confuse the two. *The score of physical actions* includes the many external moves and strategies that the actor needs to carry out the overarching purposeful action, that has been identified as necessary to the scene. The larger *score of actions* gives all the inner and purposeful actions that the character carries out from the beginning to the end of the play.

The actor tests the physical score by executing it silently, what Stanislavsky calls *the silent étude*. In such improvisation, actors perform the segment of the scene completely: they establish circumstances and activities, carry out the sequence of physical actions, and accomplish the overarching action. Unlike a standard rehearsal, however, they do so without using words. Such non-verbal acting helps physicalise the scene. Actors avoid pantomime, however, using credible gestures and blocking that could conceivably be transferred to a spoken performance. If the actors successfully communicate the key elements of the scene in a *silent étude*, they have created useful scores for performance (Kovshov 1983: 108–28; Knebel' 1971: 72–5).[14]

Steps in the method of physical actions

* Identify the inner, purposeful action of the bit on which you are working.
* Compile your score by listing all the physical actions necessary to carry out this action.
* Test your score by means of a *silent étude*, playing that bit of the scene without words.

Active analysis

Stanislavsky hammered out his last, most unique rehearsal technique in workshops conducted in his home from 1934 to 1938. He bases active analysis upon a literary assumption which he took from the Russian Formalist critics and adapted to drama: that plays encode 'structures of action'. Thus, he speaks metaphorically of the 'anatomy of the role and the play', of a role's 'skeleton', its 'arteries, nerves, pulse' (Stanislavskii 1991: 58, 131, 64, 135). One of his last students expressed this assumption well. 'The idea of any artistic work is contained not only in its words, but in its structure, and in the very medium of art' (Kovshov 1983: 45).[15]

In active analysis, actors grasp a play's anatomy before memorising lines. To do so, they read a play as if it were a system of clues that imply potential performance, just as musicians read musical scores. Stanislavsky calls these clues the *facts*, to which actors accommodate performance. Such facts can be obvious. After Duncan's murder, when Lady Macbeth (Act II, scene 2) says 'My hands are of your colour', we know that she must appear bloodied. However, facts may also entail sophisticated literary observations. In the same speech, Lady Macbeth speaks only in short phrases, broken by ends of lines and punctuation: 'Hark! More knocking./Get on your night-gown, lest occasion calls us/And show us to be watchers. Be not lost/So poorly in your thoughts' (Shakespeare 1974: 1320). This rhythm suggests that she has been running from the murder chamber and is out of breath. In this technique, the actor learns to read each line not only for semantic meaning, but also for style, literary images and rhythms, which betray the action of the scene and the personality of the character.

The 'facts' of each scene encode an *event* that occurs between the characters before the scene concludes. For each individual event, actors discover the *action* (that *incites* or moves the scene forward) and the *counteraction* (that *resists* the scene's forward momentum). When action meets counteraction *conflict* results. Consequently, actors must identify situations and problems that are *contradictory*. Take, for example, Act I, scene 7 from *Macbeth*. The scene between husband and wife occurs when Macbeth has begun to falter in his resolve to kill the King to gain the throne. The key event takes place when Lady Macbeth persuades her husband to proceed. Macbeth's action (to say 'no') meets Lady Macbeth's counteraction (to persuade him to say 'yes'). Whilst he incites the scene, her resistance ultimately carries it, producing the event. She uses a number of different active strategies – calling him inconstant in his love, naming him a coward, and finally attacking his manhood. Her verbal images embody sarcasm, taunting and challenge. Her last approach clearly weakens his position, and instead of further resistance, he questions her, 'If we should fail?' (Shakespeare 1974: 1318). This moment marks a *reversal point*, when Macbeth's action begins to be modified by his wife's, paving the way for the event to occur.

A play reveals its anatomy through the *chain of events*, which tells the story. Each event carries different weight according to its sequence and function within the play. The event that begins the play is the *inciting* event; the one which resolves the through-action is *climactic*. Others may be *main* or *incidental* depending on their relative importance to the story or to subplots within it (Kovshov 1983: 84–95; Knebel' 1971: 57–62).

Stanislavsky means active analysis to be far from a mere intellectual exercise. He asks actors to discover the play's anatomy, not through discussion, but *on their feet*. Analysis is 'active' because actors test their understanding of how characters relate to and confront each other through improvisations of scenes in the play. These *études* serve as successive 'drafts' for future performance, each draft embodying and actualising the text better than the last (Knebel' 1971: 52). 'The best way to analyse the play', Stanislavsky said, 'is to take action in the given circumstances' (Stanislavskii 1991: 332–3).

The process of active analysis

- Carefully read and assess the facts of the scene on which you are working. Determine the event, the inciting and resisting actions that create its dynamics, and notice the style, language, images and rhythms of each character's language.
- Immediately play the scene using your own words; incorporate any 'facts' that you remember. (You may also use *silent études* to test your understanding of action, counteraction and event.)
- Re-read the scene and compare it with what happened in your improvisation. Did you retain the scene's basic dynamics and sequence? What images, styles, rhythms were you able to retain, and which did you forget? Did the event occur?

- Repeat the improvisation again, and again check your work against the text. Continue this repetition until you come as close as you can to the scene without actually memorising it. Each time, add something specific from the scene, using images, phrases, lines as written.
- Now memorise the scene for performance.

Productions

Stanislavsky staged Chekhov's plays without a System. He strictly controlled the external elements of production to create realistic illusion. Three-dimensional rooms with real knobs on real doors and historically accurate props and costumes reproduced reality as closely as was then technologically possible. Blocking too helped sculpt credible space. For example, in Act I of *The Seagull* (1898) Stanislavsky places Sorin on a bench with his back to the audience, thus making the invisible 'fourth wall' palpable and reminding spectators of their role as eavesdroppers (Stanislavskii 1981: 61). These early Moscow Art Theatre productions borrowed the latest techniques in realism from European directors like Germany's Duke Georg of Saxe-Meiningen (who used an ensemble of actors and perspective to produce believable crowd scenes) and France's André Antoine (who created three-dimensional interior rooms on stage and whose theatre coined the term 'fourth wall'). In short, Stanislavsky used means familiar throughout Europe to join the aesthetic revolution of his time. His promptbooks for Chekhov's plays betray his technical approach. They describe movements, gestures, *mise en scène*, not inner action and subtext.

Moreover, in these early productions the Moscow Art Theatre overturned the star system, then current on Russian stages, in order to forge an ensemble of actors who worked together seamlessly. Grounded in Stanislavsky's oft-quoted motto, 'There are no small parts, there are only small actors' (Stanislavski [*sic*] 1952: 298), the Art Theatre's ensemble most distinguished its productions from others at the time. However, the Chekhov promptbooks tell us little of how that ensemble was forged. Sound effects best suggest Stanislavsky's attitude towards actors during rehearsal. He ended Act I of *The Cherry Orchard* with a plethora of sound: 'A shepherd plays on his pipe, the neighing of horses, the mooing of cows, the bleating of sheep and the lowing of cattle are heard' (Stanislavskii 1983: 337). Whilst his critics, including Chekhov, complained that such details cluttered the play,[16] Stanislavsky inserted them primarily for the actors' inspiration. He assumed that the more actors could believe in the reality of the play's environment, the better they would act. Therefore, all production details, and most especially sound, served to stimulate the actors' imaginations by creating distinct 'atmospheres'. In the same spirit, Stanislavsky allowed his actors to use make-up and costumes as early as two months before a play opened (Nemirovitch-Dantchenko [*sic*] 1937: 100).

In 1907 and 1908, coincident with his staging of symbolist plays,

Figure 1.2   Stanislavsky as Astrov in Chekhov's *Uncle Vanya*, 1899

Stanislavsky turned his directorial attention away from external details and towards the inner worlds of characters and plays (Soloveva 1988: 51). His plan for Turgenev's *A Month in the Country* (1909), the production for which he first used the nascent System, best embodied this change.

This Russian classic dramatises the story of Natalia Petrovna, a wife and mother who falls hopelessly in love with her son's tutor. In choosing this play, Stanislavsky was moved by a married woman who, at twenty-nine, experiences first love (Soloveva 1988: 62). He used everything in the production to express the play's central conflict: Natalia's illicit passion, frustrated by the conventional rigours of her loveless marriage. Simple and symmetrical sets portrayed the calm restraint of her environment; paintings on the wall (a storm at sea and the eruption of Mount Vesuvius) suggested her inner turmoil. In his promptbook, Stanislavsky describes Natalia's situation: 'All her life she has been corseted' (Chevrel 1979: 282). His comment is both literal and metaphorical. Stanislavsky saw the tutor, with his youthful, unfettered energy, as fresh air in Natalia's stuffy salon. The production embodied great continuity between visual and interpretative elements. Its economy of expression unmistakably showed that Stanislavsky had learned from the symbolists. He directed Turgenev as Chekhov would have wanted his own plays directed.

In sharp contrast to the elaborate blocking in his Chekhov productions, Stanislavsky now reduced gesture and movement to a minimum. In the Turgenev promptbook, Stanislavsky describes not bodily movement but states of mind for nearly every line. Moreover, by cutting extensively from long monologues, he enriches the unspoken subtext. Quoting one of Natalia's lines, Stanislavsky writes that with this production he intended to expose 'the subtlest lacework of invisible, spiritual sensations' amongst the characters (Soloveva 1988: 50). His work with the actors certainly aimed to do so. Rehearsals for *A Month in the Country* began with two months 'at the table', discussing the nuances behind every line. Once 'on their feet', Stanislavsky conducted a series of exercises on feelings, concentration and communication. At one rehearsal the actors explored remembered emotions, transitions from one feeling to another and simplicity of expression. The next day, they tested circles of attention. These exercises, as well as others on communicating with the eyes alone, speaking without gestures, and playing scenes without words (*silent études*), clearly anticipate the System's inner techniques.

The Turgenev promptbook also anticipates the System's overarching emphasis on action. Stanislavsky gives active verbs for most lines. In Act I, when the tutor enters, Natalia 'observes' him closely, 'flirts' and 'pets' her son (Stanislavskii 1988: 385). For many scenes, Stanislavsky also distinguishes between activities and actions. He notes that when the curtain opens, Natalia and her would-be lover Rakitin carry on a desultory conversation (their *activity*). However, Natalia's absorption with the tutor and Rakitin's unsuccessful flirtation form the hidden, subtextual *action*. 'She concentrates [inwardly]', Stanislavsky explains, 'and that is why she seems externally distracted' (Stanislavskii 1988: 377). Her external distractions (listening to Rakitin reading aloud, his chatter and his story about a neighbour) contrast with the objects of her real attention (her contemplation of the tutor and her dissatisfaction with her own life). She inadvertently reveals herself when she interrupts Rakitin by asking, 'Have you seen how they make lace?' She imagines lace makers 'in airless rooms, no one moving from their places. ... Lace – a beautiful thing, but a gulp of fresh water on a hot day is a much better thing.' Her remark shakes Rakitin out of his chatter and forces a moment of true communication between them. In performance Rakitin, together with the audience, understood that Natalia spoke about herself (Stanislavskii 1988: 382–3).

Stanislavsky's last production, Molière's *Tartuffe*, opened posthumously in

December 1939 under the direction of Mikhail Kedrov, who had been assistant director and played the title role. Stanislavsky conducted rehearsals at his home between March 1936 and April 1938. His choice of material was significant. Molière's story of Tartuffe, the cunning religious hypocrite who hoodwinks the trusting Orgon, is told in rhyme; the play could not be further from Chekhov. Whilst psychological realism had been the style for which Stanislavsky had become best known, he always resisted association with any particular style. That his System be perceived as universally applicable became an obsession in his last four years. In choosing a classic seventeenth-century comedy in verse, he insisted on the wide applicability of his techniques.

Stanislavsky used this production to explore rehearsal techniques other than affective cognition. He had complained that, after long discussions 'at the table' and individual visualisations, 'the actor comes on stage with a stuffed head and an empty heart, and can act nothing' (Stanislavskii 1991: 325–6). He therefore replaces 'analysis of feelings' with 'active analysis', obviating the need to translate imagination into actuality. From the first, the actors were on their feet. Stanislavsky began by asking the cast to turn their rehearsal space into Orgon's house. They located each room, arguing over which area would be better suited for dining, or sleeping (Stanislavskii 1991: 69–74). Thus, collective fantasy replaces individual imagination. Such initial work makes the play more palpably present. 'Here, today, now', resounds throughout Stanislavsky's writing from this period (Stanislavskii 1991: 331).

Rehearsal records show that Stanislavsky dissected the play, ascertaining its 'anatomy'. He divided the cast into two camps, one led by Tartuffe (with Orgon in tow), the other composed of those who see through Tartuffe's chicanery (Orgon's wife, his daughter, brother-in-law, and clever servant). Each camp's set of problems were chosen to conflict with those of the other camp, thus prompting actions and counteractions. Stanislavsky then broke the play into twelve bits, each one defined in terms of a key event that embodies struggle. He includes 'a protest against the oppression of Tartuffe', '[the servant's] counteroffensive', 'Orgon's counterattack by his promise to marry [his daughter] to Tartuffe' (Stroeva 1977: 374). The war-like metaphors reveal that conflict is the essence of dramatic structure for him.

Improvisations served to recreate both the world of the play and its dynamic structure. In early rehearsals, Stanislavsky encouraged improvisations on any aspect of the play's story: how Orgon's family dines, how they play cards, Orgon's first meeting with Tartuffe. Whilst these events do not occur in the play proper, they establish context and environment. As rehearsals continued, Stanislavsky turned to the exact structure of Molière's play for true active analysis. The actors paraphrased each scene over and over again to discover each action, counteraction and event within the scene. With each paraphrase, they incorporated more of the text (images, style, rhythms, even lines) until, as one of Stanislavsky's actors reports, 'We could move on to the next step of rehearsal work, a step where the text became necessary. Our improvisations had reached the point where they demanded greater expressiveness through the author's words' (Toporkov 1979: 165).

Just as Stanislavsky's System for actor training remained experimental and dynamic to the end, his rehearsal methods reflect his ever-changing views on how best to establish connection between actors and their roles. From his early work on Chekhov which features directorial control over the external aspects of production, he turned his attention to the inner realm of non-verbal communication. His last experiments connected the actor with the text through a unique process of dramatic analysis.

Throughout his career, Stanislavsky believed that there are three basic drivers behind creativity: 'mind' (for analysis and understanding), 'will' (for control), and 'feeling' (which fosters passionate and zestful relationships with the characters we create). At various times, both in classrooms and in rehearsal halls, he focused on one or another of these drivers. Ultimately, however, he saw them as inextricably linked to each other in a tightly wound 'knot' or 'bundle' (Stanislavskii 1989: 395, 417). The successful actor, by whatever path, arrives always at the same place, where mind, will and feeling together produce a satisfying performance. 'How astounding a creation is our nature!' he writes. 'How everything in it is bound together, blended, and interdependent!' like a 'harmonious' musical chord, in which one false note creates disharmony, all elements of the system work together (Stanislavskii 1991: 314).

The System's techniques suggest various pathways for actors to follow as they strive towards successful performances. In choosing a path, each actor reinvents and personalises the System. This reinterpretation and adaptation is exactly what Stanislavsky hoped to inspire in actors. He hated the dogmatic teacher who insists upon a single correct way. Thus, in his last years he advised his students that:

> The System is a guide. Open and read. The System is a handbook, not a philosophy.
> The moment when the System begins to become a philosophy is its end.
> Examine the System at home, but forget about it when on stage.
> You can't play the System.
> There is no System. There is only nature.
> My lifelong concern has been how to get ever closer to the so-called 'System', that is to get ever closer to the nature of creativity.
>
> (Stanislavskii 1990: 371)

The history of twentieth-century actor training can be seen as a series of explorations, inspired by Stanislavsky's guide, and each probing a different pathway into the actor's unique creativity as a performer.

Notes

1 Stanislavsky adopted the name of his favourite Polish ballerina. In one surreptitious production, he met his future wife; she too was acting on the sly as Maria Lilina.
2 No wonder the Moscow Art Theatre adopted a seagull as its visual logo.
3 These productions were Hamsun's *The Drama of Life*, Andreev's *The Life of Man*, and Maeterlinck's *The Blue Bird*.
4 This house has since become one of Moscow's museums.
5 Stanislavsky's manuals were published in English versions, that abridged longer Russian texts: *An Actor Prepares* (1936), *Building a Character* (1949) and *Creating A Role* (1961). Stanislavsky had intended that the first two volumes be a single long book, entitled *An Actor's Work on Himself*. Because of its excessive length, Stanislavsky reluctantly divided it into two; *Part I* was published in Russian in 1938 (two years after the English), and *Part II* in 1948. The third manual was compiled from incomplete drafts for a projected work entitled *An Actor's Work on the Role*. For a complete publication history of these books, see Carnicke 1998: Chapter 4. I base my analysis of the System and the following exercises on the Russian language manuals and on recently published drafts and notebooks in K. S. Stanislavskii, *Sobranie sochinenii* [*The Collected Works*], Moscow, 1988–95. I also draw upon my work as assistant director and interpreter for Sam Tsikhotsky of the Moscow Art Theatre whilst he was in residence at the Actors Studio (New York) in 1978, and classes at the Moscow Art Theatre School and the Russian Academy of Theatrical Arts.
6 This grouping of exercises is mine. All cited exercises are adapted either from Stanislavsky's published acting manuals or recently published notes on training (Stanislavskii 1990).
7 Stanislavsky borrows these anecdotes from Ribot (1897: 152–3). Whilst The Method would later turn them into models for its famous affective memory exercise, Stanislavsky uses them as mere examples of the range of emotional recall discovered by Ribot.
8 Notice that the exercise on hearing assumes the actor's ability to use 'circles of concentration'.
9 I observed the following exercises at Moscow's Russian Academy of Theatrical Arts (formerly GITIS), 1989; see also Gordon (1987: 69–70).
10 All examples from *Macbeth* are my own.
11 'Beats' may derive from the 'bits' of the play strung together like 'beads' on a necklace, when pronounced in English with a Russian accent by émigré teachers.
12 The Russian word, *zadacha*, which has been translated as 'objective' in the classic English language texts, is more commonly translated as 'problem' or 'task'. Stanislavsky explains this term by comparing the actor's *zadacha* to an arithmetic problem that must be solved (Stanislavskii 1989: 212). Therefore, I favour 'problem' as the best translation.
13 Lee Strasberg rejected this formulation, adopting what he thought to be Evgeny Vakhtangov's modification: 'What would motivate me, the actor, to behave in the way that the character does?' This question allows the actor to replace the play's circumstance with a personal one, called a 'substitution' (Strasberg 1987: 85–6).
14 I observed master teacher Natalia Zvereva and director Leonid Kheifetz teach *silent études* and other aspects of active analysis in Paris at the international symposium, 'Le Siècle Stanislavski' (Centre Georges Pompidou, 2–6 November 1988) and at their home institution in Moscow, the Russian Academy of Theatrical Arts (formerly GITIS) during 1989 and 1990.

15 The Group Theatre's use of the word 'spine' also reflects Stanislavsky's metaphor.
16 In retaliation, Chekhov threatened to write an opening line for his next play that reads, 'How wonderful, how quiet! Not a bird, a dog, a cuckoo, an owl, a nightingale, or clocks, or jingling bells, not even one cricket to be heard' (Chekhov in Benedetti 1990: 135).

Bibliography

All translations from Russian sources are the author's unless otherwise indicated.

Benedetti, Jean (1990) *Stanislavski: A Biography*, New York: Routledge.
Carnicke, Sharon Marie (1998) *Stanislavsky in Focus*, London: Harwood Academic Publishers, Gordon and Breach International.
Chevrel, Claudine Amiard (1979) *Le Théâtre Artistique de Moscow (1898–1917)*, Paris: Editions du CNRS.
Filippov, Boris (1977) *Actors Without Make-Up*, trans. Kathelene Cook, Moscow: Progress Publishers.
Gordon, Mel (1987) *The Stanislavsky Technique: Russia*, New York: Applause Theatre Book Publishers.
Hecht, Leo (1989) 'Stanislavsky's Trips to the United States', paper for the American Association of Teachers of Slavic and East European Languages, Washington, DC.
Knebel', M.O. (1971) *O tom, chto mne kazhetsia osobenno vazhnym* [What Seems Most Important to Me], Moscow: Iskusstvo.
Kovshov, N. (1983) *Uroki M.N. Kedrova* [The Classes of M.N. Kedrov], Moscow: Iskusstvo.
Nemirovitch-Dantchenko [*sic*], Vladimir (1937) *My Life in the Russian Theatre*, trans. John Cournos, London: Geoffrey Bles.
—— (1948) *O Stanislavskom: Sbornik vospominanii* [About Stanislavsky: A Collection of Reminiscences], Moscow: VTO.
Ribot, Théodule (1897) *The Psychology of Emotions*, London: Walter Scott, Ltd.
Shakespeare, William (1974) *The Riverside Shakespeare*, Boston, MA: Houghton Mifflin Co.
Smeliansky, Anatoly (1991) 'The Last Decade: Stanislavsky and Stalinism', *Theater*, 12, 2: 7–13.
Soloveva, I.N. (1988) 'Puti iskanii' ['The Paths of Inquiry'], in K.S. Stanislavskii, *Rezhisserskie ekzempliary K.S. Stanislavskogo*, vol. 5, Moscow: Iskusstvo.
Stanislavski [*sic*], Constantin (1948) *An Actor Prepares*, trans. Elizabeth Reynolds Hapgood, New York: Theatre Arts Books.
—— (1952) *My Life in Art*, trans. J.J. Robbins, New York: Theatre Arts Books.
—— (1961) *Creating a Role*, trans. Elizabeth Reynolds Hapgood, New York: Theatre Arts Books.
Stanislavskii, K.S. (1923) Untitled Draft, Bancroft Library, University of California, Berkeley, Typescript.
—— (1961) *Sobranie sochinenii*, vol. 8 [letters], Moscow: Iskusstvo.
—— (1981) *Rezhisserskie ekzempliary K.S. Stanislavskogo*, vol. 2 [directing plans], Moscow: Iskusstvo.
—— (1983) *Rezhisserskie ekzempliary K.S. Stanislavskogo*, vol. 3 [directing plans], Moscow: Iskusstvo.

—— (1986) *Iz zapisnykh knizhek* [*From the Artistic Notebooks*], vol. 2, Moscow: VTO.

—— (1987) *Stanislavskii repetiruet: Zapisi i stenogrammy repeticii* [*Stanislavsky Rehearses: Notes and Transcripts*], I. Vinogradskaia, ed., Moscow: Soiuz teatral'nykh deiatelei.

—— (1988) *Rezhisserskie ekzempliary K.S. Stanislavskogo*, vol. 5 [directing plans], Moscow: Iskusstvo.

—— (1989) *Sobranie sochinenii*, vol. 2 [*An Actor's Work on Himself, Part I*], Moscow: Iskusstvo.

—— (1990) *Sobranie sochinenii*, vol. 3 [*An Actor's Work on Himself, Part II* and notes on exercises], Moscow: Iskusstvo.

—— (1991) *Sobranie sochinenii*, vol. 4 [*An Actor's Work on the Role* and *From the Artistic Notebooks*], Moscow: Iskusstvo.

—— (1993) *Sobranie sochinenii*, vol. 5, part 2 (*From the Artistic Notebooks*), Moscow: Iskusstvo.

Strasberg, Lee (1987) *A Dream of Passion: The Development of the Method*, Boston, MA: Little, Brown and Company.

Stroeva, M.N. (1977) *Rezhisserskie iskaniia Stanislavskogo: 1917–1938* [*The Directorial Inquiries of Stanislavsky*], Moscow: Nauka.

Tolstoi, L.N. (1964) 'Chto takoe iskusstvo?' ['What is Art?', written in 1897] in *Sobranie sochinenii*, vol. 15, Moscow: Khudozhestvennaia literatura.

Toporkov, V.O. (1979) *Stanislavski in Rehearsal: The Final Years*, trans. Christine Edwards, New York: Theatre Arts Books.

Vernadsky, George (1969) *A History of Russia*, New Haven, CT: Yale University Press.

2   Meyerhold and biomechanics

Robert Leach

> Training! Training! Training! But if it's the kind of training which exercises only the body and not the mind, then No, thank you! I have no use for actors who know how to move but cannot think.[1]

Throughout his career, Vsevolod Meyerhold sought to train the brains and bodies of actors so that they would be able to participate in his lifelong quest for a theatre which would not attempt to reproduce the surface reality of living, but would be, rather, 'theatrical'. Yet largely because of accidents of history, which cruelly silenced him and fortuitously aided the ideas of his mentor, colleague and ideological rival, Konstantin Stanislavsky, the significance of his quest is, even at the end of the twentieth century, rarely recognised or acknowledged. His contemporaries believed that he was Stanislavsky's equal, and that this was as true for his ideas about actor training as about stage production. It is probably fair to say that virtually all those scholars, especially Western scholars, who have discussed his work since his 'rehabilitation' in 1955, have underestimated the importance of his pedagogy.[2] But many of his ideas were preserved through dark times by his pupils, and his pupils' pupils, who are now promulgating them energetically, and the time has perhaps come for a new assessment of Meyerhold's work on training actors.

Meyerhold's own troupe, the Comrades of the New Drama, was founded in September 1902 when Meyerhold was twenty-eight years old. His experimental and pedagogical practices developed alongside his mainstream production work, notably through his work with Stanislavsky's Theatre Studio on Povarskaya Street, Moscow, in 1905, then from 1906 until 1908 at Vera Komissarzhevskaya's Dramatic Theatre in St Petersburg, and in his own Studio on Borodinskaya Street, St Petersburg, between 1913 and 1917. After the Bolshevik revolution he developed a course on stage production in Petrograd (which, however, seems never to have operated meaningfully); then in 1921 the Meyerhold Free Workshop was established in Moscow, and this was absorbed into the Meyerhold Theatre when that became a reality in 1923. From then until its liquidation in 1938, the Meyerhold Theatre school trained actors conscientiously and in significant numbers.

Meyerhold cared passionately about his pupils. Erast Garin, one of his star graduates, painted an unforgettable picture of the Master overseeing his students:

> He would appear in the doorway with a green military greatcoat flung carelessly over his shoulders. ... The studio was never properly heated, but we were young, and involved in energetic exercises, so we didn't mind. Meyerhold sat by the round, tiled stove, smoking...and watching us as if he was studying each one of us.[3]

Meyerhold's own acting career began as a founder member of the Moscow Art Theatre. At that time, Stanislavsky had not even developed his 'round the table' method of analysing text, though his insistence that every stage action must be justified, or motivated, and that each character must have an 'objective' was already present in his work method. Meyerhold always held to these principles, even as he energetically rejected the Moscow Art Theatre's search for a life-like naturalism. The turn of the century was the period when Symbolism dominated avant-garde literature and art, especially in Russia, and Meyerhold sought a stylised means of staging the works of Symbolist dramatists. In 1906, however, his production of Alexander Blok's *The Fairground Booth* completely destroyed stage Symbolism. In the play, dreamy mystics and starry-eyed lovers confront the old theatrical masks, Harlequin, Columbine and Pierrot, and their spurious emotionalism is (literally) swept away by the theatrical games of the commedia dell'arte. Harlequin 'jumps through the window. The distance, visible through the window, turns out to have been painted on paper. The paper bursts. Harlequin flies head over heels into nothingness.' A few moments later, as the hitherto-agitated 'Author' joins the hands of Columbine and Pierrot, 'suddenly all the scenery rolls up, and flies away'.[4]

This production signalled Meyerhold's rejection of mysticism in the theatre. From then on, as Erast Garin wrote later, Meyerhold's 'point of departure' became the 'liquidation of the awe-inspiring, shamanistic aura surrounding the art of the actor'.[5] It led to his discovery, through the commedia dell'arte, of the grotesque as an artistic principle, that is the bringing together of matters, actions, ideas, which are not thought to natu-rally cohabit. At his Studio on Borodinskaya Street, under the pseudonym of 'Doctor Dapertutto', he experimented with the interplay of character and action as it had operated in various historical and exotic contexts, not only in Renaissance Italy, but also in eighteenth- and nineteenth-century France and in Shakespeare's England, in China, Japan and elsewhere. The work consciously combined actor training and experimental performance.

Meyerhold's ideas were drawn together and, in some senses, formalised in his syllabus for the course on stage production which he worked out with Leonid Vivien in Petrograd immediately after the 1917 revolution.[6] But his practice in the training of actors continued only when he moved to Moscow, first at his Free Workshop from 1921, and then at the school attached to his own theatre. As his system acquired a more integrated and theoretically justified basis, he gave it the typically Soviet, but not inappropriate, name of 'biomechanics', implying its connection with a technology of the body. Throughout the next two decades Meyerhold continued to adapt, refine, promulgate and demonstrate the biomechanical system, but in 1938 the Stalinist dictatorship closed his theatre. He was arrested the following year and judicially murdered in 1940 in gaol. Just at the time when Stanislavsky's ideas were receiving their greatest acclaim and support, both in Russia and in the USA, Meyerhold's career and work were wiped from the record, and his ideas consigned to oblivion. For fifteen years it was as if he had never existed. From 1955, when he was officially 'rehabilitated', his achievements were gradually rediscovered and made public again; at first cautiously through the Communist period, and then more expansively, so that by the end of the century his true position as one of the enduring colossi of the stage could again be legitimately argued.

From the time of his break with Stanislavsky (for whom, however, he retained the warmest admiration), Meyerhold's constant question was: what is 'theatrical' about the theatre? It was a question typical of its time, and may be compared with Kandinsky's contemporary search for the 'painterly' in painting, or the Russian Formalist critics' argument that it was the 'literariness' of literature that was its real strength and appeal. Stanislavsky's system was rooted in an earlier time, for it was designed to make stage action 'lifelike'. For Stanislavsky, 'theatricality' was a negative concept. Meyerhold, however, wanted a system which could cope with all styles (including naturalism, though he regarded this as something of an irrelevance; for him, Chekhov's appeal, for instance, did not lie in his 'truth to life'). The actor for the task which Meyerhold was to set – the ability to perform farce and tragedy, melodrama, pantomime and circus-style skits, to name but some of the genres he was interested in – needed a rigorous and long-lasting training: 'An actor must study as a violinist does, for seven to nine years. You can't make yourself into an actor in three to four years.'[7]

Beginning with the formulation that: 'Every art is the organisation of its own material', Meyerhold asserted that: 'In order to organise his material, the actor has to have a colossal reserve of technical resources.' The reason for this need was that the actor, unlike other artists, 'is at one and the same time the material and the organiser'.[8] This was formulated algebraically by Meyerhold as:

$$N = A_1 + A_2$$

(where N = the actor; A_1 = the organiser of the material; and A_2 = the material). The actor must therefore be able to move and to think.

But what – or rather, how – is the actor to think? He is not to identify with the part, wondering what the character is feeling or trying to identify his or her wants. Rather, the actor's brain is to decide on the physical formulation of the moment. Igor Ilyinsky, one of Meyerhold's most impressive actors, noted that: 'If the physical form is correct, the basis of the part, the speech intonations and the emotions, will be as well, because they are determined by the position of the body.'[9] Another of Meyerhold's protégés, the film director, Sergei Eisenstein, concurred: 'The pulse of the emotion (its curve) is the result of spatial-plastic placing. It is excited as a result of the quality of the treatment and training of the material' (that is, the 'A 2' of the actor).[10] Therefore, the actor's training was, for Meyerhold, devoted largely to an understanding of the body in space, or as he called it, 'scenic movement'. Following his work on *The Fairground Booth*, his scenic movement class focused most closely on the 'play' of the commedia dell'arte. 'It is not necessary [for the actor] to feel, only to play, to play', Meyerhold exclaimed in 1913.[11] The actor was thus to be seen as akin to the child when he or she is playing: for the child, the play is 'real', but it involves, initially, recreating the motion of the action, not seeking the Stanislavskian objective of the character in the 'play'. Understanding, which may include an understanding of feelings, becomes accessible to the child, but through the doing. Jonathan Pitches, one of the few British performers to have trained with a Russian biomechanics Master, and then to have put what he learned into practice, noted that 'to experience biomechanics practically is to understand it...I developed a sensitivity for detail. I noticed which foot was leading, where the actor's weight was situated, the rhythmic pattern of each action'.[12]

In his Studio in St Petersburg in the 1910s, Meyerhold experimented tirelessly and in great depth; first with the commedia, the strengths of which lay not only in 'play', but also in the traditional characters – Harlequin, Pantaloon, Columbine and the rest – 'masks' whose characterisations derived most significantly from their individualised movement and gesture patterns. The characters were literally masks: the performers wore masks over their faces, partly to focus attention on their characteristic movements, but also because masks eliminated passing or fleeting emotions, and because they fixed and expressed specific attitudes, or mental or spiritual states.

The investigation of commedia dell'arte led to further explorations of clowns, puppets and marionettes, as well as of other theatrical traditions from both Europe and the Far East. These in turn led to a bewildering and eclectic array of exercises and other practical acting work, from which much of interest and importance emerged. For instance, the relationship between the stage and the proscenium or forestage was examined; the oriental concept of 'self-admiration' (a kind of self-watching or monitoring) was introduced; and actors found a fulfilling excitement in emitting a cry or shout at moments of intensity. Costume was explored as a decorative ornament rather than a utilitarian necessity, and the hat as something to be doffed, not just worn. A prop – a tambourine, for example, or a flower – acquired significance when it became an extension of the hand (which itself was an extension of the arm, and thus an extension of the whole body: the resonance of the body as a whole being important); and stage furniture, such as the screen, was used in various ways. Entrances and exits were also play-fully explored. All these made an unsurpassed range of technical acting devices available to the Meyerholdian performer, not to be used merely for the recreation of past theatrical styles from which they were derived, but now as weapons in her or his armoury for contemporary stage compositions.

Meyerhold's 'scenic movement' covered all these experiments at this stage of his career (immediately before the Bolshevik revolution), and created a grotesque 'polyphony' on the stage. But the exercises may be said to have had their focus in concepts of rhythm – spatial rhythm as much as temporal rhythm. His student actors improvised prolifically to develop physical agility and physical responsiveness to others on the stage (spatial rhythm), and then what he called 'musicality' (temporal rhythm). Thus, actors might be asked to hum whilst they moved, or they might treat speech and dialogue as musical scores. These concerns with rhythm found their confluence in the pause or 'silhouette', the expressive moment when the movement was spatially and/or temporally broken.

Many surviving photographs of Meyerhold's productions show a picture-like composition, the theatrical equivalent to the still frame from a moving film, where the dynamic of the scene is reflected in the bodily postures of the performers, and their interrelationship in space. It was something not unlike Brecht's 'gestic interruption', but more self-referential, initially at least having more to do with the onward movement of the scene than with the socio-political structures in the outside world to which it might be refer-ring. Meyerhold told Gladkov two decades later that: 'The swifter the text, the more distinct the breaks must be, the transitions from one segment to another, from one rhythm to another. Otherwise the motivation is lost, the living breath of meaning vanishes.'[13]

In his work at the Borodinskaya Street Studio, he found that this concern with what might be called the 'through rhythm' could be most easily explored in the improvised pantomimes he occasionally presented and with which he frequently worked. The specific learning cycle which he developed at the Studio began with exercises. These were often developed into 'études', whose purpose was mainly to do with developing the actor, and then further expanded to become self-contained pantomimes suitable for public consumption. Such were most of the items in the presentations by his students.[14] Other examples were the traditional Chinese 'black comedy' improvisation, when actors pretend it is a dark night and creep furtively about on the brilliantly illuminated stage; and the three-minute version of *Antony and Cleopatra* which they showed to the visiting Italian Futurist, Filippo Marinetti.

By the time of the Free Meyerhold Workshop, and the establishment of his own school attached to the Meyerhold Theatre in Moscow, the 'polyphony' and the almost endless variety of explorations were becoming more focused and integrated. A new social awareness was also apparent in the work, and Meyerhold's students were now expected to have a sense of social responsibility which would inform his or her work. Thus, in Meyerhold's thinking about characterisation, instead of relying on the old traditional masks, he now developed the concept of the 'emploi' belonging to the 'set roles' of the actor, which extended the boundaries of the mask by relating it in new ways to what might be termed 'real life'.[15] At any given moment, Meyerhold's actors were asked to present a theatricalised 'mask' to the audience. But as the plot (or intrigue) developed, the character required a new mask. Their 'set role', and consequently their 'emploi' (what they did, or how they behaved), also changed.

As illustration, we might consider Hamlet. When he finds Claudius praying, his set role is that of the Revenger; but moments later, in his mother's bedroom, his mask is that of the disobedient child. Characterisation was, therefore, no longer simply a device of the pantomime, it was more like our experience of life, for, like Hamlet, we change: we behave as a child when with our parents, whatever our age; and – at least to some extent – we behave as a supplicant to our Bank Manager, as a 'good fellow' to our acquaintances in the pub, as a conscientious worker to our boss, and so on. The actors' 'set role' changed through the production, so that instead of a consistent through-line, Meyerhold's creations were grotesque, paradoxical and associative. They theatricalised the action and were the agent for the expression of emotion. Thus they effectively became action-functions. The actor's 'emploi' – how she or he expressed the 'set role' – was therefore not quite psychological, nor was it a stylistic peculiarity of the production, though it owed something to both of these. Rather, it was the exposure of the driving force of the specific image at a particular point in the production, the theatricalisation both of the specific motive (the objective, in Stanislavsky's term) and of the state of the relationship.

This helped Meyerhold to develop the learning sequence from exercise–étude–pantomime as practised in the Borodinskaya Street Studio to exercise–étude–acting: in other words, this greater awareness and flexibility enabled the work to be utilised more easily for all sorts of acting work for the public stage. But it still depended primarily on Meyerhold's 'scenic movement', now called biomechanics, which Ilyinsky described powerfully and precisely. In biomechanics, he wrote, the actor

> seized his partner's body as it was stretched in the sun, threw it over his shoulder and carried it off. He dropped this body. He threw a discus and traced its imaginary course. He gave his partner a slap in the face, and received one back. He leaped on his partner's chest, and received him on his chest. He jumped onto his partner's shoulders, and his partner ran, carrying him. Certain exercises were very simple: to take the partner's hand and pull his arm, then repulse the partner, then seize him by the throat. ... Although we sometimes gave demonstrations of these

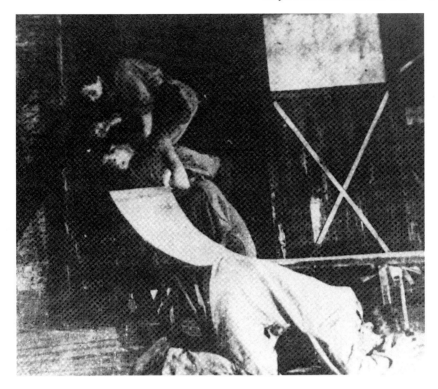

Figure 2.1   Biomechanics in action: *The Magnanimous Cuckold*, 1922
Source: Photo from the collection of Robert Leach

exercises, we did not need to transpose them literally to the stage: they served to give us the taste of conscious movement on the stage. The exercises combined the gymnastic, the plastic and the acrobatic; they developed in the students an exact 'eye'; they enabled them to calculate their movements, to make them meaningful and to coordinate them with their partners; and...they helped them to move more freely and with greater expressiveness in the stage space.[16]

The 'exact eye' is the 'self-admiration', or self-awareness, referred to above. In a theatre such as Meyerhold's, the actor needs to be extremely sensitive to what his body, his gestures, his movements are connoting. He needs a kind of in-built mirror.

Biomechanics is not arbitrary. It requires of the actor, and it trains: (1) balance (physical control); (2) rhythmic awareness, both spatial and temporal; and (3) responsiveness to the partner, to the audience, to other external stimuli, especially through the ability to observe, to listen and to react. It is worth pausing for a moment to consider these as they were

Figure 2.2   Biomechanics in action: *DE*, 1924
Source: Photo from the collection of Robert Leach

experienced by Jonathan Pitches. His experience of the étude, 'Throwing the Stone', for instance, was that it developed

> the solidity of the physical base by introducing falls, jumps, runs and exaggerated body positions and demanded the same movement away from the centre of gravity before finding this centre anew. The etude required a constant shifting of weight from left to right and, at one moment, from the lower body to the upper body. As the hieroglyphic body shape was adopted for the etude, one's balance was further tested, particularly by the jumps included in the exercise.

Pitches similarly found that the biomechanical exercises developed spatial awareness and the ensemble, noting particularly that the work with its emphasis upon collective, collaborative action, insists that each element of the ensemble comes together with a shared point of intense concentration whilst retaining each person's uniquely individual stamp as a physical body on stage. There can be no progression until each person has found the appropriate rhythm and mastered the skills within each action. The ensemble is in effect bound by a common cause which breeds a humility in relation to the work.[17]

These are large claims, but by examining a few of Meyerhold's exercises and études in detail, and relating them to performance, it may be that we shall be able thoroughly to justify them.

Perhaps the first and simplest of the exercises is that with the stick, a straight piece of broom handle or dowel about a metre long. Stand with the legs about 30 centimetres apart, the knees slightly bent, the stick held three-quarters of the way down in one hand. Bend the knees to obtain momentum, and rise, and as you rise, toss the stick easily up so that it arcs over. Keep your eye on the other end of the stick, and catch it, letting it fall into your hand. Do not grab at it. Repeat. Continue to repeat each exercise many times. Now toss the stick so that it arcs twice and you catch the same end as you threw. Toss it so that it arcs once and catch it in the other hand. Toss it so that it arcs twice. Three times. Four times. Always bend the knees and toss as you straighten them. The exercise should be performed in as relaxed a manner as possible: easily, lightly.

Now hold the stick in the middle, vertical to the ground. Toss it from one hand to the other. Hold it horizontally, with the back of your hand upwards. Bend the knees, straighten them, and as you straighten them lift your hand and open your fingers so that the stick flies out. Bring your hand down, catch the stick, the back of your hand still upwards. Repeat, letting go with one hand, catching with the other. Pass the stick from one hand to the other under one leg; then under the other. Pass it behind your back.

Place the stick in the palm of the open hand. Toss it up. Catch it, without closing the hand. Catch it on the other palm, without closing the hand. When the stick is in the air, turn the hand over, 'bat' it up again with the back of the hand or the back of the wrist. Catch it on the open palm. Place the stick on the index and middle finger. Balance it. Push up with the index finger, 'catch' the stick between the middle and fourth finger. Push up with the middle finger, 'catch' it between the fourth and little finger. Continue, involving the index finger again, till you can twirl the stick.

Balance the stick on the palm of the hand so that it is perfectly still. Balance it on the back of the hand. Balance it on one finger. On the wrist. The elbow. The shoulder. Balance it on the foot, the knee, the back of the neck, the forehead. Keep the eye on the end of the stick. The aim is for it to be absolutely still at all times. The number of stick exercises is enormous: these few simple beginnings will give some idea of the richness of the work. It is also useful to work in pairs, tossing the stick in various ways from one to another. Make sure your feet form a solid base, and concentrate on making the stick feel soft and light: never grab it, let it land in the hand. The stick is an indication of your own balance and co-ordination, especially when you balance it. Any movement in the stick indicates that you have not found your centre of gravity.

The remaining biomechanics exercises and études are more complex, and more strict, but each is carefully calculated to produce the kind of effect described here. The first exercise is the Dactyl, a sequence of moves designed to put the student-actor into a state of physical and mental readiness. A 'dactyl' is a verse foot, comprising of long beat, followed by two short beats. This is mirrored in the exercise:

The Dactyl

Stance: stand firm, alert, but relaxed, feet about 30 centimetres apart, arms loose at sides, head up, facing front. There are no pauses in the exercise, the whole movement flows through the seven points isolated here. The tempo of the exercise may vary, but initially at least it is quite slow and relaxed, flowing from point to point until movement 4 below, when the movement speeds up and points 4–6 are performed with a degree of taut intensity.

1   Both arms swing in a wide arc from in front of the body backwards, knees bend, torso leans forward, head forward.
2   Both arms remain straight as they swing forward and up high, the knees straighten, the feet remain firm on the ground.
3   The arms are brought straight down in front of the chest with bent elbows, the torso inclines forward, the head begins to bend.
4   As the hands reach a point about level with the groin, they clap energetically.
5   Immediately after the clap, the body partially straightens again, the elbows bend, the hands are drawn up towards the chest, the head lifts.
6   Immediately the body bends again, the head lowers, the elbows straighten and the hands drop, clapping energetically again at about the level of the groin. The effect is of two quick, strong claps closely following one another.
7   Relax to starting stance.

This preparatory exercise is performed by student-actors before, and often at the end of, other exercises. It requires them to stretch the spine and bend it, to 'open' and 'close', and to be physically alert and responsive. Erast Garin noted that the movement of the hands 'transfers itself into the torso, imparting elasticity to the whole body'.[18]

There are other exercises, which lead on to études, and then into performance, including 'Pushing the Kneeling Partner with the Foot', 'Throwing the Stone', the 'Stab with the Dagger' and 'Shooting from the Bow', all of

1.

2.

3.

4. + 6.

5.

Figure 2.3   Meyerhold's exercise: The Dactyl

which are preserved on contemporary film from the 1920s in what are clearly Meyerhold's authorised versions. Others include the 'Leap on the Chest', the 'Slap in the Face', 'Dropping the Weight', the 'Leap on to the Partner's Back', and more. Meyerhold himself did not codify a specific series, and used them more or less as the situation seemed to demand. Modern practitioners such as Alexei Levinsky often argue that only five of the exercises are really essential for a biomechanical training: 'Throwing the Stone', the 'Slap in the Face', the 'Leap on the Chest', 'Shooting from the Bow' and the 'Stab with the Dagger'.

However that may be, it is interesting that a comparison between Levinsky performing, say, 'Shooting from the Bow'[19] and the same exercise performed by Meyerhold's actor in the 1920s reveals Levinsky's considerably more complex structure. The exercise itself is described in detail below, but an analysis of Levinsky's performance of it shows that he has twenty-eight discrete units, each segmented from the others by a pause. The earlier version recorded under Meyerhold's supervision includes only eighteen distinct movement units, and several of these run together with no pause between them. Moreover, Levinsky's performance gives an impression of deliberation, each move being considered and measured, and actually performed in almost the same tempo throughout. Meyerhold's actor changes tempo frequently, some of their actions being performed *presto*, others clearly *largo*.

This is not pointed out in order to detract from Levinsky's work; on the contrary, it shows that the exercises are capable of great personal variation as between one performer and another, as well as how the exercises have proved capable of development. Levinsky learned from Mikhail Kustov, who himself joined the Meyerhold Theatre's school around 1930. His version of this exercise is therefore likely to be later, and more 'developed' than the earlier version.

The exercise of the 'Leap on the Chest' was one which allowed Meyerhold to delight his own students. In its simplest version, it is precisely what its name implies: one student-actor stands firms, one foot in front of the other, braced ready to catch the second student-actor. The second then runs straight at the first, and leaps up, placing his knees on the catcher's chest, and binding one arm round his neck, whilst the first actor wraps his arm (or arms) round the back of the leaper's knees. If the student-actor who is to perform the leap concentrates on leaping up, and not on his catcher, the exercise is quite easy.

It is then developed into an étude, which was what Meyerhold showed off. Based on the 'Stab with the Dagger', it was a miniature melodrama, which shows how Meyerhold was keen to theatricalise everything the students did. Erast Garin recalled:

> He chose a student who was strongly built, and showed him how to hold himself firmly, gripping the table behind him, and imparting 'give' to his body. Then he [Meyerhold] acted a pantomime of creeping up to the student, when he leaped upon his chest, his right knee against the student's ribs. With his right hand he then drew out an imaginary dagger from his belt, stabbed his partner in the neck, and leaped down. The wounded figure slumped to the floor, while the attacker straightened up.[20]

The exercise was transferred into performance precisely as a leap on to the chest in Meyerhold's 1922 production of *The Magnanimous Cuckold* by Fernand Crommelynck, when the Cooper rushed through a door and leaped on to the unsuspecting Bruno's chest. More interestingly, perhaps, a version of the étude was performed in Eisenstein's 1947 short dance, *The Last Conversation*, performed by members of the Bolshoi Ballet. This dance was perhaps the film-maker's last creative work, and was based on the final act of Bizet's *Carmen*. In it, the faithless heroine was murdered in a danced, almost dreamlike sequence which ended when she was stabbed. Eisenstein did not simply reproduce the étude, however, but made his own version of it, and this at a time when Meyerhold's name was obliterated in the USSR and when any mention of him was dangerous. He created a piece which seemed on one level almost like his leave-taking, his regretful but desperately necessary breaking-away from his Master, with its unexpectedly moving finale. The choreography was a dynamic testimony to the enduring power and versatility of Meyerhold's creation.[21]

The exercise of 'Shooting from the Bow' is one of the best known in biomechanics, but it is much less easily transferred to the stage than the 'Leap on the Chest'. Student-actors at Meyerhold's school in the 1920s first learned a simplified version of the exercise:

> The left hand mimes carrying a bow, the left shoulder leading. When the student sees the target, his body stops, with the weight equally disposed between both feet. The right hand moves back in an arc to take the imaginary arrow from a quiver on the back. The movement of the hand is conveyed to the body as a whole, and the weight is shifted to the back leg. The hand finds the arrow, and brings it to the bow. The weight shifts again to the front leg. The arrow is aimed. The imaginary bow is drawn back, the weight shifting again to the back foot. The arrow is loosed, and the exercise is completed with a leap and a cry.[22]

Later, they discovered the full version (which, however, was shorter than Alexei Levinsky's as noted above). The exercise was preceded and concluded with the 'Dactyl'.

Shooting from the Bow

Stance: as Dactyl (see above).

1 Slow swivel to left on right toe and left heel, arms by sides.
2 Bend and straighten knees, rapidly flick left hand to left shoulder, completely bending left arm, then extend the arm downwards and point with the finger (at imaginary bow on ground).
Pause.

3 Slowly bend knees, keep torso vertical, arms by sides.
4 Left hand moves rapidly to the floor (to pick up imaginary bow), takes the weight of torso which is now parallel to ground; right arm extended vertically, legs bent, weight on left leg.
Pause.

5 Return to position 3.
6 Slowly stand, weight on both feet, arms by sides, spine straight.
7 Slowly bend left arm so hand touches left shoulder, then extend left arm, hand vertically upwards, weight on right foot.
Pause.

8   Right arm makes a big arc parallel with the ground to draw imaginary arrow from belt at left hip, left arm bends to shoulder, weight is transferred to left foot, torso swivels left.

9   Right arm is raised to vertical above head, left arm extended, hand upwards, torso leans left, head half down, weight on left foot, right foot on toes, right leg bent, left leg straight.

10 Right arm rapidly bends, touches right hip, and extends vertically upwards again, torso bends left to be parallel with ground, left arm remains thrust out.

Pause.

11 Rapidly shift weight to right foot as right arm arcs back to horizontal, torso is brought back to vertical, head up, left arm still thrust out.

Pause.

12 Slowly, left arm is bent, hand nearly to shoulder, as right arm is brought in big arc over head to beside left arm, weight shifted to left foot.

13 Right arm 'draws bow', left arm extends horizontally, weight on left foot still.

14 Return to position 12.

15 Rapidly swivel torso to right and down, weight on right foot, both arms vertically down (as if 'firing' bow at right foot), torso bent over to right, head down.

Pause.

16 Rapidly swivel the torso to left and up, both arms raised, head up, weight on left foot, back arched.

Pause.

17 Bend knees, then rapidly straighten them and leap, left foot then right, pulling right arm down rapidly to vertical, whilst stretching neck and spine upwards; at end, weight equal, both feet firm on ground after leap.

18 Slowly bring left arm to side, face front, as at start of exercise. Stand.

This exercise led into the étude, 'The Hunt', in which the hunter shot the bow at a wild animal. The actual hunt could take various forms, depending on the individuals performing it, and the animal being hunted. Meyerhold was used to taking his students to the zoo for an afternoon to study the animals, which were then used as models for this étude. As 'Shooting from the Bow' is itself, at least in its most extended form, almost an étude, so 'The Hunt' is almost a pantomime: it is certainly instructive to watch good students perform it, since at an advanced level, it does allow for the improvisation associated with the public presentations of the Borodinskaya Street

Figure 2.4 Meyerhold's exercise: Shooting from the Bow

Studio days. But after the Revolution in Moscow, it informed several production sequences, including the spectacular chase of Tarelkin by the police in *The Death of Tarelkin*, for which Eisenstein was the assistant director, in 1922. Most notable, perhaps, was the adaptation of 'The Hunt' in the fourth episode of *The World Turned Upside Down* by Sergei Tretyakov, first performed in 1923, in which Erast Garin played the cook, whom he made into a sort of clown:

> In a white jacket and hat, and with a large knife in my hand, I had to chase a live cockerel which was to be put into the pot. I had to stumble

and the cockerel flew out of my grasp. (It was secured by a long black string, since nobody completely trusted the way the cockerel might develop its part.) Then the chase began, full of comic improvisation. Once, before a packed house, I could see Meyerhold on the front row at the right hand side of the stage. The audience was enjoying the chase. The cockerel stopped, blinded by the stage lights, and looked round. I jerked the string so as to get hold of it, but it flapped its wings madly, broke away from my grip and flew off towards the audience. The string had broken. Shame, misery. ... Suddenly Meyerhold leaped from his chair like a cannonball from a cannon, a look of grim determination on his face. He caught the cockerel in mid-air, and tucked it under his arm. Then, with some difficulty but as nonchalantly as a stage attendant, he walked through the audience to the stage, and handed the cockerel up to me. I put it under my arm and exited hastily to wild applause![23]

Amusing, even exhilarating, as this is, it only indicates part of the true value of biomechanics for the actor, which Jonathan Pitches hinted at in his assessment:

At the beginning of the process there was no conceivable link between the workshops and the rehearsals on Gogol's text – the work on the etude merely acting as a diversion from the real matter in hand. It was my belief that as the pressure built on the schedule we would be forced pragmatically to lose the 'luxury' of the biomechanical training in order to devote all our time to the blocking of the text. But this scenario did not play itself out. As the language of the etude began to establish itself the biomechanics became progressively invaluable. The rewards of the training in terms of concentration, ensemble discipline, rhythmic understanding and gestural expressivity were too great to be lost. We had no choice but to continue with the two hour workshop right up to the week of performance, a total of four months.[24]

It is clear from such an evaluation that Meyerhold's biomechanics do indeed uncover what is 'theatrical' in the theatre, and how it can be true to itself. The Russian critic, Nikolai Pesochinsky, observed how it may in fact transcend Stanislavsky's system: 'In the power of the [biomechanically trained] actor, there resides not only the imitation of ordinary life, but also the way towards its subconscious image-association, the embodiment of the metaphor.'[25] For Pitches, his biomechanical work showed how the training enabled the actor to 'maximise the theatrical potential of every moment in performance as the physical quality of the body itself is defamiliarised and estranged onstage via an approximation of the Meyerholdian grotesque'.[26] Because it has seemed strange in an age dominated by the naturalistic acting styles associated with Stanislavsky, Strasberg and their followers, the virtually limitless potential of biomechanics has long been obscured. Perhaps it will become apparent again in the new millennium.

Notes

1 Gladkov, Aleksandr (1997) *Meyerhold Speaks, Meyerhold Rehearses*, Amsterdam: Harwood Academic Publishers, p.104.
2 The most significant works in English about Meyerhold are: Braun, Edward (1995) *Meyerhold: a Revolution in Theatre*, London: Methuen; Hoover, Marjorie (1974) *Meyerhold – The Art of Conscious Theater*, Boston, MA: University of Massachusetts Press; Leach, Robert (1989) *Vsevolod Meyerhold*, Cambridge: Cambridge University Press; Rudnitsky, Konstantin (1981) *Meyerhold the Director*, Ann Arbor: Ardis.
3 Garin, Erast (1974) *S Meierkhol'dom*, Moscow: Iskusstvo, p. 34.
4 Reeve, F.D. (ed. and trans.) (1973) *Twentieth Century Russian Plays*, New York: Norton, pp. 174, 175.
5 Garin, Erast, op. cit., p. 30.
6 See Leach, Robert, op. cit., pp. 50–1 where the basic syllabus is reproduced.
7 Gladkov, Aleksandr, op. cit., p. 108.
8 Meyerhold, Vsevolod, Biomechanics course notes, 1921–2, quoted in Titova, G.V. (1995) *Tvorcheskii teatr i teatral'nyi konstrukivism*, St Petersburg: MKR, p. 198.
9 Ilyinsky, Igor (1961) *Sam o sebe*, Moscow: Iskusstvo, p. 154.
10 Eisenstein, S.M., Notes from a lecture by V.E. Meyerhold, 1921–2, quoted in Bushueva, Svetlana (ed.) (1992) *Russkoe akterskoe iskusstvo XX veka*, St Petersburg: Russian Institute of History of the Arts, p. 141.
11 Verigina, Vera, in Valenti, M.A. (ed.) (1967) *Vstrechi s Meierkhol'dom*, Moscow: VTO, p. 57.
12 Pitches, Jonathan (1997) 'The Actor's Perspective', in Shrubsall, Anthony and Pitches, Jonathan, 'Two Perspectives on the Phenomenon of Biomechanics in Contemporary Performance', *Studies in Theatre Production* 16, December, p. 101.
13 Gladkov, Aleksandr, op. cit., p. 104.
14 An example was the presentation on 12 February 1915, the programme of which is reproduced in Leach, Robert, op. cit., pp. 48–9.
15 Meyerhold's list of 'set roles' for the 1922 biomechanics class is published in Leach, Robert, op. cit., p. 75.
16 Ilyinsky, Igor, op. cit., p. 155.
17 Pitches, Jonathan, op. cit., pp. 105, 119.
18 Garin, Erast, op. cit., p. 35.
19 Levinsky's work may be seen on Arts Archive, the Third Archive, video number 10, *Meyerhold's Biomechanics: A Workshop*, Arts Documentation Unit, Exeter, 1997.
20 Garin, Erast, op. cit., p. 36.
21 The short ballet, *The Last Conversation*, was reconstructed by Sally Banes, and the performance recorded by her on video available from the Department of Theatre and Dance Studies at the University of Wisconsin-Madison, USA.
22 Garin, Erast, op. cit., p. 36.
23 Valenti, M.A., op. cit., p. 310.
24 Pitches, Jonathan, op. cit., p. 103.
25 Bushueva, Svetlana, op. cit., p. 104.
26 Pitches, Jonathan, op. cit., p. 125.

Bibliography

Benedetti, Jean (1988) *Stanislavsky: A Biography*, London: Methuen.

Bergen, Ronald (1997) *Sergei Eisenstein: A Life in Conflict*, London: Little, Brown.

Braun, Edward (ed.) (1969) *Meyerhold on Theatre*, London: Eyre Methuen.

—— (1995) *Meyerhold: a Revolution in Theatre*, London: Methuen.

Garin, Erast (1974) *S Meierkhol'dom*, Moscow: Iskusstvo.

Gladkov, Aleksandr (1997) *Meyerhold Speaks, Meyerhold Rehearses*, Amsterdam: Harwood.

Gourfinkel, Nina (1963) *Vsevolod Meyerhold – Le théâtre théâtral*, Paris: Gallimard.

Hoover, Marjorie (1974) *Meyerhold – The Art of Conscious Theater*, Boston, MA: University of Massachusetts Press.

Ilyinsky, Igor (1961) *Sam o sebe*, Moscow: Iskusstvo.

Leach, Robert (1989) *Vsevolod Meyerhold*, Cambridge: Cambridge University Press.

—— (1994) *Revolutionary Theatre*, London: Routledge.

Meyerhold, V.E. (1968) *Stat'i, pis'ma, rechi, besedy*, 2 vols, Moscow: Iskusstvo.

—— (1976) *Perepiska 1896–1939*, Moscow: Iskusstvo.

Picon-Vallin, Beatrice (1990) *Meyerhold*, Paris: CNRS.

Rudnitsky, Konstantin (1981) *Meyerhold the Director*, Ann Arbor: Ardis.

Schmidt, Paul (ed.) (1980) *Meyerhold at Work*, Austin, TX: University of Texas Press.

Valenti, M.A. (ed.) (1967) *Vstrechi s Meierkhol'dom*, Moscow: VTO.

van Gyseghem, Andre (1943) *Theatre in Soviet Russia*, London: Faber and Faber.

Zolotnitskii, David (1976) *Zori teatral'nogo oktyabrya*, Leningrad: Iskusstvo.

3 Jacques Copeau
The quest for sincerity

John Rudlin

The context

Jacques Copeau entered professional theatre as a practitioner relatively late in life: he was thirty-two years old when he first became involved in directing his own adaptation of Dostoevski's *The Brothers Karamazov*, and it was not until two years later that he finally relinquished a promising literary career for a hazardous theatrical one. In 1913, with the help of friends from the *Nouvelle Revue Français* (of which he was a founder and the first editor), he set up the Théâtre du Vieux Colombier on the left bank of the Seine. The building had previously been a variety hall called l'Athénée St-Germain. Copeau not only re-named it – with deliberate simplicity – after the street in which it sat, but also stripped out its tawdry hangings and gilded plaster-work, and eventually even its proscenium arch.

This *mise à nu* was typical of his approach to all aspects of French theatre as he found it, and he had observed more of it than most, having spent eight years as a drama critic for several Parisian magazines. In review after review he had pointed out the detrimental effects of the star system and its basis in commercial exploitation. Such a critique had been of little consequence, however, and he considered it was now time for remedial action. He called his self-appointed task 'Dramatic Renovation'. As in the restoration of a work of art, he intended a peeling away of layer upon layer of over-painting so as to reveal, say, a Molière underneath, unembellished and in its original colours:

> It is often said that I intend to break with tradition. The exact opposite is true. I am seeking to bring works closer to the 'true tradition' by freeing them from the contributions loaded on them for three centuries by the official actors [of the Comédie-Française]. The important tradition is the original one.[1]

Copeau was in a sense, therefore, a pre-modern post-modernist. He did not believe in '-isms', or artistic movements and cultural revolutions, but in a renewable, re-discoverable entity, the medium of theatre. It was not that he had an antiquarian interest in the old, but that he considered the theatre had fallen into such disrepair that it could no longer offer a solid platform on which new works could be presented. His literary collaborators, many of whom were uncertain whether to write novels or plays, were hopeful that he would provide them with a radical but elementary outlet for their essays in various theatrical genres. Copeau is, indeed, often instanced as the champion of respect for the text in the production process. Some of his early *mises en scène* seemed, in fact, to be little more than dramatic readings: but rather that, in his view, than actors offering phoney emotions and nineteenth-century tricks-of-the-trade, the whole gamut of what he called *cabotinage*:

> a disease that is not only endemic to the theatre. It's the malady of insincerity, or rather of falseness. He who suffers from it ceases to be authentic, to be human. He is discredited, unnatural. … I am not only speaking of the 'so-called stars', of those phenomena, those poor monsters whose deformities are too obvious to require description. I am speaking of all actors, of the most unimportant of them and of his [or her] slightest gesture, of the total mechanisation of the person, of the absolute lack of profound intelligence and true spirituality.[2]

It was to prove, however, a deal easier to strip encrustations off walls than actors. He chose his company with care, and took the actors away into the countryside, to his family house, Le Limon, near the tiny village of La Ferté-sous-Jarre in Seine et Marne to 'de-urbanise', as he called it. There they rehearsed in the open air with daily warm-ups based on 'rhythmical exercises' together with sight-reading and sports such as swimming, fencing and ball games. In this natural environment he sought a natural simplicity and spontaneity from his performers consisting of authenticity of gesture to impulse, well-spoken text and a sense of collective playfulness leading to a unity of dramatic purpose. By the end of their first season together, this preparatory work had undoubtedly paid off: Paris was queuing to get into the Vieux Colombier production of *Twelfth Night*. In 1917, with Parisian theatres closed for the duration of the war, Copeau reflected:

> Why did I succeed, in the eight months from October 19th 1913 to May 1914, in that Paris which is said to be blasé, in forcing on an ever-growing audience a repertoire made up entirely of French and foreign classical masterpieces and of the boldest plays of the present generation? It was because I was surrounded by fellow-workers, men and women, whose pure souls and minds remained unsullied.[3]

Regrettably, they did not remain so for much longer: some never returned from the war, some proved to have concealed their true nature, and others

Figure 3.1   Copeau: gymnastic class in the garden at Le Limon
Source: Photo from the Marie-Hélène Dasté collection

left the company. Six years later, in 1923, Copeau remarked to his assistant, Michel Saint-Denis, after rehearsal:

> Did you see them today? I always know in advance what they are going to do. They cannot get out of themselves; they love only themselves. They reduce everything to the level of their habits, their clichés, their affectations. They do not invent anything. It is all sheer imitation of imitation.[4]

Nevertheless, Copeau was never antipathetic to actors: in fact he became one himself, copying the practice of his acknowledged masters – Molière, Stanislavsky and Antoine – so that he was able to perceive the performer's difficulties from the inside out as well as, directorially, from the outside in. He described the underlying problem of acting as 'the freezing of the blood':

> The actor tells his arm 'Come on, now, arm, go out and make the gesture', but the arm remains wooden. The 'blood' doesn't flow; the muscles don't move; the body fights within itself; it's a terrifying thing. To someone on the outside this sounds like verbalisation or poetry. But we know, because we have often felt what it means to stand on the stage, we know that what you are doing is not what you mean to do, that you

meant to move your arm differently and you meant to come over to the audience with ease and warmth, and instead you're standing there like a stick.[5]

Yet even worse than such paralysis, in Copeau's view, was the over-facility of an actor such as David Garrick, who on a visit to Paris once sat in a drawing room and, for the amusement of friends including Denis Diderot, let his face run through a catalogue of emotions without, seemingly, feeling anything himself. In a preface to an edition of Diderot's *Paradoxe sur le Comédien*, Copeau wrote:

> the actor...applies his monstrous sincerity to being what he is not – not to expressing what he does not feel, but to feeling the make-believe.

> What upsets Hamlet the philosopher, as much as his other hellish apparitions, is the diverting of natural faculties in the human being to a fantastic use.

> The actor takes the risk of losing his...soul...which, having been too often upset by acting, too often carried away and offended by imaginary passions, contorted by artificial habits, feels irrelevant before reality. The whole being of the actor carries the stigmata of a strange relationship with the human world. When he returns among us, he looks as if he were coming from another world.

> An actor's profession tends to pervert him. It's the consequence of an instinct which pushes a man to abandon himself and live a pretence. And consequently it is a profession that people despise; they find it dangerous, immoral, and they condemn it for its mystery. This pharisaical attitude, which has not been eliminated in even the most tolerant societies, reflects a profound idea. That is, that the actor is doing something forbidden: he is playing with his humanness and making sport of it.[6]

Copeau continually demanded personal sincerity from his actors as an antidote to the *cabotinage* which continued to dominate the boulevards and the Comédie Française (whose Conservatoire, incidentally, offered the only available actor training in France before the opening of the Vieux Colombier School). He sometimes stayed behind after rehearsal to watch the carpenters working on stage. What they did seemed purposeful, rhythmical, incidentally sincere. Whereas the actions of the actors in rehearsal had been unnatural and forced – lacking in a sure tradition of craftsmanship.

Between 1917 and 1919 Copeau was able to re-assemble some of his company in New York. After the Great War, he re-opened the Vieux Colombier in Paris in 1920, but with some reluctance. By this time he was only too aware that he had compromised his quest for theatrical renovation by putting, as the French say, the cart before the oxen. What was needed was not remedial work with established actors during rehearsals, but preliminary work in an attached school where the problem of sincerity could be addressed before the protective devices of *cabotinage* became ingrained: a separate place in which to educate, rather than train (or re-train), actors from the earliest possible age. Such performers would be then free of the egotism required by the star system and would have their allegiance to an ensemble emergent from their common apprenticeship. Copeau called this unity of spirit and commonalty of technique '*Choeur*', which translates roughly as both 'choir' and 'chorus'. In order to get on with the business of 'dramatic renovation', however, he had had to give the opening of the Vieux Colombier Theatre precedence over its School.

In 1915, whilst the Vieux Colombier was closed, he had visited Edward Gordon Craig in his school in Venice (also shut for the duration of the war). He noted:

> In founding a school, Craig does not feel the same need as I do, does not pursue the same goal. He does not even pursue any immediate goal. He is not a theatre director. He is not trying to form a company of actors to fulfil the requirements of a repertoire. The actor does not interest him [but only] his theory of the 'Über-Marionette'.[7]

Craig told him that he had refused the directorship of the Théâtre des Arts in Paris unless the building could be closed to the public for ten to fifteen years whilst he prepared pupils for a renewed art of the theatre:

> You will ask how it is that I did not follow Craig's advice and open a School before opening a Theatre. I did not do it because I was not able to do it, because I had neither the authority nor the means to do so. If, in October 1913, I had proposed the founding of a School, no-one would have listened to me. ... Craig was being logical. If I had been so, I should have remained in oblivion. I was deeply convinced that it was imperative to exist first of all. We had to familiarise the public with our utopian ideas. We had to give proof of what a company of actors, mostly novices, could give in a year's work in common, under direction. ... So, it is true that I started by making a concession to life's demands. But it was through caution, not ignorance. ... The idea of the School and the idea of the Theatre are one and the same; they were conceived together and described as such in my *Attempt at Dramatic Renovation*.[8]

The Vieux Colombier School proper opened in December 1921 after an initial try-out period between December 1920 and June 1921, and a number of short-lived experiments previous to that, both in France and America. The director was the novelist and playwright, Jules Romains, and the principal teacher was Copeau's *aide*, *confidante* and *amante*, Suzanne Bing, who was up to that point a leading actress with the company. Copeau himself was rarely seen at the School, except for giving a semi-public lecture course, but was able to monitor progress via his association with Bing. In 1922 he took over the directorship of the School himself, but was still prevented by a punishing production and performance schedule from being more than an occasional presence. Although the School had three divisions, it was the 'apprentice group' which more and more dominated his horizon. It consisted initially of a group of six pupils,[9] of both sexes, from fourteen to twenty years old, apprenticed for a minimum of three years. At the end of that time the intention was for a new, even younger group to be initiated. The key course was 'Dramatic Instinct', taken by Suzanne Bing. Copeau's only brief to her was to follow her own instinct, with the proviso that the students spoke no dialogue before the third year. At the end of 1923 he summed up the project so far:

> The first year is particularly concerned with the acquisition of funda-
> mental concepts; the second with a common general and vocational
> cultural development; the third concentrates on specific abilities and
> individual excellence; performance work is undertaken for the first time.

> The teaching is based on *education of the body* (musical, gymnastic, acro-
> batic, dancing, games of strength and skill), with a progressive
> initiation into *craft skills* (drawing, modelling, decorative art, costume
> and props), *singing*, both choral and solo, *exercises in dramatic expression*
> (mask-work, physical games, physiognomy, mimicry), then to *improvisa-
> tion* (*plastique* and with dialogue), to *elocution*, *diction and declamation*, to
> *general education* and to *dramatic theory* (laws of dramatic expression,
> study of the great epochs, scenic arts and crafts).

> Ultimately, *free play* gives way to small-scale productions for which
> people are left entirely to their own devices, as creators and workers.
> Working and living communally, not excluding specialisation according
> to individual capabilities, has rapidly made a real little company…with
> healthy ideals, a solid professional working basis, a remarkable *esprit de
> corps* and self-sufficiency.[10]

Here is an example of how one of the 'small-scale productions' emerged. As a development of the 'Follow My Leader' game, masked students would take the expressive focus in turn, with the rest of the masks responding sympa-thetically – though not necessarily reduplicating what the lead mask was doing. Often no theme would be given and intuitive discoveries made through initially abstract improvisation led to simple situations, such as that of village women in a wash-house gossiping whilst working. One such involved the gathering of a crowd to welcome home a ship. The quality of this piece, amongst others, intensified Copeau's dilemma over his future priority – to devote his time to the school or the company:

> A group of pupils come to the front of the stage. They produce, despite their masked faces, a vision of a strand and of fisher-folk peering out upon a stormy sea. Their bodies create not alone their own emotion, but by a subtle fugue the heave of the water. A rowboat comes up. It is created by two actors in a rhythmic unison of propulsion. They leave their boat and mount the stairs to the apron. They have news of the drowning of a comrade: the news transfigures the group. The scene shifts to what is an interior of a fisher cottage. The wife and children await the master. The friends come in with the tragic tidings.[11]

What was to be the future of this little group? In a year's time, some might have been subsumed into the Vieux Colombier company, others would have had to make their own way. Little by little the intensity of their collective experience would have been dispersed and diluted and Copeau would have had to continue in rehearsal his daily struggle with the 'problem of the actor'. On 15 May 1924, two weeks after the first semi-public presentation of the work of the apprentice actors from the School, Jacques Copeau did a remarkable thing, for which he has often been castigated and rarely sufficiently lauded; he closed the Vieux Colombier which had seemed by now to be a success established *en permanence*. He himself now acted instinctively and with no forward planning:

> persuaded that our compromises with the times would produce nothing fertile, tired of standing still and having rejected the 'boulevard' theatre since 1913, we resolved to reject the so-called 'avant-garde' theatre, which is already infected by counterfeits and lies. At the end of 1924, we decided to risk everything. We wanted this 'renovation' that we had tried for so long to define and to understand, to at least mean something for ourselves. We started over again. We turned backwards in order to check what we knew, learn what we did not know, experiment with what we vaguely felt, no longer proceeding without our sense of vocation, doing something that was not true, but building, moderately but purely.[12]

By September of that year he was established in the Château de Morteuil, 10 kilometres from Beaune in the heart of Burgundy, with the apprentice group, together with four young professional actors from the company and their families, plus two more performers living nearby, one technician, and a poet.

The 'château' was merely a large, imposing farm house situated in a damp hollow. It was filthy, had no electricity and the stoves did not work. Copeau himself was mentally and physically exhausted, suffering the first effects of an undiagnosed and debilitating disease. But there he was, with his furniture, his library, his own (extended) family, the contents of the Vieux Colombier costume store, and an excited coterie of dramatic voyagers ready to discover a new world of theatrical initiative, 'exactly like old man Noah on his ark, surrounded by a crowd of young faces quizzing my feeble looks'.[13]

On 4 November *Le Patron*, as he was universally known, brought them all together for an introductory talk. Someone noted down what he said:

> He explained why he had come and that he had abandoned everything in order to do so. He said he regarded it as his last chance in life and that we should realise the responsibility that placed us under; our sense of that responsibility would show itself in a perfectionist attitude to work and a dignified life style. He laid great emphasis on the morality of the artist and the discipline needed to aspire to it. He had not obliged anyone to come: we were all volunteers and would have to accept poverty as a condition of discipleship. There would be no question of erasing our personalities, rather of disciplining, managing and conserving our individuality. We would need respect for others, discretion and deference; above all, sincerity, charity, intelligence and good humour. He himself was not infallible, but he would never do anything knowing it to be unjust. We would never bore him. His powers were all coming back to him. He went on to explain how these general principles would be worked out in practical detail in the rules for the school and for the house. He could only work if these rules were observed, since freedom would only come from regulation and observance.[14]

It is worth pausing to appreciate the courageous admixing of family and working lives, the proposed *kibbutzim*-style attempt to live, work and play *ensemble*. The high moral tone, however, reflected Copeau's own recent re-embracing of the Catholic faith at a practically Jansenist level. Unfortunately, his personal spiritual crisis was still deepening, the château was damp and unhealthy and the funds expected to underpin the enterprise did not materialise. At the moment of nadir, five months later in February 1925, Copeau dissolved the community. Nevertheless, a few of the actors proposed to stay on at their own expense and, together with those members of the apprentice group that were part of Copeau's own extended family, to form a troupe that would perform in the villages and towns of Burgundy. It was, however, to be a training company and not a school that occasionally performed. Nevertheless, *Le Patron* became gradually drawn into its work and took over the reins in June of that year, acting, directing and providing texts, whilst Suzanne Bing and others such as Jean Dasté were again largely responsible for the training programme. There were happier times and happier climes as the company, now named *Les Copiaus* after the local dialect pronunciation of *Le Patron*'s name, moved from the misty hollow to a large house on a sunny hillside in the nearby village of Pernand-Vergelesses. The renewed spirit of the *Copiaus*, he wrote, stemmed from their education in the 'dramatic instinct', which continued to be based on

> a conscientious examination of the principles of their craft and on a personal investigation of the elements of dramatic creation. Their teachers guide them towards those innermost discoveries that are necessary to the possession of any technique. Their sense of discipline consists of avoiding nothing, of never pretending, of never expressing or even thinking of anything that they cannot personally and authentically think and express. They apply themselves to finding principles within themselves, to implanting in their bodies, hearts and minds a direct experience of the laws of theatre and the feeling for their necessity. Thus, they are brought back to a naïve state that is not an artificial or literary attitude, but is their natural position before a world of possibilities where nothing is corrupted by habits of imitation, nor perverted by an acquired virtuosity. ... That is where they stand, and they aspire no further at the moment. Far from priding themselves on their sufficiency, they remain at the starting point. In my opinion this is a positive conquest.[15]

They played Molière farces, and adaptations by Copeau of Goldoni and Lope de Rueda. They also developed their own original pieces, increasingly depending on the new masks for commedia dell'arte which they had devised. Playing first at local fêtes and fairs, they gradually began to establish a national and international reputation. Perhaps their most typical piece was *L'Illusion* since, although ostensibly written by Copeau after Corneille and Fernando de Rojas, it contained large amounts of material culled from improvisation. The text reveals the extent to which their performance style was interpenetrated by a 'naïve', albeit idealised, representation of their individual and collective lives. In the prologue, Copeau playing The Actor virtually as himself, ruminating on the 'freezing of the blood', was joined on stage by The Actress, played by Suzanne Bing:

ACTRESS: If we remain silent too long, if we remain too long in the contemplation of our thoughts, shall we retain the power of some day giving birth to the Illusion? I am only an actress. I don't care very much for reality. I don't like myself very much. I don't wish to be invaded by everything I am. My passions, my desires, my jealousy, my deceits: give me back Comedy so its fire will consume them and purify me.
(*On this last line Maiène* [Copeau's daughter, Marie-Hélène] *enters.*)
ACTOR: I was trying to invent something...a manner of acting, full of thwarted movements, of young faces, of love and music, and for you, a character overflowing with poetry which would make you love me as I love you. But I am haunted by nothing but sombre images...

(*Maiène approaches the Actor.*)

MAIÈNE: Good morning.

ACTOR: (*Kissing her.*) Good morning, my child.

MICHEL [Saint-Denis, Copeau's nephew]: (*Entering.*) Good morning.

ACTOR: Good morning, youth.

VILLARD [Jean Villard, former Vieux Colombier actor]: (*Entering.*) Are you ready, Actor? The young people are waiting.

ACTOR: What do these young people want of me?…

MAIÈNE: To be what we are.

ACTRESS: Actors who live by Comedy, free and poor, from morning to night, kneading the dough of their craft with their own hands.

ACTOR: My young companions, my young companions, are you going to give me back the courage necessary for forming a world each day out of nothing, and hanging it above reality, a world which falls apart even as it is being created? Will you have the strength, the constancy, the saintly humility? … I had folded up my hope. My memories had faded away. Even the loveliest of them. … Why do you come to make my head swim, like birds in a garden in the month of May?[16]

After the prologue the action began with a youth called Petit Pierre (a derivative of the Pedrolino/Pierrot figure of the commedia dell'arte) joining the company to escape the wrath of his old father. Once on stage he is able to join in because the drama is improvised and there are no lines to learn. However, the father is in the audience – is their only audience, in fact. He watches his son – in the part of Calixte – fall in love with Melibée and win her (with supernatural assistance!). This all happens whilst Melibée's father, Plébère, is away. When he returns, the spectator/father leaves and the actors stop the play and argue as to the continuation of the plot. They decide that Plébère should deal with Calixte in a traditionally heavy-handed manner; the illusion is about to begin again when the father, who has not left after all, rushes on stage and lectures Plébère about the undesirability of parental harshness. Father and son are reconciled and go home. The actors pack up their effects, put them in their cart and leave singing the Copiaus' theme song.

The mood of the piece was almost whimsical, yet, in line with the desire not to have actors express any sentiments they had not themselves experienced, Copeau (Plébère) was making deliberate reference to the courtship of his own daughter, Maiène (Calixte), by Jean Dasté (Petit Pierre). Was this incorporation of reality into illusion the ultimate resolution of the quest for sincerity? Copeau called the piece 'pure theatre', neither a drama nor a comedy, but a theatre game. *The Times* of London noted:

> You feel as you watch them that they are indeed a community *de famille et d'amitié* who are earnestly bent on re-discovering the childhood – or is it the second childhood? – of the theatre. An odd quest that would soon

become tedious if pursued at length; but if we must have 'pure theatre', may it always come with the grace and polish of Pernand-Vergelesses.[17]

This astute appraisal presaged yet another severance in Copeau's career. The quest was not 'pursued at length'; the underlying tension between his desire to have Les Copiaus train for two-thirds of the year and their desire to

Figure 3.2   Jacques Copeau as Plébère in *L'Illusion*

perform as much as possible, capitalising on their new-found acclaim, became too great. Rather than compromise his vision of the Vieux Colombier School any further, he suddenly broke with the company in June 1929. Led by Michel Saint-Denis, the Copiaus became La Compagnie des Quinze and toured Europe with great success until the mid 1930s. The last phase of Copeau's career as freelance director, playwright and man of letters does not concern us here since he undertook no further actor training.

The training

Discovering dramatic principles within oneself, embracing the naïve without intellectual reservation, developing an authenticity of gesture to emotional impulse – how did Copeau attempt to unfreeze the blood of his apprentice actors without their becoming insincere? Here are some notes on some of the methods used by him, and by Suzanne Bing and others at his instigation.

Breath and text

Breathing, because it is an involuntary, essentially natural, life-sustaining activity, was for Copeau the *primum mobile* in his quest for gestural sincerity and vocal concord. The taking of voluntary control of the involuntary activity provided a resolution of the 'monstrous sincerity':

> Breathing controls everything.
>
> A voice which does not breathe becomes dull, collapses on itself and becomes sad. It flounders like someone drowning. It is dragged along by the text. It fails to dominate it and cannot articulate it either. It is breathing which ensures that our sensibility has the faculty to move in any direction. On it depends natural laughter and heartfelt emotion. From it comes nobility and authority, which give weight to one's presence. Inadequate breathing creates disorder. Vigorous breathing brings freedom.
>
> Reading out loud requires perpetual *tours de force* of breathing. Above all, when a dramatic text demands constant switching from one tone to another, from one movement to another, from one character to another, to different ages and sexes.
>
> One has continually to get a grip on oneself, to master one's own sincerity, change attitude and tonality, posture and rhythm, never let

oneself get wrapped up in the text. The gymnastics, say, of the play-wright.

Breathing makes lightness possible, which is one of the supreme virtues of the artist. That is to say that even in paroxysm one should not go to the end of one's powers: leave a little margin which allows the supposition that one could, if one had wanted, have gone further, that there is still a reservoir, a reserve. There is a sort of distinctiveness and reverence which is dictated by taste and made possible by lightness.

In this lightness there can be found a certain faculty of skimming over the text, a coming together of the eyes and of the mind in order to be always ahead of the tongue. A well-trained reader gives the impression of knowing the text by heart.

One does not know it by heart. That would be too easy. And it would be much less effective – one is saying by heart many things which one is understanding at that very moment, which one has just discovered and which are still fresh in one's mouth.[18]

During his first attempt at 'de-urbanisation' in the garden of Le Limon, Copeau, as we have seen, separated movement from text during the daily warm-up before rehearsal. Up to two hours were devoted to sight-reading out loud. Being himself a sought-after public reader, Copeau returned repeatedly to this exercise in his later schools. Often he would send two actors off with a non-dramatic work of literature, one to read and one to listen. This not only obliged the listener to listen with personal intent (and not just for their cues), but also to develop a critical faculty by which they learnt from the other's mistakes. For the reader, the alertness and speed of reaction required, often with the eyes reading a line ahead of what was actually being vocalised, helped break down habits of phrasing and inflection. And for both participants there was the slightly discomfiting knowledge that shortly it would be time to swap roles. The selection of suitable texts also extended the range of the participants' cultural awareness:

Our graduated exercises in reading out loud, at first sight, pursue a double goal of increasing intellectual flexibility at the same time as perfecting vocal articulation. In order to read well, whilst at the same time paying attention to diction and to the register of one's voice, one needs continual mental alertness, never to 'let oneself go', to understand quickly and to express oneself with precision. Thus actors have the possibility of avoiding their natural penchant for falling into ready-made inflexions, and also avoiding the difficulty they usually have, that of a slowness, a certain laziness in getting into the spirit of the text, something which obliges the director, during the first rehearsals, to pre-masticate all their dialogue for them ...

A good sight-reading, devoid of affectation, that is the open ground on which to build a healthy interpretation [of a role].[19]

Natural gymnastics

In referring to the interplay of mind and voice as 'gymnastic', Copeau was only too aware that the oral (and aural) training of sight-reading was the adduction of the literary man. A physical complement was needed. As a stop-gap at Le Limon, he tried to balance verbal exercises with physical ones. As noted above, daily rhythmical limbering was taken by one of the actors, Roger Karl, and sporting activities were encouraged. What Copeau ultimately sought, however, was not just a means of attaining a desirable level of fitness, balance, control and physical confidence, but a physical training which would be integral to the development of the actor as instrument. After a visit to Jacques Dalcroze in 1915, he tried to adopt the latter's system of eurythmics. But by 1921, after experimenting with three different teachers, he decided that it was 'another language, a speciality and consequently a deformation. [Eu]rhythmics leads to a personal idolatry of the body.'[20] Eventually the Vieux Colombier School adopted Georges Hébert's method of 'natural gymnastics', designed primarily to develop strength and flexibility for sporting rather than dramatic activities. However, thanks to monitor Jean Dorcy,[21] the method gradually became geared to the students' needs:

At first these exercise sessions were poorly attended and quite limited. Dorcy finally complained that they were doing nothing but jumping, and did his best to expand the program. As class leader in the absence of M. Moine [Hébert's instructor], Dorcy made sure also that students did more than the exercises they did best. Some of these exercises were: marching, leaping over obstacles, balance-bars. Out-door work at St. Cloud once a week was more varied and rigorous, including jogging, high-jump contests, push-ups, throwing a medicine ball, obstacle courses, military endurance exercises, and even some trapeze work.[22]

When work began again in November 1923, it was largely Dorcy who worked with the group. All noted improved agility and flexibility and balance, acquiring a 'relaxed tonality through work with solid obstacles'.[23] Later, in Burgundy, it was Jean Dasté who took over the role of monitor; later still Dasté's own scion, Jacques Lecoq, used the Hébert method in his school in Paris: 'pull, push, climb, walk, run, jump, lift, carry, attack, defend, swim. These actions trace a physical circuitry in sensitive bodies in which emotions are imprinted.'[24]

Lecoq himself came from a sporting background, and his is perhaps a larger claim for the potential of the method than Copeau would have believed possible. He would certainly have found such a development of it desirable.

Corporeal music

Music was a mystery to Copeau, which is perhaps why he continually sought to incorporate it in the training. Students at the Vieux Colombier School learned choral and solo singing, reading music and the basics of an individual instrument. However, Copeau did not want any part of the instruction to be an island, a specialism. He intended music to be integrated with movement studies, primarily with the dance course given by Mlle Lamballe.[25] This class was begun in late November and was given somewhat sporadically. Mlle Lamballe worked with the students on classical ballet positions and exercises, as well as steps like the *pas de bourrée*, *saut du chat*, slides, *jetés*, and dances like the minuet and gavotte. It was Suzanne Bing, as usual, who took on the task of applying such dance concepts to dramatic expression. She often held her course in 'Musique Corporelle' just after ballet class, discussing and working with such concepts as time and duration, space, shape, force, speed, volume, intensity and weight.[26]

Bing began by focusing on breathing and filling a particular duration with breath. Next she added movements, to be accomplished in the same duration. These simple exercises grew into movements on beats, with more complex assignments given to fill time sequences with improvised dialogue or mimed action. She then had the students analyse and explore the relationships between emotional quality of a gesture and its time of preparation – first with breathing, then movement, using various parts of the body, stressing imagination, continuity and unity of direction. This method of developing a gesture was then continued in ensemble movement and in movement sequences. Later they played 'Follow my Leader' in order to become instinctive at performing actions together within the same time sequence.

One of Bing's exercises was to begin an action and then interrupt it with a brief movement. The students then worked to juxtapose two different tempos – the arms keeping the beat whilst the feet walked in a circle on the measure, accompanying themselves with the voice instead of music. Examples of everyday phenomena were found to illustrate different tempos: a sewing machine as quick, percussive, a lift as sustained. Early in the New Year rhythms were introduced based on regular intervals as exemplified in drawing, poetry and prose, architecture and music. The group clapped different rhythms, imitating each other, then putting poly-rhythms together. Clapping was then replaced by simple verbal exclamation – 'Ah!' for example. Subsequently they played musical charades, using rhythms whose musical qualities were simple and clear – then afterwards they had to guess what the music was. They discussed the effects of quality, duration, silence, and made up rhythmic examples to illustrate each.

Group compositions were performed in silence, then with accompanying piano music – an addition which highlighted plastic rather than the dramatic qualities. These were followed by a study of dynamics – visualising loudness and softness in space for example. Eventually these exercises were used in the creation of dances. Exercises in 'taking possession of space' were also an important element, to which was added expansion in sound and the exploration of shapes – individually and in a group. Later they did exercises related to obedience to a particular rhythm, standing in a circle and using a ball thrown in patterns to reinforce the concept. Then came study of spoken phrases and the analysis of differing meanings conveyed through the use of pause. In application they worked with three different types of phrases: spoken, in movement and musical – discussing the different means of differentiating between phrases, accents, silence, contrasts. For movement phrasing, elements to use might be: changes in direction, weight, duration, level, using different parts of the body. A complex exercise in the use of space exploring phrases and sentences was performed with three groups: the first ran and stopped in position; the second group took a complementary position; the third group completed the figure. They then tried the exercise with their eyes closed.

Thus Bing utilised the study of a particular style of movement – ballet – to help students discover more general characteristics of style that they could apply to their own work. Using an approach somewhat reminiscent of Laban and modern dance exploration, Bing stressed both analysis and play. Work was often facilitated by music on the piano, accompanying exercises such as the mirror game or the miming of opening a door. The students discovered the difference between choreographed movement to music, or dance, and that which is performed with an internal rhythm and no music, i.e. corporeal mime. Music gave their movements greater purity and abstraction, but often blurred the dramatic sense. Bing was sometimes bothered by the students' inability to concentrate on pure movement and their insistence on using anecdotal material. They sometimes lost sight of an objective she had proposed, or did not experiment enough with abstract concepts. She noted, incidentally, that Copeau's occasional presence seemed to paralyse the students – a freezing of the blood again![27]

Neutrality

'*The point of departure of an expression.* The state of repose, of calm, of relaxation or decontraction, of silence or simplicity.'

> To start from silence and calm. That is the first point. An actor must know how to be silent, to listen, respond, keep still, begin a gesture,

develop it, return to stillness and silence, with all the tones and half tones that those actions imply.[28]

Such a state of neutrality should not be construed as being negative, it has nothing to do with being neutered. It means simply 'Putting oneself in a state of readiness' (*Décontraction préalable*).

Much more is known today about relaxation than in the 1920s and to offer a résumé of Copeau's practice would be of academic interest only. Were he working today, I am personally convinced that he would borrow from the disciplines of Yoga and T'ai Chi, provided that they did not leave a stylistic imprint on the performer. Suffice, then, to say that from a state of maximum possible relaxation in the whole body (i.e. one in which phasic muscles receive no unnecessary support from voluntary ones), Copeau's students learned to isolate energy in different parts of themselves. That area was then encouraged to lead a particular expression.[29] The back, for example, was used to express astonishment, disquiet, grief-strickenness, anger, remorse, courageousness or the regaining of hopefulness. The face (as simply another part of the body) was used to express subtle gradations of emotion which the rest of the apprentice group tried to guess by name. This exercise was not meant to emulate Garrick's party tricks – the return to the neutral state between expressions was considered crucial to the honest development of the next intention. After one such session in silent improvisation Copeau concluded that:

> There are two kinds of manifestations in an actor's playing: discontin-uous manifestations that seem intentional, phoney, theatrical, and continuous manifestations that give an impression of modesty and internal sincerity, of real life and power. Continuity and slow pace are conditions of powerful and sincere playing.[30]

Slow motion was henceforward incorporated in the training. As usual, it was Bing who developed the detail of the exercise. After the state of decontrac-tion (which is physical), she proposed mental states: pre-formation of the expressive idea; suspense, i.e. not immediately giving in to the impulse; then attack, i.e. a complete commitment of the body to the pre-formation; then the return to the neutral state.

As an aid to the discovery of the neutral state, the neutral mask has been developed by Jean Dasté, Jacques Lecoq and others from Copeau's use of the 'noble' mask, outlined below. I have sometimes had students approach me to 'borrow some of those neutral masks for the show we're doing'. The whole point of such masks is that they are not expressive and have no performative validity. They afford a tool with which to deepen an under-standing of the neutral state, which in itself is only a foundation and no longer visible as part of the expressive edifice of performance. The absence of such a foundation is precisely why Copeau wanted a school attached to his theatre, but separate from it.

The noble mask

Copeau became aware of the potential of the mask, both in actor training and, ultimately, in performance during his visit to Craig. It made its appearance in his work almost by accident – whilst rehearsing a scene at the Vieux Colombier he despaired of an actress who found herself repeatedly physically blocked during a scene and unable to move – a literal freezing of the blood. Copeau took his handkerchief and covered her face, noting that her body was immediately released as an expressive instrument. It was her face which had been making all the effort. This experiment was immediately put to work in the School, using stockings as well as pieces of cloth. Jean Dasté later noted:

> When the face is masked or hidden, one is less timid, feels freer, more daring and insincerity is quickly apparent. ... The mask demands both a simplification and an extension of gestures; something forces you to go to the limit of the feeling being expressed.[31]

An invaluable tool had been discovered to aid the work on neutrality. Eventually the students made their own 'noble' masks based on maquettes of their own faces, modelled in clay to remove individual characteristics and regularise the features. Copeau called them 'noble' after the expressionless masks worn by the aristocracy up till the eighteenth century when wishing to pass incognito in the street. In order to enhance rather than interfere with the neutral state, a ritual was developed for putting on the mask:[32]

(a) Well seated in the middle of the chair, not leaning against the back of the seat. Legs spaced to ensure perfect balance. Feet flat on the ground.

(b) Stretch the left arm horizontally forward, shoulder high; it holds the mask, hanging by its elastic. The right hand also stretches out, thumb holding the chin, index and second finger seizing the opening of the mouth.

(c) Stretch out the elastic over the top of the head and put the mask on the forehead.

(d) Lower the mask over the face.

(e) Simultaneously inhale, close the eyes and shoe the mask.

> In all this, only the arms and hands are active. They carry out the small movements necessary to fasten the mask on the face, arrange the hair, verify the proper adjustment of the elastic, so that the mask will cling well and hold without slackness.[33]

(f) Simultaneously, breathe and place forearms and hands on the thighs. The arms, as well as the elbows, touch the torso, fingers not quite reaching the knees.

(g) Open the eyes, inhale, then simultaneously close the eyes, exhale and bend the head forward. While bending the head, the back becomes slightly rounded. In this phase, arm, hands, torso, and head are completely relaxed.

(h) It is here, in this position, that the clearing of the mind occurs. Repeat mentally or utter, if this helps, during the necessary time (2, 5, 10, 25 seconds): 'I am not thinking of anything, I am not thinking of anything...' If, through nervousness, or because the heart was beating too strongly, the 'I am not thinking of anything' is ineffective, concentrate on the blackish grey, steel, saffron, blue, or other shade found inside the eye, and extend it indefinitely in thought: almost always, this shade blots out conscious thought.

(i) Simultaneously, inhale and sit upright, then exhale and open your eyes.

Now the masked actor, sufficiently recollected, can be inhabited by characters, objects, thoughts; he is ready to perform dramatically.

When the actor is not seated but standing, nothing changes; however (see h), the back should not be rounded, for the weight of the head would draw the torso forward.

All these phases are for beginners. Later, the technique may be altered. But...it should never be neglected.[34]

Once 'in' the noble mask, students were given initially very simple transactions to explore, simultaneously and without reference to each other. Words or phrases were called out and the students, after pre-forming and suspending the impulse, would let the mask 'attack', moving in slow motion to an intuitively felt physical position which expressed this word or phrase. They then held that position for a brief moment to confirm the impression before returning to a de-contracted, neutral stance.

The first exercises were composed of sets of tasks dealing with the exploration of the five senses. Then the students were asked to let the mask handle imaginary objects, making them as concrete and specific as possible by exploring weight, texture, shape and function. Next, they had to experience certain physical sensations such as fatigue, heat and cold. Then they were asked to explore actively the five senses more fully, followed by an exercise in which they were deprived of one sense, such as being deaf. Next came simple physical actions such as throwing, lifting and pulling objects. Finally they were required to give bodily expression to some simple emotions.

The second set of exercises involved making combinations from the first set. For example, a simple emotion was combined with a simple physical activity, or an exploration of one of the senses was paired with the handling of an imaginary object. In a third set of exercises, the students were asked to physically represent inanimate objects. Following this came the final and most difficult exercises: the embodiment of moral and abstract ideas such as 'glory' or 'strength'.[35]

From these silent exercises the students went on to non-verbal sound explorations in the mask. The voice was used 'not in speaking or in singing but in a sort of primitive gamut of autopoetic sounds. ... The voice, at the beginning, is a kind of arabesque like the castanets of the classic Spanish dance.'[36] These sounds were later developed into 'grummelots' – elements of gibberish language which have all the phrasing and inflection of real speech, but do not turn a physical improvisation into a word-driven one.

Copeau perceived spontaneity as another key to collective creativity. Working in this case without allowing time for premeditation, he would call out a word such as 'Paris!', 'Storm!', 'Goal!', etc. The (unmasked) students 'immediately, without an instant of reflection, had to react by one or more gestures, by a state of being, by a sequence of movements, etc.'.[37]

Play and games

Such exercises in spontaneity bring me to the last area of Copeau's pedagogical practice that there is space to consider, which is arguably one that should have been discussed first, since without it the spirit of élan and freedom of expression which enlightened the work of the apprentice group cannot be understood. In the first draft prospectus for the School he wrote:

> It is through play, in which children imitate more or less consciously all human activities and sentiments, which is for them a natural path towards artistic expression and for us a living repertoire of reactions of the most authentic kind – it is through play that we wish to construct, not a system, but an educational experience. We seek to develop the child, without deforming him or her, through the means which the child provides, towards which he or she senses the greatest inclination, through play, in playing, in games which are imperceptibly disciplined and exalted.

Since he was unable to take children from as early an age as he would have liked, when the play instinct was still naturally present, he compromised by working with adolescents and tried to re-open for them the door to the enchanted garden. Again, it was Suzanne Bing to whom he handed the key. During the Vieux Colombier's stay in New York, from 1917 to 1919, she had taught at The Children's School which embraced the latest educational theories to do with freedom of choice and creative expression for children of primary-school age. There she used, in particular, games based on animal mimicry and later took the same classes in the Vieux Colombier School without making any adjustment for the greater age of the pupils. Today there are any number of books on the use of dramatic games in the classroom and elsewhere, right up to their political and therapeutic use in the work of Augusto Boal. In the face of such sophistication, any listing here of the actual exercises used by Bing would seem simplistic. The important thing to note is that Copeau sought to gain nothing from play a priori except those things which belong to it naturally.

> We observe the children at play. They teach us. Learn everything from children. Impose nothing on them. Take nothing away from them. Help them in their development without their being aware of it. All this is difficult to describe because it is still in a state of experimentation, nothing dogmatic. Inspired from life and human contact. Full of promise. Labour of patience already begun. Aim for making the actor not only the medium, but the source of all dramatic inspiration.[38]

He said that in 1917. Throughout the period of the Vieux Colombier School and of the *Copiaus*, he created a culture where imaginative play informed the work and did, as he had promised, lead to 'small-scale productions for which people are left entirely to their own devices, as creators and workers'.[39]

As much as he believed in *laisser jouer*, however, he could not bring himself to let it happen without absenting himself altogether. Bing could do it for him, but in the end he let her go too. In 1929 she, and the Copiaus, were indeed left to their own, separate, devices. Copeau took his ball and stayed at home. He had always maintained that his work was provisional and preparatory: prophetic, one might say, rather than messianic. It may be that the future came too close, or that he had a temperamental preference for disillusion and preferred to leave it to others to claim the domain which he had helped to discover.

Of his actors, Charles Dullin and Louis Jouvet went on to become the most influential French directors of the inter-war years. Of his pupils, Jean Dasté carried the banner of decentralisation in his work as director of the Comédie de St Etienne, whilst Michel Saint-Denis continued the pedagogy, founding the London Theatre Studio and The Old Vic School, the National Theatre School of Canada and the Drama Division of the Juillard School, New York. Following another star, Etienne Decroux became the father of modern corporeal mime. Copeau's real legacy, however, has been to put the playfulness back into plays and the quest for sincerity back into playing them. This quest has been disseminated latterly throughout the world via countless of his and Suzanne Bing's drama exercises and their derivatives.

Notes

1 From 'Comment mettre Molière en scène', interview in *Lecture pour tous*, January 1922; translated in *Copeau, Texts on Theatre* (1990), edited and translated by John Rudlin and Norman Paul, London: Routledge, p. 145.

2 From an address to the Washington Square Players, New York, 20 April 1917, Rudlin and Paul, op. cit., p. 253.

3 *Vanity Fair*, April 1917, p. 49.

4 Michel Saint-Denis (1982) *Training for the Theatre*, New York: Theatre Arts, London: Heinemann, p. 31.

5 Lee Strasberg (1965) *Strasberg at the Actors Studio*, ed. Robert H. Hethmon, New York: Viking Press (quoted in T. Cole and H.K. Chinoy (eds) (1970) *Actors on Acting*, New York: Crown, p. 624.

6 From *Réflexions d'un comédien sur le Paradoxe de Diderot*, Plon, 1929, translated in Rudlin and Paul, op. cit., pp. 72–3.

7 From 'L'Ecole du Vieux Colombier', unpublished notebook, translated in Rudlin and Paul, op. cit., p. 21.

8 From an unpublished notebook 'L'École du Vieux Colombier No. 2', 1915–20, translated in Rudlin and Paul, op. cit., p. 28. 'An Attempt at Dramatic Renovation' is the correct English translation of Copeau's 1913 manifesto for Le Vieux Colombier, 'Un Essai de Rénovation Dramatique'.

9 In 1922–3 the number went up to twelve, then shrank again to nine in 1923–4.

10 From: 'L'Ecole du Vieux Colombier', in the Vieux Colombier programme for *La Locandiera*, January 1924, translated in Rudlin and Paul, op. cit., pp. 46–7.

11 Waldo Frank (1925) 'Copeau Begins Again', *Theatre Arts Magazine*, IX (September), pp. 585–90.

12 From an open letter to the Swiss press, May 1928, translated in Rudlin and Paul, op. cit., pp. 168–70.

13 Copeau (1931) *Souvenirs du Vieux Colombier*, Nouvelles Editions Latines, Paris, p. 106.

14 These notes are taken from *Le Journal de Bord des Copiaus* (1974), Paris: Gontard, pp. 45–6.

15 Letter to the Swiss press, op. cit.

16 Translated from the manuscript in the *Fonds Copeau* of the Bibliothèque de l'Arsenal, Paris, in Rudlin and Paul, op. cit., pp. 172–6.

17 30 November 1928.

18 Copeau, quoted in 'Copeau l'Eveilleur', ed. Pavis and Thomasseau (1995) *Buffoneries* 34: 15–16, no source given.

19 From Copeau's first plan for the Vieux Colombier School, 1916.

20 Undated notes in Copeau's Journal, translated in Rudlin and Paul, op. cit., p. 67.

21 Jean Dorcy, later to found the Danse et Culture School, whose pupils included Marcel Marceau, was an actor in his mid-twenties, attached to another division of the Vieux Colombier School.

22 Barbara Anne Kusler (1974) 'Jacques Copeau's Theatre School, 1920–1929', Doctoral thesis, University of Wisconsin, p. 133.

23 Livre de bord, quoted Kusler, op. cit., p. 144.

24 Jacques Lecoq (1997) *Le Corps Poétique*, Paris: Actes Sud, p. 82.

25 Lucienne Lavalle, of the Opera Ballet Company, was first in her class in 1923. She danced such roles as Coppelia, the cat in *Sleeping Beauty*. In Paris and on tour she was especially cited for her technique in *Romeo and Juliet*. She later taught at the Paris Opera.

26 This weekly class lasted from November 1921 to June 1922.

27 For this section I am indebted to Barbara Anne Kusler, op. cit., pp. 132–3. She in turn relies on the class notes taken by Bing and Marie-Hélène Copeau, which are not available to me at the time of writing.

28 *Notes sur le Métier d'un Comédien*, notes taken from the diary and writings of Jacques Copeau by Marie-Hélène Dasté (Paris: Michel Brient, 1955, p. 47), translated in John Rudlin (1986) *Jacques Copeau*, Cambridge, p. 46.

29 This study of 'isolations' was later greatly to be developed by Copeau's pupil, Etienne Decroux.

30 Rudlin, op. cit.

31 Jean Dasté, from an article for the programme of the *Cahiers de la Maison de la Culture de Grenoble*, 3 November 1945, translated Rudlin and Paul, op. cit., p. 236.

32 The French word used was '*chausser*', meaning to put on a shoe. This has no single equivalent in English and the usually adopted translation of 'shoeing the mask' to my mind conjures up images of horse hooves and farriers.

33 A conflation of notes by Jean Dorcy and Jan Doat, as suggested by Sears Eldredge (1975) 'Masks: Their Use and Effectiveness in Actor Training Programs', Doctoral thesis, University of Michigan, 1975, p. 179.

34 Jean Dorcy (1975) *The Mime*, trans. Speller and Marceau, London: White Lion, pp. 108–9.

35 *Précis* from Jan Doat (1944) *L'Expression Corporelle du Comédien*, Paris: Bordas, pp. 53–5.

36 Waldo Frank (1925) 'Copeau Begins Again', *Theatre Arts Magazine*, IX (September), pp. 585–90.

37 Letter from Marie-Hélène Dasté to Barbara Anne Kusler, December 1973.

38 From Copeau's notes for his third lecture (given in French) at The Little Theatre, New York, 'L'Ecole du Vieux Colombier', 19 March 1917, translated in Rudlin and Paul, op. cit., p. 12.

39 See note 10.

Bibliography

Borgal, Clément (1960) *Jacques Copeau*, Paris: l'Arche.

Doisy, Marcel (1954) *Jaques Copeau ou l'Absolu dans l'Art*, Paris: Le Cercle du Livre.

Frank, Waldo (1918) *The Art of the Vieux Colombier*, Paris, New York: Editions de la NRF; reprinted in his *Salvos*, New York: Boni and Liveright, 1924.

Kurtz, Maurice (1950) *Jacques Copeau, Biographie d'un Théâtre*, Paris: Nagel.

Lerminier, Georges (1953) *Jacques Copeau, le Réformateur*, Paris: PLF.

Levaux, Léopold (1933) *Jacques Copeau*, Louvain–Paris: Rex.

Paul, Norman H. (1979) *Bibliographie Jacques Copeau*, Société des Belles Lettres, Université de Beaune.

Pavis, Patrice and Thomasseau, Jean-Marie (eds) (1995) 'Copeau l'Eveilleur', *Buffoneries* 34: 15–16.

Rudlin, John (1986) *Jacques Copeau*, Cambridge: Cambridge University Press.

Anthologies, Catalogues

Jacques Copeau et le Vieux Colombier (1963) Catalogue for exhibition at Bibliothèque Nationale.

Bing, S., Copeau, J. and Chancerel, L. (1974) *Le Journal de bord des Copiaus*, Gontard, Denis (ed.), Paris.

Cabanis, A. (ed.) (1976) *Registres II. Molière*, Paris: Gallimard.

Dasté, Marie-Hélène and Maistre Saint-Denis, Suzanne (eds) (1979) *Registres I. Appels*, Paris: Gallimard.

—— (1979) *Registres III. Les Registres du Vieux Colombier I*, Paris: Gallimard.

—— (1984) *Registres IV. Les Registres du Vieux Colombier II, America*, Paris: Gallimard.

—— (1993) *Registres V. Les Registres du Vieux Colombier III, 1919–1924*, Paris: Gallimard.

Rudlin, John and Paul, Norman H. (eds and trans.) (1990) *Jacques Copeau, Texts on Theatre*, London and New York: Routledge.

4 Michael Chekhov on the technique of acting

'Was Don Quixote true to life?'

Franc Chamberlain

The context

As an outstanding actor and author of one of the best actor training manuals ever published in the European tradition,[1] Michael Chekhov (1891–1955) is one of the key figures in twentieth-century theatre. His ability to transform himself onstage was celebrated by some of the major directors of the century, including Stanislavsky, Vakhtangov, Reinhardt, and Meyerhold: whilst his practical advice continues to inspire actors through his writings and through schools in Russia, Lithuania, Holland, Denmark, Germany, Great Britain and the USA.

The nephew of the playwright Anton Chekhov, Michael Chekhov was only seven years old when Nemirovich-Danchenko and Stanislavsky formed the Moscow Art Theatre (MAT) in 1898, including his uncle's play *The Seagull* in their first season. In a diary entry written in the same year, Vsevolod Meyerhold recorded a conversation between some of the MAT actors and Anton Chekhov. Bemused to hear of plans to introduce country-side noises offstage in *The Seagull* in order to make the environment more 'realistic', the playwright laughed, asserting that the theatre was art and that the additions were superfluous.[2] Stanislavsky's approach, at this time, was to attempt to create as detailed an imitation of life onstage as possible.

By contrast, Meyerhold, inspired by the symbolist plays and theories of Maeterlinck and Bryusov, was interested in the idea of a stylised theatre which emphasised 'atmosphere' or 'mood' over naturalistic detail. Atmosphere, for Meyerhold, was generated by the actors and, despite his reservations regarding Stanislavsky's concern for naturalistic production values, he felt that the MAT actors had managed to evoke the appropriate mood of *The Seagull*. The importance of the actor as a creative artist was picked up by Bryusov, who argued that it was the theatre's task to assist the actor in manifesting this creativity in a way that would be understood by the audience. Working with these symbolist influences for a decade, Meyerhold attempted several productions of Maeterlinck, searching for a technique which would use movement as 'plastic music' in order to construct an 'external depiction of an inner experience'.[3]

The search for a new approach to acting which would emphasise the creativity of the actor was being undertaken across Europe. Even Craig, whose polemical attack on actors is well known, argued that actors should 'create...a new form of acting' in order to revitalise their art.[4] Stanislavsky had always aimed to break the fixed habits of actors and to develop acting as a creative art. His failures to stage Maeterlinck in 1904 and 1908, however, together with his resistance to the proposed solutions of Meyerhold and Craig, led him to explore new directions by setting up the experimental First Studio under Sulerzhitsky in 1912.

The themes of atmosphere, actors' creativity, physicalisation of inner experience, and the question of style, which were to become important elements in Michael Chekhov's method, can be seen to have been part of the theatrical milieu for over a decade – well before 1912, when he joined the MAT. As part of the First Studio, Chekhov developed his skills under the tutelage of Sulerzhitsky, who instructed the actors in the basic elements of Stanislavsky's method: relaxation, concentration, naiveté, imagination, communication and affective memory. Chekhov was eventually to reject Stanislavsky's emphasis on memory but the other aspects of the Studio's work were to find a place in his own method, although somewhat transformed.

Between 1912 and 1918 Chekhov developed his reputation as a talented actor in a number of roles, despite occasional conflicts with Stanislavsky and some of the other members of the company. A part of the problem appears to have been the expression of his creativity as an actor. In one of his earliest roles at the MAT, in *Le malade imaginaire*, Stanislavsky criticised Chekhov for having too much fun with the role, and on another occasion Stanislavsky held him up before the rest of the company as 'the ulcer of our theatre'.[5] It was in Boleslavsky's production of *The Wreck of the 'Good Hope'* (1913), however, that Chekhov first attracted critical attention when he transformed the minor role of Kobe from a stereotypical 'idiot fisherman' into a 'sincere and morbid seeker of the truth'.[6] When his interpretation of the role was challenged on the grounds that it was not what the playwright had intended, Chekhov asserted his creative individuality by claiming that he had found the 'true' character by going beyond both text and author.

By 1918, despite his success at the Studio, Chekhov's life was falling apart. He was drinking heavily, his wife divorced him and took their daughter away, his mother died, and he was sinking into suicidal depression. He was unable to act, and on one occasion left the stage in the middle of a performance. Interpreting his extreme state as a spiritual crisis, Chekhov began to investigate the anthroposophy or spiritual science of Rudolf Steiner, which was attracting the interest of a number of Russian artists including Andrei Bely and Wassily Kandinsky. Steiner, like Kierkegaard and others before him, drew a distinction between the everyday self with which we normally identify and the higher ego which is our more authentic and creative self. Anthroposophy enabled Chekhov to gain a distance on his personal troubles and to put them in a different perspective from which he saw himself as a 'drunken egotist'.[7] He began an intense study of Steiner's teachings as a means of liberation from his self-indulgent and self-destructive tendencies. Steiner's theories were to form the basis of Chekhov's personal belief and would have a significant impact on his theory of the actor.

It is after 1918 that Chekhov comes out most strongly against Stanislavsky's use of personal experience and emotion, arguing that this, in effect, binds the actor to the habits of the everyday self which was not the way to liberate the actor's creativity. Furthermore Chekhov argued that the emphasis should be on the character's feelings, not the actor's – not 'how would I feel?' but 'what does the character feel?' – and that this would enable the actor to transform into the character rather than reducing the character to the personality of the actor. Chekhov gives a very good example of what he means by this. In a scene where a character's child is ill, the Stanislavskian actor will focus on the child and see 'only the things seen by the character residing within him'.[8] The Chekhovian actor, on the other hand, will focus on the character and observe how the character responds to the child. Chekhov believed that Steiner's higher ego, which he interpreted as the 'artist in us that stands behind all of our creative processes',[9] was the key to this approach. Chekhov eventually identified four ways in which a sensitivity to this higher ego would help the actor's work: (1) it was the source of the actor's 'creative individuality', which explained why different actors played the same role differently, and which helped the actor to go beyond the text; (2) it was possessed of an ethical sense which enabled the actor to feel the conflict between 'good' and 'evil' in the play; (3) it enabled a sensitivity to the audience's perspective on the play in performance; and (4) it brought a sense of detachment, compassion, and humour into the actor's work by conferring freedom from the 'narrow, selfish ego'.[10]

Chekhov also drew on Steiner's explorations into movement and speech through eurythmy and his theories of speech as invisible gesture, and both found their way into his system.[11] Once the work of Steiner was added to the influences from the Moscow Art Theatre and his own reflections on the actor's art, Chekhov began to construct a coherent system of training that was distinct from Stanislavsky's. Between 1918 and 1921 he ran workshops in his flat in Moscow to explore the possibilities opened up by his new interests, although these experiments were only popular with a minority, and financial difficulties led to the closure of the workshop. Chekhov's recovery from his illness led to his blossoming as an actor from 1921 to 1927. His performance of a number of major roles, both at the First Studio (which became the Second Moscow Art Theatre in 1924) and at the MAT, confirmed his exceptional talent.

During his time at the First Studio, Chekhov built a strong friendship with Evgeny Vakhtangov, who was initially very taken by Stanislavsky's notion of emotion memory, but who eventually argued for a combination of

Stanislavsky and Meyerhold's thinking, which he called 'fantastic realism'. Vakhtangov felt that Stanislavsky was too attached to naturalism and missed the significance of theatricality in the theatre, whilst Meyerhold's fascination with stylised physicality had led him to ignore the importance of feelings – it was necessary to combine both approaches to create a theatre which was both 'live' and 'theatrical'.[12] One of Chekhov's major acting triumphs was when he appeared in the leading roles in Vakhtangov's production of Strindberg's *Erik XIV* at the First Studio in 1921.

Erik XIV tells the story of a weak and deranged sixteenth-century Swedish king who imprisons and murders the nobility, is deposed in a rebellion led by his brothers, and after marrying his mistress attempts to flee the country. Strindberg saw Erik as a Swedish Hamlet, and Chekhov's *Erik XIV* was full of internal conflict, revealed through sharp contrasts in physical and vocal dynamics. In his search for a physical means to represent the weakness of the character, Chekhov was inspired by Vakhtangov, who visualised Erik trapped within a circle from which he constantly tried to escape. Stretching out his hands beyond the circle in hope, Erik would find nothing and leave his hands dangling in misery. Chekhov felt that the essence of Erik's character was expressed in Vakhtangov's gesture, and claimed that from that moment he had no difficulty in playing the character with all of the appropriate nuances throughout the whole of the play.[13] This condensation of the essence of the character into a single full-body gesture is the prototype of Chekhov's psychological gesture, and he reports another example from his work with Stanislavsky on Gogol's *The Government Inspector* at the MAT in the same year.

Chekhov describes a rehearsal with Stanislavsky where the director is giving him suggestions for playing Khlestakov. He 'suddenly made a lightning-quick movement with his arms and hands, as if throwing them up and at the same time vibrating with his fingers, elbows, and even his shoulders'.[14] Once again, Chekhov understood the whole of the role from this condensation. What both of these incidents show is that the idea of expressing the essence of the role in a gesture was familiar to Stanislavsky and Vakhtangov, and that the idea was not Chekhov's as such. None the less he was the one who developed the idea of the psychological gesture and made it an important aspect of his training as an intuitive, rather than an analytical, approach to character.

In contrast to the brooding melancholy of Erik, Chekhov's Khlestakov in *The Government Inspector* was light and mischievous. Critics were stunned by the scene in which Khlestakov improvises fantastic lies in the Mayor's house, because Chekhov would play it differently each night. Opening to the higher ego involved a means of accessing the creativity and spontaneity that Stanislavsky had been searching for, and provided an alternative approach to his creative state of mind. The problem for Chekhov was that when creative energy was unleashed, the actor was inclined to overstep necessary boundaries, and there was a need to develop a way of ensuring that the limits of the performance were respected.[15] By the time of the performance, Chekhov was able to keep the basic shape of the scene but earlier in rehearsals he had got so carried away improvising with an apple that he lost contact with the objective of the scene and the other actors before Stanislavsky called a halt. The ability to improvise within set limits was another aspect of the performer which Chekhov wanted to develop through his teaching.[16]

Vakhtangov died in 1922, and Chekhov was offered the directorship of the First Studio which became the second MAT in 1924. He continued to act as well as to teach and direct, and in the 1924–5 season he directed and performed the title role in a critically acclaimed production of *Hamlet*. Despite the acclaim Chekhov received for *Hamlet*, however, there was concern that the second MAT was not producing revolutionary plays. By 1927 Stalin's clampdown on experiments in the arts was beginning, and Chekhov was accused of being a mystic and a 'sick' actor who would spread corruption. Anthroposophy was banned in the Soviet Union and Chekhov was warned that he was about to be arrested. Chekhov left Russia in 1928 and his work was discredited in the Soviet Union. It was not returned to the official curriculum until after 1969.

Accepting an invitation from Max Reinhardt, Chekhov moved to Berlin in 1928. During the same period he continued his studies in anthroposophy, and directed the Habima in *Twelfth Night*. Chekhov was unhappy with Reinhardt's theatre, but had a strong experience of his higher ego in the role of Skid in *Artists*, when he saw the character as if he were viewing it from the perspective of the audience or the other actors. Skid was indicating to Chekhov how he should sit, move and speak.[17] Meeting Stanislavsky in Vienna soon after the performance in 1929, Chekhov insisted on the importance of the imagination and attacked Stanislavsky's emphasis on emotional recall for being dangerous.[18] In a lecture during 1941 he repeated his attack and argued for the importance of a divided consciousness:

> When we are possessed by the part and almost kill our partners and break chairs, etc., then we are not free and it is not art but hysterics. At one time in Russia we thought that if we were acting we must forget everything else. Of course, it was wrong. Then some of our actors came to the point where they discovered that real acting was when we could act and be filled with feelings, and yet be able to make jokes with our partners – two consciousnesses.[19]

By the time Chekhov gave this lecture, however, Stanislavsky had already acknowledged the significance of the actor's dual consciousness in his writings, although this was not to appear in English until 1946, eight years after Stanislavsky's death.[20]

In 1931 Chekhov moved to Paris where, together with Georgette Boner, he set up another studio but encountered a number of difficulties. Chekhov had hoped that he would find support for his work from the large Russian émigré community in Paris, but in this he was disappointed. He staged an adaptation of Tolstoy's fairy tale *The Castle Awakens*, working with eurythmy and other ideas from Steiner, but the production was a commercial failure. In 1932 and 1933 he worked at the state theatres in the still independent Latvia and Lithuania, but the unstable political situation sent him back to Paris.

In 1934–5 Chekhov put together a company of exiled Russian actors for a short tour of the USA with seven plays and an evening of stage adaptations of Anton Chekhov stories. He also gave a lecture-demonstration to the Group Theatre at the invitation of Stella Adler. In this lecture-demonstration, Chekhov suggested that when approaching a character the actor must first identify the archetype on which the character is based. He also outlined his theory of centres and the imaginary body, and considered the notion of personal atmosphere.[21]

It was in New York that Chekhov met Beatrice Straight and Deirdre Hurst du Prey, who invited him to the experimental community at Dartington Hall in Devon. Chekhov accepted the invitation and the Chekhov Theatre Studio was established at Dartington in 1936. The arrangement was ideal for Chekhov because there were no commercial pressures and he was free to develop his system of training. Chekhov planned a three-year course which would include the development of concentration and imagination, eurythmy, voice and speech (drawing on Steiner), and musical composition. Folk tales were to be studied as a means of freeing the imagination, and students would start with short scenes and improvisations, gradually building to longer and more difficult pieces. By this time the main components of his system were in place: imagination and concentration, higher ego, atmospheres and qualities, centres, imaginary bodies, radiance and style. Chekhov also added what came to be known as the 'Four Brothers', a series of linked exercises that focused on feelings of ease (to replace Stanislavsky's relaxation), form, beauty and the whole.

Chekhov was in an enviable position, but the outbreak of war with Germany in 1939 caused him to move once again – this time to Ridgefield in Connecticut – taking a number of his students with him. Unfortunately there was more financial pressure on Chekhov in Connecticut than there had been in Devon, and he was forced to stage performances too early. Initial productions were not well received, but the Chekhov Studio production of *Twelfth Night* attracted positive reviews on Broadway in 1941. It was during this period that Chekhov began to formulate his ideas on the psychological gesture which had been in the process of gestation since the 1920s. Inevitably war once again interrupted his work and in 1942 the Studio was forced to close because of the draft. In 1943 Chekhov moved to Los Angeles and began a film career in Hollywood which included an Oscar nomination for his role in Hitchcock's *Spellbound* in 1945. His film career was interrupted by a heart attack during filming in 1948, and ended after a second heart attack in 1954. Whilst in LA Chekhov continued to teach, and

Figure 4.1   Michael Chekhov in the Dartington Studio with students
Source: Dartington Hall Trust

included Jack Palance, Mala Powers, Marilyn Monroe and Anthony Quinn amongst his students. After a career constantly interrupted by personal, financial and political difficulties, Michael Chekhov died of a heart attack in Los Angeles in 1955 at the age of sixty-four.

Theory and practice

In 1942 Chekhov completed his manual for the actor entitled *To the Actor*, but it was not until 1953 that it was published in a seriously modified form.[22] In 1991 a new edition entitled *On the Technique of Acting* restored Chekhov's original manuscript. This most recent volume contains eighty-seven exercises covering all of the main aspects of the technique. The volume is not exhaustive, however, as Chekhov was inventing new exercises until his death, and the basic principles of the technique will allow as many varia-tions and creations as there are creative individualities. The following material offers a 'taster' of Chekhov's work, focusing on a small number of key elements and exercises.

Imagination and concentration

Chekhov's fascination with the imagination stayed with him throughout his life. He felt that any artist needed to be able to work in a disciplined way with the images that appeared in hypnagogic and dream states, as well as those that appeared in response to engaging with an artwork. What fasci-nated Chekhov about hypnagogic images was that they transformed themselves independently without any conscious intervention from the indi-vidual. The task for the actor is to become an active participant in the process of imagination rather than just a passive dreamer, to bring the world of the imagination on to the stage and give it life. In order to do this, the actor – according to Chekhov – has to develop a feeling for artistic construc-tion, and this can be done by studying 'great works' of the past and imaginatively altering certain aspects of them. How would it be if Mona Lisa's smile was a little broader? If Hamlet had killed Claudius whilst he was at prayer? By asking such questions, the actor begins to develop a sense of the rules of composition, and this understanding will help in making appropriate choices. At the same time this questioning assists in developing an awareness of the 'flexibility of images'. By imagining fairy tale or dream-like transformations (a frog into a prince, a flamingo into an elephant) and by paying close attention to the stages of the transformation, the actor will develop both concentration and a facility for working with images. The actor also has to be able to let go of the images, to allow them to sink into the subconscious, and to welcome the changes in them when they return transformed. By recognising and accepting the independence of the world of the imagination, the actor begins to soften the boundaries of the everyday self and 'confront the Higher Ego'.[23] This takes the actor away from the

Stanislavskian 'true to life approach'. As Chekhov pointed out: 'what if the character's psychology and inner life are *not* true to life? Was Don Quixote true to life?'[24]

The actor has eventually to begin to embody these images and, in addition to a well-developed and flexible imagination, Chekhov required the actor to have a body which was sensitive to inner impulses, noting that 'every actor, to a greater or lesser degree, suffers from some of [the] body's resistance'.[25] Chekhov proposes a number of useful exercises for increasing the body's flexibility and responsiveness, but he notes that the exercises in concentration, atmosphere and imagination also assist in this process of sensitisation.

Atmosphere

Although Meyerhold and Bryusov discussed the importance of atmosphere at the beginning of the century, Michael Chekhov developed the idea in theory and practice more extensively than anyone else, and it became one of the major elements in his technique.

An atmosphere can be considered as the dominant tone or mood of, amongst other things, a place, a relationship, or an artwork. An old ruined castle, for example, has a different atmosphere from a busy casualty department, and each atmosphere will have a different effect on individuals in contact with them. Chekhov used the example of walking along and arriving at the crowded scene of a street accident; we will be aware of the atmosphere before we realise exactly what has happened. Each individual in the scene will have their own response to the situation, but there will be a dominant atmosphere which is experienced as a whole and as an external phenomenon. In this sense Chekhov considered atmospheres to be 'objective'.

A more orthodox Stanislavskian approach would involve the actor focusing on their own emotional response to a previously experienced street accident or analogous circumstance. Even in Stanislavsky's later period, when he was working on his method of physical actions as a less direct approach to the actor's emotions, the question for the actor would have been: 'What would *I* do if *I* were in this situation?'[26] Chekhov's emphasis is on the evocation of the overall tone of the situation, and he considered atmospheres to be the equivalent of musical keys. A sensitivity to atmospheres and the ability to create them onstage is a key skill for the Chekhovian actor, and one which forges a connection between actor and audience.

Chekhov encouraged actors to practise creating atmospheres in their imagination by reading through scenes from plays, getting a sense of the overall atmosphere and then imagining the characters acting and speaking in tune with it. Rather than doing this just once, Chekhov proposes that the exercise is repeated until the inner performance is satisfactory, and then suggests that the atmosphere is altered. The following exercise focuses on emotional atmospheres, and is Chekhov's alternative to Stanislavsky's affective memory work:

Exercise 1

Imagine the air around you...filled with the Atmosphere that you have chosen. It is no more difficult than imagining the air filled with light, dust, fragrance, smoke, mist, and so on. You must not ask yourself, 'How can the air be filled with fear or joy, tenderness or horror?' You must try it practically. Your first effort will show immediately how simple it is. What you have to learn is how to sustain the imaginary Atmosphere that now envelops you. Your main aid will be a developed Concentration. ... In this exercise you do not need to imagine any special circumstances or events to justify the Atmosphere. It will only distract your attention and make the exercise unnecessarily complicated. Do it as simply as described above.

After a certain period of time, when you feel sure of being able to imagine and sustain the Atmosphere around you, proceed to the next step. Try to relate the reaction inside you to that of the imaginary Atmosphere outside. Do not force yourself to feel anything, simply realize the reaction, which will appear of itself if the first part of the exercise has been carefully and patiently done. The whole value of this exercise will be lost if you impatiently impose the reaction upon yourself, instead of letting it grow freely. In the beginning the exercise may take time, but very soon you will see that the process of creating the Atmosphere and reacting to it is almost instantaneous. Gradually the Atmosphere will penetrate deeper and deeper into the realm of your emotions.[27]

The next phase is to speak and move in harmony with the atmosphere and to begin to radiate the 'inner life' stimulated by the atmosphere back into the space, thereby setting up a kind of feedback loop which amplifies both the atmosphere and the inner response.

Once actors develop a basic facility in creating atmospheres they can explore transforming them and breaking them. According to Chekhov, two strong atmospheres cannot exist in the same space; one will always be dominant. If a group of clowns surrounded by an atmosphere of playfulness were to chance upon the street accident mentioned above, one of the two atmospheres would have to change.

The Four Brothers

A group of exercises known as The Four Brothers are significant because they focus on qualities which pertain to all other work in the Chekhov technique. They are the feelings of ease, of the whole, of form and of beauty. The feeling of ease involves performing any action with a sense of lightness and ease, no matter how 'heavy' the situation or subject matter. This replaces Stanislavsky's exercises in relaxation, and Chekhov considered it to be a crucial aspect of art as well as being connected to humour.[28] The feeling of the whole requires an awareness that every action, every piece of stage business, every speech, has a beginning, middle and end which needs to be clearly defined, however subtly. The feeling of form develops an ability to perceive one's own actions from an aesthetic viewpoint, to become aware of the shapes made in space and their appropriateness. The feeling of beauty is an inner sense which involves a feeling of deep satisfaction in the work and is to be distinguished from 'showing off'. Chekhov gives the example of someone profoundly engaged in a physical task flowing effortlessly. Each of these qualities fosters a sense of aesthetic distance in the work encouraging the actor to take a view from outside rather than inside.

The psychological gesture

The psychological gesture (PG) is a means of expressing the entire character in condensed form through an intuitive grasp of the character's main desire. The PG was Chekhov's answer to an analytical approach to role which could offer keen insights but leave the actor without a means of embodying them. The PG is perhaps Chekhov's single most original contribution to twentieth-century actor training. Drawing on the work of Steiner, Chekhov notes that we often use gestural language when talking of psychological processes. For example we 'grow pensive', 'draw conclusions' or 'grasp ideas'. Chekhov considers that these phrases suggest a 'tendency to produce such a gesture'[29] exists at these moments, and can stimulate us to make the physical gesture if necessary. The following exercise does not involve a focus on language, however, but on an imaginative and intuitive search for the character's objective (in the Stanislavskian sense). None the less, once the psychological gesture becomes invisible the character still speaks in accordance with it, and this makes the link to Steiner's idea that gesture disappears into speech:

Exercise 2

Imagine [any play] as we have described before, without choosing any part for yourself. Continue imagining until the events and characters of the play become a living performance for you. While doing so, fix your attention on moments which...seem significant or expressive to you. Concentrate on the character that appears central in the moment you have chosen. Ask this character to act before you in your Imagination and follow its action in all details. Simultaneously, try to 'see' *what* the character is aiming at, *what* is [the character's] wish, desire? In doing so, attempt to avoid reasoning, but rather seek to penetrate as clearly and as vividly as possible into the character's *what* by means of the image before your mind's eye. As soon as you begin to guess what the character is doing, try to find the most simple Psychological Gesture for it. Do it physically, looking at the same time at your image.

Improve the Psychological Gesture in its simplicity and expressiveness by exercising it. Do not ask your imaginative character to do the Psychological Gesture for you. It is useless. The character must only act in terms of the play. Hamlet, for instance, when the curtain is raised, can sit motionless in the throne room. This is your imagination. But Hamlet's Psychological Gesture might be a large, slow, heavy movement with both arms and hands, from above downward toward the earth. You may find this Gesture right for Hamlet's dark, depressed mood at this time of his life. And this Gesture is what you must do in reality, while you are watching your image. Then try to act and to speak like Hamlet, having now the Psychological Gesture only in the back of your mind as it were.

Do the Psychological Gesture and the acting alternately, until it becomes evident to you that behind each internal state or movement in acting is hidden a simple and expressive Psychological Gesture that is the essence of the acting. ... The Psychological Gesture will appear

Figure 4.2   Michael Chekhov's students at work in the garden at Dartington
Source: Dartington Hall Trust

before your mind's eye and, after being practised, will always remain with you as a kind of inspiration while you are acting.[30]

There is some confusion as to whether or not the PG should be visible to the audience; in this example it is suggested that it should be invisible. Earlier in the same chapter, however, Chekhov uses the term to refer to 'visible (actual) gestures as well as to invisible (potential) gestures' (1991: 60).

Into production

Chekhov argued for a plurality of theatrical styles and the variety of work he engaged in – from Moscow to Hollywood – indicates the range to which he thought his technique could be applied. Each project will require its own 'special technique', but will keep to the basic principles of the 'general technique'.

The most readily available material on Chekhov as director is on his production with the Actors Lab in *The Government Inspector* in 1946, published in Charles Leonard's *Michael Chekhov's To the Director and Playwright*. This material is not particularly helpful in developing an understanding of Chekhov's directorial approach, and part of the problem is that Chekhov was working with actors who were not trained in his system, and whom he did not have time to train. Nor is it clear whether the chapter in *To The Actor* on the 'Composition of the Performance', which uses *King Lear* as its example, has any direct connection to Chekhov's production. In fact this is unlikely, as he comments that Shakespeare's plays should be shortened and restructured in order to give them a 'driving force' appropriate to the times, but chooses not to indicate how this would be done.[31] The material in Leonard and in *To the Actor* does, however, illustrate Chekhov's ideas on how a text should be examined for its main and auxiliary climaxes.

In this material, Chekhov suggested that a piece should have a threefold structure in which a conflict is generated, unfolds and concludes, with the main qualities of the opening being transformed into their opposite by the end. Each of the three major sections will contain a moment of maximum tension or climax and will also have a number of moments of lesser tension (auxiliary climaxes). Chekhov believed that these climaxes should be discovered through the 'artistic intuition' developed in the training.

A clear sense of the form of these key moments and the rhythmic ebb and flow of energy is important for the composition of any performance. Outside of the climaxes and auxiliary climaxes there are smaller moments of significance known as 'accents'. These are lines or actions which provide impulses for transformations, or clarify past or future occurrences. A further element in the structure of a piece is the use of repetition. Any aspect of a production might repeat and either recur unchanged or transformed, and each kind of repetition has different effects on the spectator's perception.

This emphasis on the structure has a more abstract and analytical flavour than most of Chekhov's work and, whilst offering some useful guidelines, it seems as something of an afterthought to his main body of theory. The chapter entitled 'The Four Stages of the Creative Process', which appeared for the first time in the 1991 edition of Chekhov's manual, offers a clearer sense of the relationship between training and production. Unlike the material on *The Government Inspector* or *King Lear*, there is no reference to any specific production or text, but a description of Chekhov's ideal process. The first key to this process is that actors and director should have trained in the technique and be able to share a working language.

Chekhov claims that an understanding of the four stages will free the actor 'from the slavery of accidents, personal moods, disappointments, and nervous impatience',[32] and thus generate a sense of 'assurance'. He argues for the importance of the basic pattern but does not dictate what must happen at any moment: 'the rehearsals can at any time take any course that may be required to further the work'.[33]

The first stage of the production process involves the actors reading the text and beginning to get a sense of the general atmosphere of the play. Chekhov described this stage as 'musical', and likened it to the act of listening to a distant piece of music and gradually being able to pick out its different aspects. At this point, even though the play has been cast, it is important for the actors to pay attention to the entire work, and not focus solely on their own character. In addition to the general atmosphere, the actors need to get a sense of the style, the 'dynamic of good and evil' and the social significance of the piece. This work is done in the actor's imagination, and Chekhov indicates that the 'more conscientious' the actors have been in practising the method the 'more successful'[34] their results will be. Entering into the general atmosphere of the play the actors should read it again and again, allowing various images to arise without interference. Chekhov suggests that the actors keep a 'diary' of this part of the process, noting down the visions which attract them most in words and images. As this stage progresses the actors will become more focused on their specific characters but still keep a sense of the whole.

The second stage involves the conscious elaboration of images and the beginning of the working conversation between director and cast. Now that the actors have familiarised themselves with the text and have allowed their imaginations to engage with it, they are ready for a mutual exchange of visions with the director. The director has overall responsibility, but it is important that the creativity of all parties is respected. Chekhov recognised the director as a creative artist but never abandoned the importance of the actor's creativity. It is during this period that the cast show the psychological gestures for their characters, and may begin to move and speak with them. Different scenes in the play are explored for different points of view: ease, form, style, atmosphere and so on.

During the first two stages material and ideas are generated and a working relationship developed. The third, and longest, stage is that of incorporation, when the work starts to become more embodied. For Chekhov the 'best way to proceed' at this stage is

> to create a series of Incorporations of the characters with short moments from the play. The director may ask [the] actors such questions as the following: What do the arms, the hands, the shoulders, the feet of your character look like at such and such moments? How does the character walk, sit, or run in other moments? How does it enter, exit, listen, look? How does it react to different impressions received from other characters? How does it behave when enveloped in a certain Atmosphere?[35]

The actors perform their answers for the director who offers feedback and other suggestions as the exploration develops. This dialogic approach is helped in Chekhov's model by the requirement that the director has been trained in the technique and understands the processes of acting. Chekhov suggests at one point that the 'best way' for the director to communicate what is required is to act it. If the actors have been appropriately trained, Chekhov believed they would 'grasp the essence' and would 'not need to copy their director outwardly'.[36]

The third phase is the rehearsal stage proper and involves the repetition of scenes and the development of the performance score. Chekhov suggests that different segments of the play are explored with different 'grounds', by which he meant that the sequences should be explored whilst emphasising different aspects of the technique.

The fourth and final stage commences towards the end of the rehearsal process and is the phase of inspiration and divided consciousness. At this point in his description Chekhov leaves behind questions of text, ensemble and actor–director relationships, and focuses primarily on the individual actor. If the actor has worked through the process conscientiously then it is at this point that the actor can stand back from the character and admire it as an aesthetic object. Chekhov quotes Rudolf Steiner at this point in a brief passage that makes clear the relationship between the theories of the two men: 'The actor must not be possessed by his role. He must stand facing it so that his part becomes objective. He experiences it as his own creation.'[37]

Chekhov's recipe for the creative process, together with the great detail and wealth of exercises offered in his writings, offers a practical and experimental approach that demystifies the art of acting. For Chekhov the last thing an actor should worry about is talent:

> The actor should never worry about...talent, but rather about...lack of technique...lack of training, and...lack of understanding of the creative

process. The talent will flourish immediately of itself as soon as the artist chisels away all the extraneous matter.[38]

Acknowledgements

The 3rd Michael Chekhov International Workshop at Emerson College, Sussex, in 1994 was such a rich experience for me that I cannot possibly thank by name all of those who helped me. I benefited greatly from the generosity of former Chekhov students by participating in workshops, having my own work audited, listening to anecdotes and memories and through conversation. I am indebted to Mala Powers, Jack Colvin, Deirdre Hurst du Prey, Mary-Lou Taylor, Hurd Hadfield, Ford Rainey, Joanna Merlin, Paul Rogers and Daphne Field. At the same event Professors Andrei Kirillov and Marina Ivanova were stimulating in debate and possessed a tremendous depth of knowledge concerning Chekhov's life and work in Russia. I hope that the demands of this task have not led me into any unforgivable errors.

Notes

1 Whilst this is a personal view it is one supported by practitioners as diverse as Richard Hornby and Eugenio Barba.
2 Vsevolod Meyerhold (1969) 'The Naturalistic Theatre and the Theatre of Mood' in Braun (ed.) (1969) *Meyerhold on Theatre*, p. 30.
3 Vsevolod Meyerhold (1907) 'The New Theatre Foreshadowed in Literature', in Braun (ed.) (1969) *Meyerhold on Theatre*, p. 36.
4 Craig (1980) *On the Art of the Theatre*, p. 60.
5 Reported by Chekhov biographer Professor Marina Ivanova at the 3rd Michael Chekhov International Workshop (MCIW), Emerson College, 1994.
6 Gordon (1987), p. 119.
7 Gordon (1987), p. 124.
8 Michael Chekhov 'The Teachings of the Great Russian Directors' in Leonard (1984), p. 51.
9 Chekhov (1991) *On the Technique of Acting*, p. 16.
10 Chekhov (1991) *On the Technique of Acting*, p. 24.
11 Eurythmy, not to be confused with Dalcroze's Eurhythmics, has been described as the 'difficult task of interpreting speech in movement' (Raffe *et al.*, 1974, p. 14). This does not mean that the text is interpreted through movement but is based on the idea that sounds themselves have fundamentally physical qualities. Whilst eurythmy is a dance form in its own right, Steiner considered that the actor's task was to internalise these movements so that the gesture is 'taken back into the word' and alters the quality of the speech. The combination of these ideas with the Stanislavskian 'objective' led to Chekhov's technique of the 'psychological gesture'.
12 Vakhtangov (1922) 'Fantastic Realism', in Cole and Chinoy (1963), pp. 185–91.
13 Chekhov (1991) *On the Technique of Acting*, p. 89.
14 Chekhov (1991) *On the Technique of Acting*, p. 89.

15 Chekhov (1985a) *To The Actor*, p. 97. This idea is missing from the section on Creative Individuality in *On the Technique of Acting*.
16 Deirdre Hurst du Prey (1983) 'Working with Chekhov', *The Drama Review*, 27(3): 89.
17 Gordon (1987), p. 148.
18 Gordon (1987), p. 149.
19 Chekhov (1985b) *Lessons for the Professional Actor*, p. 102.
20 Stanislavsky refers to the experience in positive terms in *Building a Character* (1979), p. 21, although the book was written after Chekhov discussed his experience with Stanislavsky. Although Chekhov appears to experience divided consciousness for the first time in the role of Skid, it is a well-discussed phenomenon in Western actor training since Diderot. Coquelin's version of the idea was very much part of the debate on the actor's art during the first part of the century and was also explicitly referred to by Irving and Meyerhold. See also Chapter Eight of Hornby's (1992) *The End of Acting*; Copeau 'An Actor's Thoughts on Diderot's Paradoxe' in Rudlin and Paul (eds) (1990) *Copeau: Texts on Theatre*, pp. 72–8; and Leach (1997) 'When He Touches Your Heart...– The Revolutionary Theatre of Vsevolod Meyerhold and the Development of Michael Chekhov', *Contemporary Theatre Review*, 7(Part 1): 67–83.
21 Gordon (1987), pp. 155–9.
22 Chekhov's 1942 text was rejected by publishers. Chekhov felt that his written English was to blame and translated the work into Russian. He then re-translated the work into English only to suffer rejection once again. In 1952, Chekhov gave Charles Leonard permission to edit the manuscript in any way he saw fit, and Leonard's reduced version of *To the Actor* was published in English in 1953. It is through Leonard's version that Chekhov's work became widely known. A special issue of *TDR* devoted to Chekhov in 1983 followed by the publication in 1985 of Deirdre Hurst du Prey's transcription of Chekhov's 1941 classes *Lessons for the Professional Actor* sparked a renewed interest in Chekhov's work. In 1991 Mala Powers, ex-student of Chekhov and executrix of the Chekhov estate, re-edited the 1942 manuscript and it was published by HarperCollins as *On the Technique of Acting*.
23 Chekhov (1991) *On the Technique of Acting*, p. 15.
24 Chekhov in Leonard, 1984, p. 38.
25 Chekhov (1985a) *To The Actor*, p. 2.
26 Benedetti (1988) *Stanislavski: A Biography*, p. 338.
27 Chekhov (1991) *On the Technique of Acting*, pp. 32–3.
28 Chekhov (1991) *On the Technique of Acting*, p. 48.
29 Chekhov (1991) *On the Technique of Acting*, p. 59.
30 Chekhov (1991) *On the Technique of Acting*, pp. 64–5.
31 Chekhov (1985a) *To The Actor*, p. 101.
32 Chekhov (1991) *On the Technique of Acting*, p. 146.
33 Chekhov (1991) *On the Technique of Acting*, p. 151.
34 Chekhov (1991) *On the Technique of Acting*, p. 147.
35 Chekhov (1991) *On the Technique of Acting*, p. 151.
36 Chekhov (1991) *On the Technique of Acting*, p. 154.
37 Chekhov (1991) *On the Technique of Acting*, p. 155.
38 Chekhov (1991) *On the Technique of Acting*, p. 155.

Bibliography

Barba, Eugenio (1995) *The Paper Canoe: A Guide to Theatre Anthropology*, London: Routledge.

Benedetti, Jean (1988) *Stanislavski: A Biography*, London: Methuen.

Black, Lendley (1987) *Mikhail Chekhov as Actor, Director, and Teacher*, Ann Arbor, MI: UMI Research Press.

Braun, Edward (ed.) (1969) *Meyerhold on Theatre*, London: Eyre Methuen.

Bridgmont, Peter (1992) *Liberation of the Actor*, London: Temple Lodge.

Chekhov, Michael (1985a) *To the Actor*, New York: Barnes and Noble.

—— (1985b) *Lessons for the Professional Actor*, New York: PAJ Books.

—— (1988) 'The Golden Age of the Russian Theatre', *Alarums and Excursions* 2, Los Angeles.

—— (1991) *On the Technique of Acting*, New York: Harper Perennial.

Cole, Toby and Chinoy, Helen Krich (eds) (1963) *Directors on Directing: A Source Book of the Modern Theatre*, New York: Bobbs-Merrill Company.

Craig, E.G. (1911, 1956) *On the Art of the Theatre*, New York: Theatre Arts Books (reprinted 1980, London: Heinemann Educational Books).

Gordon, Mel (1987) *The Stanislavsky Technique: Russia. A Workbook for Actors*, New York: Applause Books.

Green, Michael (1986) *The Russian Symbolist Theatre: An Anthology of Plays and Critical Texts*, Ann Arbor, MI: Ardis.

Hornby, Richard (1992) *The End of Acting: A Radical View*, New York: Applause.

Innes, Christopher (1998) *Edward Gordon Craig: A Vision of the Theatre*, Amsterdam: Harwood Academic Press.

Kirillov, Andrei (1994) 'Michael Chekhov – Problems of Study', *Eye of the World* 1, St. Petersburg.

Leach, Robert (1997) 'When He Touches Your Heart...– The Revolutionary Theatre of Vsevolod Meyerhold and the Development of Michael Chekhov', *Contemporary Theatre Review* 7(Part 1): 67–83.

Leonard, Charles (1984) *Michael Chekhov's To the Director and Playwright*, New York: Limelight Editions.

Meyer, Michael (1987) *Strindberg*, Oxford: Oxford University Press.

Nietzsche, Friedrich (1993) *The Birth of Tragedy*, London: Penguin Classics.

Raffe, Marjorie, Harwood, Cecil and Lundgren, Marguerite (1974) *Eurythmy and the Impulse of Dance*, London: Rudolf Steiner Press.

Rudlin, John and Paul, Norman H. (eds) (1990) *Copeau: Texts on Theatre*, London: Routledge.

Schopenhauer, Arthur (1966) *The World As Will and Representation*, Vol. 2, trans. E.F.J. Payne, New York: Dover.

Senelick, Laurence (1981) *Russian Dramatic Theory from Pushkin to the Symbolists*, Austin, TX: University of Texas Press.

Stanislavski, Constantin (1979) *Building a Character*, London: Eyre Methuen.

Steiner, Rudolf (1960) *Speech and Drama*, London: Rudolf Steiner Press.

—— (1964) *Knowledge of the Higher Worlds and its Attainment*, California: Health Research.

—— (1987) *Secrets of the Threshold*, London: Rudolf Steiner Press.

Vakhtangov, Eugene (1922) 'Fantastic Realism', in Cole and Chinoy (eds) (1963) pp. 185–91.

Zarrilli, Phillip B. (ed.) (1995) *Acting (Re)Considered*, London: Routledge.

Journals

The Drama Review (1983) 27(3), Fall, is an issue devoted to Michael Chekhov's career and legacy.

Video

Mason, Felicity (1993) *The Training Sessions of Michael Chekhov*, Exeter: Arts Documentation Unit.

Audio tapes

Grove, Eddy (1992) *The Nature and Significance of Michael Chekhov's Contribution to the Theory and Technique of Acting*, New York: Eddy Grove.

Powers, Mala (1992) *Michael Chekhov: On Theatre and the Art of Acting – A Guide to Discovery with Exercises*, New York: Applause.

5 Brecht and actor training

On whose behalf do we act?

Peter Thomson

Context

Brecht was sixteen years old and living in his parents' home in Augsburg when the Archduke Franz Ferdinand was assassinated in remote Sarajevo. He was twenty when the war that was the consequence of that untidy assassination ended. The blustering, posturing adolescent of 1914 was, by 1918, an angry young man. Anger is something that must always come into the reckoning when Brecht's theatrical career is under scrutiny. Anger at the way things are provides the impetus for political or social campaigning, and Brecht's approach to acting cannot properly be divorced from his campaign to change the world. That campaign found its eventual rationale in Marxism, but it began with the impulse to contradict. Given the conventional Christian upbringing of a bourgeois provincial in traditionally Protestant Augsburg, Brecht responded with confrontational pragmatism:

> What business have they got putting that stuff about Truth in the
>   catechism
> If one's not allowed to say what is?
>
> (Brecht 1976b: 16)

These are the concluding lines of a poem written shortly after his twentieth birthday and obliquely addressed to his mother – worried about his dirty linen and dirtier language. It was time for Brecht to get away from Augsburg into the headier atmosphere of Bavaria's cultural capital, Munich. In the months following the signing of the Armistice on 11 November 1918, he travelled regularly between Augsburg and Munich, where he was trying to establish a literary foothold. It was a period of extraordinary political turmoil in Bavaria, and Brecht was caught up in it.

The King of Bavaria had abdicated a day before the German Kaiser, and a revolution designed to sever the link between Bavaria and Prussia (Munich and Berlin) had established a new government, led by a socialist intellectual, Kurt Eisner. Eisner's admirable attempts to inaugurate a new order in Bavaria were thwarted by reactionary nationalists on the one hand and left-wing revolutionaries on the other. He was too radical; he was not radical enough. On 21 February 1919, shortly after making a speech at the reconstituted Second International in Berne, Eisner was shot dead by a young aristocrat. In illogical revenge, his deputy was shot and severely wounded by a communist worker at the opening session of the Bavarian parliament. In the chaos that followed, Munich was briefly in the hands of a socialist soviet, but the soviet was ousted by the better-programmed communist faction. Predictably, the threat of communism galvanised the powers of the battered German nation into counter-revolutionary action. The army moved against Munich, and by the beginning of May the Bavarian political adventure was over. The decisive military advance began in Augsburg.

Brecht's published correspondence is largely silent about these events, though he is known to have been an active supporter of Eisner's social democrats, and may have been a fellow-traveller with the soviet. The most abiding outcome was a lifelong scepticism about acts of quixotic heroism, a scepticism which ran alongside his animosity towards the grandiose human aspirations of German expressionism. Ernst Toller, prominent amongst expressionist playwrights, was one of the leaders of the Munich soviet. In his autobiographical retrospect on political history, he writes of the ordinary Bavarians who wanted peace, but found themselves suddenly invested with power: 'Would they learn to keep their power?' (Toller 1934: 133). They did not, and the failure helped to guide Brecht towards the mature conviction that an effective revolution, political or theatrical, must be achieved through reason and scientific principle. Quite unlike Toller in most ways, Brecht shared with him a curiosity about what they considered a moral paradox. Toller expressed it in this way: 'Men could be good with so little trouble, yet they delight in evil' (Toller 1934: 26). Brecht wrote a short poem about it:

> On my wall hangs a Japanese carving
> The mask of an evil demon, decorated with gold lacquer.
> Sympathetically I observe
> The swollen veins of the forehead, indicating
> What a strain it is to be evil.
>
> (Brecht 1976b: 383)

Given what we know of their respective lives, most people would be more surprised to find Brecht in heaven than to find Toller there. But the fundamental question addressed in the work of both men is the one Toller remembers asking himself after the death of an uncle: 'what is a good man?' (Toller 1934: 8). Was Galileo good? Is Grusha? or Shen Te? or dumb Kattrin? or the Young Comrade in *The Measures Taken*? How good? Good how? From early in his life Brecht developed a habit of provocation. At its political centre was a determination to take nothing for granted. We cannot, after all, hope to change what we unknowingly assume to be unchangeable. To develop a capacity to be surprised by the familiar might be a staging post on the road to Brechtian goodness. It is certainly a staging post on the road to Brechtian acting. We should recognise, in the context of this chapter and this book, that there is a difference between being good at acting and being a good actor. Whatever is exclusively of the theatre is of no interest to Brecht and little benefit to humanity. For Brecht, the world, like the disputed land in the opening scene of *The Caucasian Chalk Circle*, should belong to those who are good for it. In his own moral system, goodness could not be divided from efficacy.

Brecht entered the German theatre as a writer, and became a practitioner primarily in order to intervene in the production of his own plays. He had no training, nor was there any tradition of actor training in Germany. The simplified view of the style of acting he would have encountered, hectically delivered by Martin Esslin, is that it sought to produce 'the maximum impression of emotional intensity by indulgence in hysterical outbursts and paroxysms of uncontrolled roaring and inarticulate anguish' (Esslin 1970: 88). Clearly carried away, Esslin goes on to write of 'orgies of vocal excess and apoplectic breast beating'. He has in mind the excesses of the Court theatres of old Germany, which lingered in the celebrated performances of pre-war luminaries, and which had again come into service in the ecstatic rhetoric of the new expressionist drama.

But this declamatory grand manner was by no means the only model available to the young Brecht. Although Otto Brahm, the outstanding exponent of naturalism in Germany, had died in 1912, the impact of his advocacy of true-to-life acting did not die with him. Brecht's early loyalty to the naturalistic drama of Gerhart Hauptmann was fed by a visceral response to witnessed productions of his plays. One of his earliest published letters, dated 10 November 1914, commends Hauptmann's 'art of exalting everyday happenings to spiritual heights' and proposes Zola as a model because 'the soul of the people has not yet been explored' (Brecht 1990: 20).

Quite as influential on the development of Brecht's ideas of performance was the generally cool, presentational style of cabaret, which had already been released into drama through the work of Frank Wedekind. Wedekind himself combined the writing of plays with performing in cabaret right up to his untimely death in March 1918. Brecht was in the Munich bar where Wedekind made one of what turned out to be his last appearances, and his own sporadic cabaret performances honoured Wedekind by imitation as well as sharpening his sense of an audience. Esslin's emphatically partial account serves his argument that Brecht's approach to acting was a legitimate response to German histrionics, but of limited relevance elsewhere. It ignores the range of Brecht's theatrical experience in a country with an uncommonly rich artistic tradition.

Before making his first attempt to direct professional actors, he had observed Max Reinhardt and other Berlin directors at work in rehearsal. This was in November 1921, when Reinhardt was preparing Strindberg's *A Dream Play*, characteristically in search of its musical orchestration. The outcome was highly artificial, but certainly not an occasion of 'apoplectic breast beating'. Brecht was already too opinionated and too censorious to share Reinhardt's sheer appetite for theatre, nor had he yet developed his admiration for the craft of the actor. That became clear in the spring of 1922, when he was invited to direct his friend Arnolt Bronnen's *Vatermord* (Patricide) for the newly formed Junge Bühne in Berlin, and was so scathing about the quality of the acting that one actress was reduced to tears, the veteran Heinrich George walked out, and Brecht was replaced by the more tactful Berthold Viertel. It may be that he returned to Munich a wiser man, able to contribute to, but not dictate, the conduct of rehearsals for the first of his plays to be performed: *Drums in the Night* (Munich, September 1922), *In the Jungle* (Munich, May 1923), and *Baal* (Leipzig, December 1923).

1923 was a year of soaring inflation in Germany, and discontent in Munich had an ominously Nazi fringe. The opening of *In the Jungle* provided a pretext for nationalist protesters to release tear-gas in the auditorium of the Munich Kammerspiele. The play was dropped from the repertoire and the dramaturg, Jacob Geis, was sacked. Such glimpses of power served as a drug to one of Brecht's fellow-residents in Munich. On 8 November 1923, supported by the legendary hero Field Marshal Ludendorff, Adolf Hitler attempted to take over the city. Brecht was probably attending rehearsals of *Baal* in Leipzig at the time, and he, like all too many of his countrymen, found Hitler slightly comic for a while. His own political attention, particularly after his meeting with the activist Helene Weigel in the autumn of 1923, was turning towards Karl Marx. Before long he would embark on a full-scale programme of Marxist self-education, in open contradiction of the increasingly fascist atmosphere in Munich. In September 1924 he abandoned Bavaria for Berlin, but not before bidding a significant farewell to the Munich Kammerspiele by directing *The Life of Edward II of England*.

Brecht admired the narrative drive and psychological sparseness of Christopher Marlowe's original, and the adaptation he prepared with Lion Feuchtwanger accommodates his own peculiarly visceral poetic voice. He was at ease with the text, happy to change it, and, perhaps for the first time, able to work confidently with actors. Bernhard Reich recalls his determination that the soldiers should hang Gaveston with authority: 'Brecht...insisted relentlessly that they repeat the hanging, but to do it like experts. The audience had to get pleasure from seeing them put the noose round the fellow's neck' (Völker 1979: 72). The outcome, in the words of the contemporary dramatic critic Herbert Ihering, was innovatory: 'The actors had to account for what they did. He insisted that they keep their gestures simple. He made them speak clearly, coolly. No emotional faking was tolerated. By these means the objective, epic style was established' (Völker 1979: 72).

Brecht remained active in the Berlin theatre until Hitler's rise to power forced him into exile in late February 1933, but his activity was always governed by the pressure to produce. Ideologies of performance were in inevitable conflict with the exigency of opening nights, and, in a country lurching towards fascism, his priorities were more consistently political than aesthetic. The formulations that give Brecht right of access to a book on actor training were almost all the result of the enforced idleness of exile, and the practice that tested the theory was confined to the last years of his life with the Berliner Ensemble. The sequence of collaborations with Kurt Weill is of critical importance in the history of music theatre, but it added comparatively little to the discoveries about acting that Brecht had made during the rehearsals for *Edward II*. A Brechtian actor will know how to sustain the poise of one who might at any moment sing, but Brecht had not yet devised a rehearsal system to serve his purposes. His aim, both with Weill and in his *Lehrstück* project, was to reach a new audience, the traditionally disempowered but now alert workers of post-war Germany. The loss of access to this audience was one of the bitterest consequences of his exile.

The exile lasted more than fifteen years and included prolonged residences in Denmark, Sweden, Finland and the United States. A stranger to every language, Brecht was constantly frustrated in his attempts to gain access to theatres. His ideas about acting found expression in the plays he wrote, sporadically in his journal and conversations with fellow-exiles and friends, through encounters with active theatre groups, and in theoretical writings of which the most carefully wrought were *The Messingkauf Dialogues* (written 1937–40) and *A Short Organum for the Theatre* (completed in 1948). It is from these, and from the recorded practice of the company he founded in East Berlin in 1949, that conclusions about his approach to actor training have been most reliably drawn.

We should note, however, that Brecht was a compulsive articulator. Much of what he wrote and subsequently published was a response to immediate circumstances. Given his taste for contradiction and his advocacy of dialectics, we should not be surprised by evident inconsistencies. There is no static, once-and-for-all manifesto. The measure of Brecht's truth is efficacy: what may be thought or half-thought expressed through what is done. In that respect, the determining document is not the *Messingkauf* nor even the *Short Organum*, but *Theaterarbeit* (1952). This volume, 'an exceedingly mixed bag of essays, notes and fragments by many hands' (Willett 1964: 239), was something new in the history of theatre: an attempt to record for posterity the processes of a theatre company during its first two years of operation. The many rehearsal photographs speak, not singly but cumulatively, about acting even to those who cannot read German. *Theaterarbeit* testifies to theory's need of a practice.

Exercises

It is a prerequisite of Brechtian actor training that the trainee should be open to a study of history, including the history of the present. The tendency of historical enquiry is almost inevitably towards astonishment in the

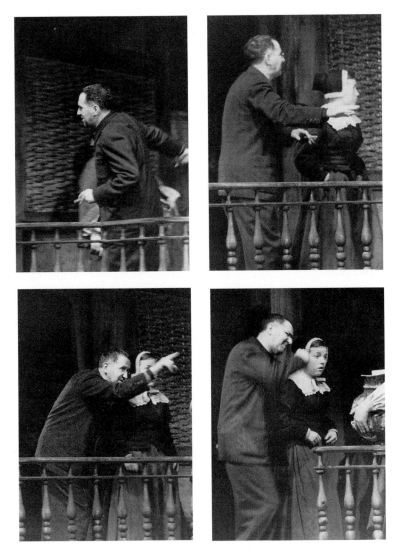

Figure 5.1 Brecht directing Regine Lutz in Heinrich von Kleist's *The Broken Jug*
Source: Photo Hainer Hill by permission of the Berliner Ensemble

enquirer. We discover details that compel us to reassess the causes of events we had previously taken for granted. When Brecht advised his actors to note for later recall their first impressions of a play, or of their part in a play, it was because he knew how rehearsal may iron flat the seams of surprise. When trainee directors at the Berliner Ensemble were invited to watch rehearsals and write down whatever they disagreed with, it was to keep alive a recognition that there is more than one way of doing the same thing.

Actors who are no longer surprised by the behaviour of the characters they play are not Brechtian actors. For Brecht, this is less a matter of psychology than of history. The fact that Galileo recanted does not make his recantation historically inevitable. The fact that life-expectancy has increased does not ensure better care of the aged. Brecht's consistent project, both as writer and practitioner, was to destabilise facts and interrogate the necessary. Significantly, he came to credit actors with sufficient curiosity to collaborate in the project. It was this that struck Peter Brook most forcibly when he visited the Berliner Ensemble:

> What Brecht introduced was the idea of the intelligent actor, capable of judging the value of his contribution. There were and still are many actors who pride themselves on knowing nothing about politics and who treat the theatre as an ivory tower. For Brecht such an actor is not worthy of his place in adult company: an actor in a community that supports a theatre must be as much involved in the outside world as in his own craft.
>
> (Brook 1972: 85–6)

The Brechtian actor's training begins with observation of the outside world. This was what Brecht chose to stress in his poetic 'Speech to Danish Working-Class Actors on the Art of Observation':

> In order to observe
> One must learn how to compare. In order to compare
> One must have observed. By means of observation
> Knowledge is generated; on the other hand knowledge is needed
> For observation.
>
> (Brecht 1976b: 233–8)

The paradoxical circularity is typical of Brecht's thinking about acting. The answer to a question is another question; the end of interrogation is interrogation. But actors cannot question what they do not notice. They must see the obvious clearly enough to mistrust it.

The question mark is Brecht's starting-point for observation. His famous essay on 'The Street Scene' (Willett 1964: 121–8) asks what an actor may learn from the way in which an onlooker describes a street-accident. But this onlooker is an exemplary actor in the everyday theatre of the street, concerned not only with *what* happened but with why and how. If we watch and listen to him carefully we will understand that the accident need not have happened. We will have our own questions about human interaction under the current dispensation. Amongst Brecht's papers there is an undated list containing a skeletal scheme of twenty-four exercises for acting schools (Willett 1964: 129). 'The street accident' is the twenty-second, and it is enigmatically glossed, 'Laying down limits of justifiable imitation'.

Brecht did not want the exercise to be used indiscriminately. It is about more than observation; critically approached, as part of the present-historical, it lays bare the functioning of society, uncritically approached its imitation is unjustifiable. The deaths of Swiss Cheese and Kattrin in *Mother Courage* are, after all, street-accidents, and they need to be accounted for as well as imitated. The first four exercises on Brecht's list, though cunningly interrogative in their way, call more straightforwardly for observation:

1   Conjuring tricks, including attitude of spectators.
2   For women: folding and putting away linen. Same for men.
3   For men: varying attitudes of smokers. Same for women.
4   Cat playing with a hank of thread.

We ask of the conjuror, how did you do that, but why are some spectators amazed and others dismissive? Do women and men do things differently? Why? Is doing things with linen a female thing? Who determines that? How can an activity as common as smoking betray the social class of the smoker? What do people play with? How do we know, when playing with a cat, that the cat is not playing with us? The observation of society ends with a question mark, too.

Almost all of Brecht's proposed exercises involve actors working together, and there is nothing surprising about that. The questions arising from observation are asked on behalf of society as a whole. The image is of interdependence. This is a point spelt out clearly in the *Short Organum*:

> the learning process must be co-ordinated so that the actor learns as the other actors are learning and develops his character as they are developing theirs. For the smallest social unit is not the single person but two people. In life too we develop one another.
>
> (Willett 1964: 197)

The social heart of an episode, which Brecht would have called its *Gestus*, is dependent on the disposition of all the characters on stage. During the Berliner Ensemble's interactive rehearsals, the actors were expected to ask where their characters stood and how they (the actors) stood towards their characters. Such questions require close attention to the totality of a text and its dramaturgy. Brecht's awareness of this is expressed in his 'Notes on Stanislavski': 'Stanislavski when directing is first of all an actor. When I direct I am first of all a playwright' (Brecht 1964: 165). Most of the exercises he used with the Ensemble were directly related to the play in rehearsal, but not necessarily to the play as it would be performed. If the actors were to work on the audience in such a way as to rob the familiar of its inconspicuousness, it might help if the familiar text could be made conspicuous to the actors.

It was in this spirit that Brecht recommended to Giorgio Strehler the rehearsal of tragic scenes for comic effect (Mitter 1992: 57). By contradicting a text, the actors might gain new insights into it. Such contradiction is not designed to open access to what Stanislavsky termed a subtext, but to surround a text with a metatext linking it to the world outside, the world that is in need of transformation. The several practice pieces for actors that Brecht wrote in 1939 with Swedish students in mind (Brecht 1976a: 339–55) are anachronistic mistreatments of the classics, which highlight the plight of an underclass disregarded in *Macbeth*, *Hamlet*, and *Romeo and Juliet*. They call attention to what is missing from the plays but present in the social order, and they invite actors to develop a critical attitude to the characters they are playing. Thus the actors become, in the language of metaphor, double agents, sometimes self-employed and sometimes employed by the character.

The metaphor is Joseph Chaikin's. He uses it to describe the performances of the man he considers the definitive Brechtian actor, Ekkehard Schall: 'I never believe he is the character by name. Nor do I believe that he is "playing himself". He performs like a double agent who has infiltrated the two worlds' (Chaikin 1991: 16). This double agency is effectively tested in one of Brecht's so-called 'exercises in temperament': 'Situation: two women calmly folding linen. They feign a wild and jealous quarrel for the benefit of their husbands; the husbands are in the next room' (Willett 1964: 129).

The manifest disparity between the orderliness of the action and the disorderliness of the speaking makes demands on the control of the actors and, at the same time, makes unusually conspicuous the commonplace activities of folding and quarrelling. Such contradictory juxtapositions are the typical ammunition of *Verfremdung*. They make strange what we might otherwise scarcely notice. A Brechtian actor must be alert to the social significance of every kind of human transaction, even the most mundane. 'I don't act emotions', explained Schall, 'I present them as ways of behaviour' (Honneger and Schechter 1986: 35).

There is a danger of distortion here. Despite what has often been said, sometimes by himself, the mature Brecht rejected neither emotion nor psychological enquiry. Angelika Hurwicz, a leading member of the Ensemble, denies that Brecht was 'hostile to drama exercises aimed at ensuring the truth to life and the warmth of the presentation of the role; in fact, he regards them as a pre-requisite' (Witt 1974: 132). In a sequel to the linen-folding exercise, for example, Brecht proposes that the game 'turn serious' (Willett 1964: 129). His departure from Stanislavskian methods was not total, but graduated. In the first stage of rehearsal actors should become acquainted with their characters, the second phase is one of empathy, 'and then there is a third phase in which you try to see the character from the outside, from the standpoint of society' (Brecht 1964: 159).

It is to the transition from the second to the third phase that the third-person exercises belong. There is an indicative journal entry, written as the opening night of the Berliner Ensemble's *Mother Courage* approached:

> I put in 10 minutes epic rehearsal for the first time in the eleventh scene. gerda müller and dunskus as peasants are deciding that they cannot do anything against the catholics. I ask them to add 'said the man', 'said the woman' after each speech. suddenly the scene became clear and müller found a realistic attitude.
>
> (Brecht 1993: 405)

This is not an exercise designed to obstruct emotional engagement, but to show that the actor's emotion does not need to coincide with that of the character. The notion of double agency is at its most complex here, but the actor's eye is on the audience. The actor both presents and scrutinises the behaviour of the character in such a way as to invite the audience's interrogation. If it is circumstance, not human necessity, that governs behaviour, actors and audience should combine to change the circumstance.

It is generally true that a Stanislavskian actor will locate in character the explanation for behaviour, whilst the Brechtian actor will look for it in circumstance. The aim of rehearsal exercises will not have been to embed action in individual psychology, but to place it in the social transactions of the group. The outcome for the audience should not be psychoanalysis but moral debate. The metaphor for a final set of exercises is that of multiple doors. You will go through only one, but you could go through any. The task is to make your choice in such a way as to indicate to the onlookers that there are other choices you could have made:

> Whatever [the actor] doesn't do must be contained and conserved in what he does. In this way every sentence and every gesture signifies a decision; the character remains under observation and is tested. The technical term for this procedure is 'fixing the "not...but" '.
>
> (Willett 1964: 137)

Brecht provides no list of 'not...but' exercises, knowing that they can be readily devised and appropriated according to context. He does, however, describe the practice, as, for example, in Helene Weigel's final moments as Mother Courage: 'Even in paying for the burial, Weigel gave one last hint of Courage's character. She fished a few coins out of her leather bag, put one back and gave the peasants the rest' (Brecht 1972: 383). If an actor can learn how to show that the choice made was not the only available choice, the audience may be encouraged to choose for change. The aim of the 'not...but' exercises is to train actors to ask why not as well as why, but Brechtian actors have always a design on the audience.

Production

John Fuegi has calculated that, before the opening of *The Caucasian Chalk Circle* on 7 October 1954, the actors of the Berliner Ensemble had rehearsed for 600 hours (Fuegi 1987: 161). It is an over-literal calculation, but it speaks appropriately of the slow pace of rehearsal once the company was fully established. Given time, Brecht explored all the elements I have mentioned:

1   Contradiction as a route to a metatext.
2   The identification of goodness with efficacy.
3   The presentational style of the actor who may at any moment sing.
4   The priority of narrative and circumstance over character.
5   The approach through history, including the historicisation of the present.
6   Observation sharpened by interrogation.
7   The ensemble working together to deliver the social *Gestus*.
8   The double agency of actor and character.
9   Speaking in the third person (sometimes augmented by speaking the stage directions).
10 Fixing the 'not...but'.

Brecht's major productions with the Berliner Ensemble, *Mother Courage* (1949) and *The Caucasian Chalk Circle* (1954), have been described in some detail by, respectively, Peter Thomson (Thomson 1997) and John Fuegi (Fuegi 1987). It is more appropriate here to set out the broader terms within which he went about making theatre.

Alone amongst the practitioners featured in this book, Brecht was a major playwright. He was also a poet, a wordsmith. Language mattered intensely to him, both the sound of the meaning and the meaning of the sound. He was quite as likely, in rehearsal, to join an actor in interrogating a sentence as in questioning a gesture. Either way, the goal of the interrogation was efficacy. An archival fragment provides a list of what he might ask of a sentence:

1   Who is the sentence of use to?
2   Who does it claim to be of use to?
3   What does it call for?
4   What practical action corresponds to it?
5   What sort of sentences result from it? What sort of sentences support it?
6   In what situation is it spoken? By whom?

(Willett 1964: 106)

The solemnity is misleading. The atmosphere at Brecht's rehearsals was normally relaxed, even expansive. His policy was to remain silent in order to provoke the actors into making suggestions, though he was typically capable of mischievous intervention. Hans Bunge remembers Brecht the director saying of Brecht the playwright, 'One cannot always be guided by what *he* says' (Fuegi 1987: 148). Changes might be made to the text if the actors came up with a preferred alternative, although the changes were sometimes obliterated in the published version. The Ensemble was incorporated in the creation of a play, not subjugated to the revival of a text, and Brecht expected the creation to be definitive. To whom will the play be of use? What practical action corresponds to it? These are metatextual matters, and only the performance can resolve them. What Shomit Mitter has called 'the tussle between text and commentary that is the hallmark of the Brechtian theatre' (Mitter 1992: 46) is fought out on the stage.

The image of struggle is entirely appropriate to any consideration of Brecht. His creative energy was always charged by disagreement. The early play, *Baal*, was provoked by the urge to counter the heroic vision of Hanns Johst's *Der Einsame* (The Loner), and the impulse to write counter-plays (*Gegenstücke*) remained with him. Not surprisingly, then, Brecht's work with actors displays aspects of a counter-practice (*Gegenpraktik*). Persuaded that traditional styles of performance, like the established dramatic repertoire, reinforced the social *status quo* by rendering the audience passive, Brecht set about changing both.

There is no reason to doubt his belief that whatever could be made visible could also be mastered, and it was certainly his conviction that Stanislavskian performances in Aristotelian drama disempowered the audience. The concept of *Gestus* became a counter to pathos, and it is a pity for those who would like to systematise Brechtian practice that Brecht himself used the word so loosely. Amongst the many attempts to define it on Brecht's behalf, one of the simplest is Mitter's. *Gestus*, he suggests, is 'a compound term which intrinsically harnesses both content and opinion' (Mitter 1992: 48).

The problem with this formulation is that it implicitly sells short the integral contribution of the actors. More recently, Meg Mumford, in an extended study of *Gestus* from the actor's perspective, has proposed it as the essential counter to Stanislavsky. For her, *Gestus* is 'the aesthetic gestural presentation of the economic and socio-ideological construction of human identity and interaction', something which 'finds ultimate expression in the corporeal and intellectual work of the performer' (Mumford 1997: xviii). However complex the understanding, there is no escaping the fact that *Gestus* is the key concept in Brechtian actor training and the defining quality of a truly Brechtian performance. Before semiotics became a recognised focus of theatrical criticism or performance theory, *Gestus* guided the productions of the Berliner Ensemble. In socio-political terms at least, it remains the most sophisticated application of semiotic principles to the preparation of actors. Carl Weber, who worked with Brecht in Berlin, recalls its relevance to individual actors:

> The *Gestus* was to be mainly determined by the social position and history of a character, and Brecht instructed his actors to develop it by careful attention to all the contradictions to be discovered in the actions and verbal text of the role…this may sound quite abstract, but it was achieved during rehearsal in a most practical, even playful manner.
>
> (Thomson and Sacks 1994: 182)

It was the business of rehearsal to anatomise what was said and done by each individual actor, however small the part. In this respect, *Gestus* is diagnosis applied to social history. The object, when it comes to production, is to present a narrative with such clarity that the audience can read, not only the behaviour of the characters, but also the provenance of that behaviour and its application to their own lives. 'The actor in Brecht's theatre', says Mumford, 'does not focus on an individual's inner life but on their *Gestus*' (Mumford 1997: 156). In his notes on particular productions, Brecht frequently records how actors embodied the *Gestus*. In the fourth scene of *Mother Courage*, for instance, after singing 'The Song of the Great Capitulation', Weigel both displayed and contradicted Courage's depravity:

> Weigel's face in this scene shows a glimmer of wisdom and even of nobility, and that is good. Because the depravity is not so much that of her person as of her class, and because she herself at least rises above it somewhat by showing that she understands this weakness and that it even makes her angry.
>
> (Brecht 1972: 362)

The Brechtian actor represents more than the self of the character. It was Brecht's contention that *Gestus*, when properly applied, would enable an audience to understand both the story of a play and its implications even if it were separated from the actors by a soundproof glass wall. To some extent, certainly, he was a pictorial director, concerned to paint meaning through costume, properties and the grouping of actors. Archive photographs, particularly of *The Mother* but sometimes even of *Mother Courage*, encapsulate the context of struggle with the starkness of Käthe Kollwitz's woodcuts.

The relationship of director, designer and actors at the Berliner Ensemble was a significant innovation. It has been finely described by Christopher Baugh (Thomson and Sacks 1994: 235–53), and is not centrally the business of this chapter. But it is important that actors should be able to visualise themselves as part of a scene, and both Caspar Neher and Karl von Appen were vital contributory members of Brecht's production team. The absence of Neher during the rehearsals of *Mother Courage* was a source of anxiety. It was Neher who originated the custom of sketching scenes in advance of their

Figure 5.2   Helene Weigel as Mother Courage, Erwin Geschonneck as the Chaplain
in Brecht's *Mother Courage and Her Children*

Source: Photo Hainer Hill by permission of the Berliner Ensemble

rehearsal. The disposition of the characters on the stage and the placing of
the attention in performance, sketched out in suggestive sequence, became a
subject of enquiry. During rehearsal these sketches could be tested, contradicted, re-affirmed. The quest was always for the *Gestus* that carried the
scene closer to reality. At the still centre of every mobile episode in a
Berliner Ensemble production there was always a signifying tableau. It is
important to recognise, though, that the spirit of contradiction operated
even here. Despite the image of the soundproof glass wall, the priority of the
visual was constantly contradicted by detailed attention to the words. We
can never afford to forget that Brecht was a writer. Attempting a third-
person summary of his unique achievement in the prose work *Me-Ti*, he
wrote:

He made use of a type of language which was at the same time stylized and natural. He achieved this by paying attention to the attitudes underlying sentences: he only incorporated attitudes into sentences and always saw that the attitudes were visible through the sentences. To this kind of language he gave the name 'gestic', since it was just an expression of people's gestures.

(Morley 1977: 120)

As a shorthand guide to Brechtian acting, it would be difficult to improve on 'paying attention to the attitudes underlying sentences' and 'an expression of people's gestures'.

Bibliography

Brecht, B. (1964) 'Notes on Stanislavski', *Tulane Drama Review* 9 (2): 157–66.
—— (1972) *Collected Plays*, vol. 5, New York: Vintage Books.
—— (1976a) *Collected Plays*, vol. 6, New York: Vintage Books.
—— (1976b) *Poems 1913–1956*, London: Eyre Methuen.
—— (1990) *Letters 1913–1956*, New York: Routledge.
—— (1993) *Journals 1934–1955*, London: Methuen.
Brecht, B. *et al.* (1952) *Theaterarbeit*, Dresden: Dresdner Verlag.
Brook, P. (1972) *The Empty Space*, Harmondsworth: Penguin Books.
Chaikin, J. (1991) *The Presence of the Actor*, New York: Theatre Communications Group.
Esslin, M. (1970) *Brief Chronicles*, London: Temple Smith.
Fuegi, J. (1987) *Bertolt Brecht: Chaos According to Plan*, Cambridge: Cambridge University Press.
Honneger, G. and Schechter, J. (1986) 'An interview with Ekkehard Schall', *Theater*, Spring: 31–43.
Mitter, S. (1992) *Systems of Rehearsal*, London: Routledge.
Morley, M. (1977) *A Student's Guide to Brecht*, London: Heinemann.
Mumford, M. (1997) 'Showing the *Gestus*: a Study of Acting in Brecht's Theatre', unpublished Ph.D. thesis, University of Bristol.
Thomson, P. (1997) *Mother Courage and Her Children*, Cambridge: Cambridge University Press.
Thomson, P. and Sacks, G. (eds) (1994) *The Cambridge Companion to Brecht*, Cambridge: Cambridge University Press.
Toller, E. (1934) *I Was a German*, London: John Lane.
Völker, K. (1979) *Brecht: a Biography*, London: Marion Boyars.
Willett, J. (1964) *Brecht on Theatre*, London: Methuen.
Witt, H. (ed.) (1974) *Brecht as They Knew Him*, London: Lawrence and Wishart.

6 Joan Littlewood

Clive Barker

Context

Although Joan Littlewood has refrained from producing works of theory, as many other directors have done, that does not mean that there is no theory behind her work. Angela Hurwicz, when asked if Brecht had spoken much about theory during rehearsals, said not at all.[1] Kurt Jooss was once asked how much theory Laban referred to in rehearsals. He said none.[2] Whatever is set out in print is only relevant if it refers directly to what happens on the stage, which is the sole place of arbitration. Peter Brook has written a great deal on his views of theatre but it contains a large proportion of rhetoric. This can be, and often has been, inspiring for the reader, but it does not always give any clear inkling as to how Brook works in rehearsal.[3] To discover that, it is probably more valuable to refer to the testimony and anecdotes of his actors.

The evidence for Littlewood's theory lies in snippets of statements in interviews and manifestos and in the memories and anecdotes of the actors who have worked with her. Although these documents, which include this chapter, have to be questioned carefully, and seen as both idiosyncratic and subjective.[4] What anyone sees and how they interpret it depends on what attitudes they bring to the work and what resources they have to contextualise it. The student handbook for London's East 15 Acting School, which was founded by a former company member, Margaret Walker (Bury), refers to Theatre Workshop as 'substantially challenging notions of repertoire, theatre propriety, actor/audience relationships and the social basis of their audience'. East 15 was founded 'to ensure the retention of *the working method*...which was never set down, codified or systematised' (my italics).

Littlewood herself has denied the existence of any method or way of working to a system.[5] If things are not set down, they nevertheless rub off. The unfortunate result of Littlewood's reluctance to set down her working methods and their theoretical backing has been that she has been accused of being a dilettante who somehow managed to hit the right button on some occasions – which is a long way from the truth. Throughout the early periods of the company, each performance was charted in long and detailed analytical notes posted the next day. There was nothing hit or miss about these notes. The slightest lapse of concentration, a failure to sustain, or the presence of cliché was noticed with what seemed an eagle eye which never relaxed.[6] Actors who have spent any time working with her are, in my experience, never in doubt as to what she intended – a clear demonstration of a shared aesthetic and technique. Richard Harris is on record as saying he learned more from one afternoon with Littlewood than in all the other time he spent at drama school.[7] I find no contradiction in Littlewood's refusal to set out her theoretical positions. There has clearly always been a deep mistrust of the word over the action. 'We know what they say but what are they doing?'[8] could be applied to the whole business of creating theatre as well as analysing a single unit in a play.

In one of the few direct statements that Littlewood has made about her view of theatre she said:

> I do not believe in the supremacy of the director, designer, actor or even the writer. It is through collaboration that this knockabout art of theatre survives and kicks. ... No one mind or imagination can foresee what a play will become until all the physical and intellectual stimuli which are crystallized in the poetry of the author, have been understood by a company, and then tried out in terms of mime, discussion and the precise music of grammar; words and movement allied and integrated.[9]

This sublime piece of theatre rhetoric merits consideration for the questions it raises about the process of making theatre, Littlewood's problems with the theatre establishment, and for the clues it offers to clarify the way she worked. Paramount is the insistence on the power of the ensemble, a group of artists with different talents, skills and minds, working and playing in a co-operative, rather than authoritarian, mode or synthetic manner.

She has consistently declined to accept a dictatorial approach, dismissing with contempt the 'genius' director, sitting in his or her study with a model of the set and some toy soldiers, working out the choreography and stage pictures of the proposed production: directing the actors, from day one of rehearsal, to carry out his or her preconceived instructions. Theatre based on such an approach results in seventeen people illustrating one person's imagination. How much more powerful to have eighteen people's imaginations working in concert! Further to this concept, she characterised the work of Theatre Workshop as a jazz combo against the classical orchestra, which was the model of established theatre practice. The quotation above is based on the understanding that it is harder to create great jazz than to play in a symphony orchestra, requiring much rigorous investigation of form, structure and style and greater instrumental flexibility and virtuosity. The British Theatre has consistently looked suspiciously at anyone who takes theatre that seriously and who appears to have faith in imagination over methodical drilling. The late Kenneth Tynan, the most influential critic at the time of

Littlewood's work, once said to me that his feeling was that British directors were afraid of actors. That could never be said of Joan Littlewood.

Background

Theatre Workshop was preceded by a sequence of other companies assembled in the 1930s by Joan Littlewood and Ewan MacColl.[10] The major feature of these companies was social commitment, often overtly political. Theatrically they consistently drew upon the rich experimentation that was taking place on the Continent in the 1920s and 1930s, which hardly touched the British Theatre at that time. A large part of this book is given over to artists who were influential in The New Movement in the Theatre, which also extended to include the United States.[11] The influences they absorbed came through personal contact and through voracious study.

Along with the new staging and lighting techniques, they took in the concepts of the ensemble, as the creative instrument of making theatre, and that of the research theatre company. Companies such as those led by Copeau, Stanislavsky and Meyerhold consistently researched the history of theatre practice from whatever sources were obtainable and through practical recreations and experimentation. The later Littlewood/MacColl companies in the 1930s, up to and into the war, mounted a systematic research of the history of theatre performance. Each actor was allocated a period or style, being expected to produce papers and lectures, to communicate his or her understanding to the others. All this apart from the personal research of Littlewood and MacColl.[12]

They were searching for an aesthetic, a philosophy of theatre, and gradually it began to emerge, basing itself on:

1   An awareness of the social issues of the time, and in that sense, a political theatre.
2   A theatrical language that working people could understand, but that was capable of reflecting, when necessary, ideas, either simple or involved, in a poetic form.
3   An expressive and flexible form of movement, and a high standard of skill and technique in acting.
4   A high level of technical sound and light into the production.[13]

Some of the major features that were absorbed and were continued through the work of Theatre Workshop consisted of a combination of both Stanislavskian techniques, to create the inner truth of the characters, and those derived from the work of Rudolf Laban, to structure the expressive techniques of performance.[14] Added to this was the use of lighting in a dramatic way. With light directed to play on textured scenic units, often three-dimensional, it was possible to paint the stage to create atmosphere and mood, and to restructure the overall space into specific isolated, or related, areas of action. This was in contradiction to the majority of British theatre practice which relied on painted two-dimensional flats, lit with bland, smooth illumination. The tendency in the 1950s and 1960s was towards smooth multi-lantern settings. Theatre Workshop used lanterns sparsely, in settings in which shadows and darkness were as important as lit areas. The settings employed levels and ramps, often built from scaffolding, and frequently opened the wings and flies of the stage to create auxiliary playing spaces. The aim was to utilise setting with the principal intention of projecting the actors into a variety of forms of relationship with the audience. This also involved a running battle with the confining and defining effect of the proscenium arch. These features were constituent parts of a major conceptual leap into style, a subject which obsessed many practitioners and theorists from around the turn of this century, united against the dead hand of naturalism.

Two aspects of this debate and experimentation mark out Littlewood and MacColl's search. Much of the experimentation of the early twentieth century was concerned with finding forms and structures in the past theatres which would offer clues to the establishment of popular theatre, accessible to a much wider audience. When Littlewood and MacColl began Theatre Workshop in 1946, their manifesto contained a recognition that all the great theatres of the past – Shakespeare, Molière and others – had enjoyed an audience of mixed classes and contained a large proportion of the working population, as well as thieves, rogues and the unemployed. All had combined song and dance within the dramatic action. Theatre Workshop wanted a way of performing the classics which made them accessible to a wide range of audiences, and put an end to elitist notions of theatre.[15]

The second feature of the experimentation which characterised the work of Theatre Workshop was the definition of style as the means through which the essence of a play was communicated to an audience.[16] Richard Findlater, writing in 1953, characterised the style of the British theatre as 'polite naturalism', and regretted that the theatre at that time showed no sign that its major innovators and world figures had ever existed.[17] The work of Theatre Workshop has never been characterised by polite naturalism or by consistent style, either overall or within the scenes and units of a play.

This is what makes the 'knockabout art' of theatre require such detailed and rigorous testing to make it survive and kick in the quotation earlier. One small but striking example is the inclusion of Chinese Theatre techniques in the sixteenth-century play *Arden of Faversham*. Act II, scenes ii and iii, take place by a river as the villains Black Will and Shakebag attempt to ambush and murder Thomas Arden. Because the ambush takes place at night the plan fails, and the villains are thwarted. Clearly, in the Elizabethan theatre, these scenes were played in broad daylight and a lot of the comedy arose out of the visible actors playing as though in the dark. Modern staging techniques make this stylised acting unnecessary and a lot of the fun is lost in modern recreations.

Figure 6.1   Henry Chapman's *You Won't Always Be on Top*

Source: Photo J.V. Spinner by permission of The Theatre Workshop Archive

Amalgamating scenes from two Peking Operas, 'The Fight in the Dark' from *The Inn at the Cross-roads* and the set piece of *Crossing the Autumn River*, Littlewood staged the scenes in two (non-existent) boats in the middle of the river. In the great theatres of the past, actors were required to undertake the double transformations of space and character. The presence of the stage designer tended to take the first of these away from the actor. The designer transforms the actual space of the stage into the virtual space of the setting and in front of this the actor creates character. This division restricts the use of the actor's imagination and physical techniques. Littlewood's restoration of the transformation of space to the actor reached its apotheosis in *Oh, What a Lovely War!*.

Preparation

Given such an approach, where each play is assessed for its intrinsic theatrical properties and values, even to the extent that productions were characterised by montages of scenes in differing styles, no two productions were ever approached in the same way. What was common was an opening period in which the text was worked over and tried out to reveal the secrets of its theatricality. Dense, classic texts were given a long time for analysis.

Figure 6.2   Littlewood's production of *The Hostage* at the Théâtre des Nations Festival, Paris

Source: Clive Barker collection

Contemporary plays were often experimented with in terms of lines and passages of dialogue spoken by a succession of different actors and pairings to discover timing and qualities of irony or social *gests*. In all cases, the social background was explored at the same time. Actors brought books and other research materials to rehearsal and the insights these gave were incorporated into the discussions.[18]

Often these insights provided the stimulus to move the play into the active, exploratory stage. The early stages of Brendan Behan's *The Quare Fellow* were filled with the actors walking round the roof of the theatre for long periods, the prisoners trying to communicate by talking out of the corners of their mouths, the warders trying to catch them doing it. *The Hostage* began with stories and songs that Behan told the company, and continued after he had left with recordings made of him holding court and developing a party atmosphere. The final text of *Oh, What a Lovely War!*, in so far as anything was ever final, grew out of the actors' own research being shaped in rehearsals.[19]

The use of games and improvisations in the early stages of rehearsal was not a simple matter, and served many functions in shaping the production. It could supply the text on occasions, or animate it as lines and dialogue were fed into the structure of the activity. The usual actor's task of learning lines was not much in evidence in Theatre Workshop – they were learned collectively during the rehearsals.[20] Action and dialogue were integrated and one informed the other. The prompter, so necessary in most theatres, was not in evidence at Theatre Workshop. If text, movement and action were integrated, the possibility of an actor 'drying' was barely conceivable and, if this happened, it was considered axiomatic that the other actors in the scene would be able to improvise from their own integrated under-standing, to carry the scene forward without difficulty.

Probably the clearest example of the importance of the games and impro-visations in Littlewood's work with actors comes from a production of Büchner's *Danton's Death*, which was never actually mounted.[21] The play was written in 1835, but was not performed until the early years of this century, and the writer made little concession to its possible staging. There are scenes of the revolutionary mob teeming through the streets of Paris. In the early stages of rehearsal, a square was drawn on the floor and the actors played a children's game called 'The Raft of the *Medusa*'. The *Medusa* was a ship which sank around the equator with inadequate boat and raft capacity to save those on board. In order to live, survivors struggled to push the weakest overboard to the sharks.

In the game, all players crowd into the square and then push and pull until only one person – the winner – is left in the square. Those who touch the ground outside the square are out. This game was played for many days before Littlewood began to introduce new rules. These, first, indicated the time that the raft had been in the sea. Five days on the equator, ten days, two weeks, etc. At each stage the energy with which the actions were played declined, and the movement slowed down and lightened. Then a copy of the painting of *The Raft of the Medusa*, by the Romantic painter Géricault, was brought in and the actors were told to play the game in the style of Géricault. Finally the square was dispensed with and the actors moved into the streets and the style of the playing was established. Out of a simple game, a complex solution, involving period style, evolved, through which to play the street scenes.

The games and improvisations became a laboratory through which Littlewood was able to explore such qualities as time, weight, direction and flow – the qualities through which Laban characterised all movements. It was also the process through which the rhythmic patterns of the perfor-mance were established. The abiding memory I have of the productions I saw and took part in is of complex interweavings of the individual actor's rhythms into the jazz ensemble to which I drew attention earlier. It was this rhythmic ensemble playing that carried the flow of the production and, again, made the presence of a prompter irrelevant.

Rehearsal techniques

A large part of the usefulness of working this way lies with the particular faculties which Littlewood brings to rehearsal. Apart from the quality and direction of her own research and her experience, she has the ability to think on her feet very fast, much faster than any of the actors. In rehearsal she was always able to change and develop the direction of improvisations, which took the pressure off the actors and propelled them into cognitive situations at a speed and with such imagination that the actor was not able to see where the rehearsal was going until it got there. This required a particular type of actor, naive and trusting, and accounts for many who were unable to respond to her direction and left early.

Littlewood has particular anathema, expressed in the Theatre Workshop time as 'Old Vic Acting', although no one could ever remember her going within miles of that institution, and 'past tense acting'. By the former she intended criticism of the conservatoire-trained actor.[22] It is common in some theatres to place no great value on the ensemble company, for the actor to work out his or her character and actions independent of the rest of the company and to rely on the director to choreograph the parts into a seeming whole. This process is one of preconception. It is all worked out in advance, very often incorporating mannerism, devices and effects which have 'worked' in other situations in the past, and then repeated in rehearsal and performance. To some degree it is a defence mechanism to save actors from the disruptive interference of poor directors. It is known as 'doing your homework', and British actors have been for a long time very good at taking responsibility for their own performances in this way.

For someone who works in an ensemble, jazz-like manner, this way of working is characterised by intractable actors. Rehearsals are reduced to synthetic, factory-like procedures. The moves are worked on, then each actor constructs a simplistic, cause-and-effect line to explain what he or she is going to do, often regardless of the others, but usually with a nod towards agreement. Then the lines are learned and in the later rehearsals the actors polish what has been set by marking through the moves and action until the final rehearsals when the actors 'let it go'. The production is then fixed and the intention is that this fixity should be repeated at each subsequent performance.

There is little or no room in this process to explore alternatives or to develop new approaches to a scene. All performances are kept within a controlled 'normal' limit. There is no room for an actor to explore the extremities of the character's psychology, pathology or creativity. Since the purpose of performance is to repeat identically the past reality of the fixed production, everything happening in the present has to be ignored. If the wall falls down, ignore it. If there is a disturbance in the auditorium, carry on regardless. Reality lies in remembering, recovering and repeating the past. It produces 'past tense acting'. This is characterised by an insensitivity to space, a slight but significant retarding of the pelvis, which alters the balance of the body and allows the mind to predominate over the physical sensations of the body, and by an absence of direct eye contact between the actors, each enclosed in their own world.

This is the antithesis of the Theatre Workshop process. It should be clear by now that productions were not conceived on synthetic lines but holistically. There was no question of adding A to B but of constantly challenging, changing and developing A. In this the work of Littlewood has affinity with that of Meyerhold, of whom it was said that every rehearsal looked like a performance and every performance like a rehearsal. At no point did a Theatre Workshop production ever become set.

There was no room in Theatre Workshop for an actor who tried out preconceived effects, or for someone who tried out the actor's defensive and evasive device of claiming, 'I don't feel it'. This brought a response on at least one occasion of: 'You're not here to fucking feel, you're here to fucking do.'[23] Experienced actors working this way reached levels of performance they could not reach elsewhere. Willing novices were preferable to the conservatoire-trained actors. The lore of Theatre Workshop ran that to join the company you should never audition but should take a job in the bar or as the boilerman.

The process of creating an ensemble and inhibiting preconceived intentions and actions went along with the process of breaking the actor down. It was not simply a question that some actors pre-planned what they were going to do and some did not, but that all actors to some extent set limits to the exploration and delay setting sail on an uncharted sea. This process is complicated, relies upon trust and self-confidence in giving up the conscious control which the actor often inhibits.[24] The intuitive actions of the subconscious are overridden in favour of conscious control, which inevitably results in the production of clichés.

Sometimes a drastic process of breaking down personality defences is necessary to allow the actor the flexibility to choose alternative ways of acting. Sexually unsure and inexperienced, and coming from a society rootedly homophobic, I was made by Littlewood to get up on stage and display femininity. I hated doing this, but as with other things it broke through my defensive inhibitions. The superb performance of the actor playing Edward II for Theatre Workshop was achieved, through great pain, by having him confront his latent homosexuality, at a time when no great sympathy or tolerance could be expected from society at large.

Often the process resulted in continual repetition of actions through a use of the *via negativa*. Seemingly endless repetition of units of action were met with a categorical rejection. Anyone who has worked with Littlewood will wince at the memory of going over single lines time and time again, each actor in turn speaking the line until the valid intonation, phasing and emphasis emerged. Units were run over endlessly until all the actor could think was: 'I have no idea what to do. I've run out of every idea I have. Oh, shit.' At this point, devoid of conscious intention, the actor would enter the stage and simply do it. This was almost invariably correct and accepted without comment.[25]

In addition to the processes outlined above, Littlewood at times has resorted to a German technique known by the French term of the *siffleuse*, the whistler. Each actor is allocated a prompter who moves behind him or her, speaking the lines half a line before the actor as a conscious prompt. The actor is not only free to explore the situation, free of having to remember the lines, but learns the text in the functional, communicative manner in which it is delivered by the prompter, close to how the line should be spoken. The use of the *siffleuse* reinstates a process close to the interactive relationship of mind and speech, which is natural to us. The use of the *via negativa* and the functional intervention of the *siffleuse* remove self-imposed and textural pressures which interfere with the action of the subconscious.

The work of the director who acts as a coach and trainer of an ensemble is more often concerned with removing obstacles to authenticity than adding to, or refining, what the actor preconceives. Directing is conceived as steering rather than ordering.[26] It should be noted that the company carried out training during the rehearsal period. The purpose, beyond that of simply keeping the instrument tuned, was, first, to condition the actor to work instinctively and also to establish a language, largely based on Stanislavsky and Laban, through which to communicate, as the process of fine-tuning in the rehearsals began.

Later rehearsals

One of the particular talents which Littlewood possesses is her ability to analyse a text in terms of work effort. I have known her put up a detailed rehearsal schedule at the beginning of the week, for the whole week, and not be more than twenty minutes out at the end. In this she sensed that certain units presented problems on which much of the later action depended. This may be related to Brecht's concept of the nodal points which pull together the previous action and from which future action flows. Her perception of these has always been a matter of judgement not accessible to analysis but singularly successful.

Rehearsals generally continued along the lines I have indicated above. Key units were worked on to explore intention and motivation. Changes were explored in terms of the Laban movement efforts being used by the actor(s). One frequent solution to problems was for the actor to sing or dance the unit, to physicalise, by extension, the line or movement. Units were often conceived in terms of another concept which springs from Laban – that of dance mime. Working actions are gradually extended in size and accentuated rhythm to transform the action into dance. A counter-process would bring the dance back down to the ground working action.

In *Oh, What a Lovely War!*, there is a scene in which soldiers portray the burial of the dead, although, as always with that play, the action is portrayed very much in the Chinese theatre fashion without any scenic attempt to represent a real graveyard with real corpses. As the action proceeds, the music comes up underneath it and the movement is gradually extended into song and dance, with shovels taking the place of skeletal partners. The result is 'The Bells of Hell Go Ting-a-ling-a-ling'. At the end, the music fades and the movement returns to the more realistic, mimetic representation it began with. This is not a unique use of this technique, which appears in several Laurel and Hardy films.[27] It was, though, particularly poignant, and it is characteristic of Littlewood's refusal to stay within naturalistic techniques but to use a wide range of stylised techniques.

Rehearsals explored counterpoint. Actors were made aware of what they brought on stage with them. Where the text made the given circumstances, the intention and the emotional mood quite clear, actors were asked to complement, or even contradict, this with other information. There was a constant use of other actors to offer, through their attitudes and movement, alternative views and interpretations of the main action. The stage became peopled with characters, each with a distinct, coherent and continuous life of their own, replete with values, hopes, ambitions, fears and judgements.

There were never any spear-carriers or supernumeraries on the stage.[28] In opposition to the synthetic, linear approach to making theatre, Theatre Workshop created a theatre rich in texture, in which every corner of the stage was alive and active. In this way it was possible to see a production over and over again and always find something new. In the sense that there were so many human beings playing out their lives in concert, no performance could ever be remotely the same in detail, but each was always bedded down in a common understanding, purpose and rhythmic technique. This interdependence and co-ordination made for a lack of self-consciousness. If the purpose of playing is not to make things happen but to let things happen, as Littlewood believes, this technique constantly strove to that state. The late Harry H. Corbett, who could stand as the epitome of the Theatre Workshop actor, said to me once that his ambition was to give one performance in which he had only one motivation, the one which took him out of the wings and on to the stage. From that point, he wanted to play only off of his reaction to the other actors. In a theatrical world where so many stages are littered with actions and questions to which no one responds, Theatre Workshop approached that ideal. In spite of poor physical and financial resources but also in the sense of 'poor theatre' (which Grotowski and Barba use to mark out a total utilisation of the actor's resources), Theatre Workshop was a rich, multi-textured theatre.[29]

The guiding principles behind this way of working are, first, that everything should come from the actor, since only the actor appears on the stage, and, second, that what the actor does on stage is determined by what has been done in rehearsal. On stage the actor can only play. This is true of all actors but not all actors have prepared to the same extent and in the same ways. In conversation Littlewood once said that any actor should be able, at the dress rehearsal, to take a direction to enter through a different door to the one which had been rehearsed. If they could not, they should not be in the theatre. But if they had not explored the material of the performance in rehearsal, there was no way they could act in any meaningful way.

There is one caveat to this. At a certain point in time, the pressure of the opening night and the consequent presence of an audience makes it inevitable that, if the actors have not at that point caught the full scale of the performance, the director must supply direction to pull the production together. In fact, working in this way leaves a mass of loose ends and a lack of overall consistency. At this point the director must head for home. In the synthetic theatre, the director begins to head for home from day one of the rehearsal period. It is in the character of Littlewood that she could delay this moment until very late: three days or so before the opening night. There has been criticism of this. Actors who have not understood these processes have complained that in the end she did what she wanted with the production regardless of what went before. Critics have noted and praised the composition of significant groupings and images in the production. There is no contradiction here. To hold back from dictatorially directing the production until such a late date depends upon a confidence in being able to pull things technically into a coherent shape, and Littlewood's early training and talent for painting facilitated her ability to rapidly choreograph stage action. However, without the complex processes which led up to that point, there would have been nothing to pull together or choreograph.

Performance

If one quality characterised Theatre Workshop performances it was high energy. There are two kinds of performance energy. One is seen when the performer goes out to 'sell' the show, blasting energy regardless of the quality, or even the nature, of the material. This was always strongly discouraged by Littlewood, who often gave instructions in terms of, 'Don't go out there to succeed, you will only fail. Go out there prepared to fail and you might succeed.' To do this involves trusting the material you have been working with, the preparation you have made during the rehearsal and, of course, the other actors. To do this involves a high level of risk and Theatre Workshop was always a theatre which encouraged risk. 'Efficiency is death', was an injunction often given.

The energy which characterised Theatre Workshop was an internal energy which sprang from engagement with the processes followed during rehearsals. This will always gain a greater response from an audience than the externally applied kick energy, which often pushes the audience back from engagement with the play. In working on the units of action, there was a continuous overlap. Before one unit ended, the next had already begun. In many lines of dialogue there was a point at which the thought could be

Figure 6.3   Brendan Behan's *The Quare Fellow*
Source: Photo J.V. Spinner by permission of The Theatre Workshop Archive

grasped without the full line being delivered. That point was the trigger to spark off the next action and the dialogue overlapped. Actors began their actions and reactions before they had a line to speak.

This gave a continuous flow of action, which heightened the concentration and stimulated energy in the actors and kept the audience continuously engaged. Actors were never allowed to become cosy, which often happens in ensembles. The actors become 'pally': personal relationships begin to stray on to the stage and soften the conflicts. Kent Baker recalls a note from Littlewood saying, 'All the actors love you and they ought to hate you'. Theatre Workshop was not a comfortable place to be and actors were often fed false opinions, slander and lies to disturb their complacency. It was the only place, said Howard Goorney, where you could stay a week and write a book on your experiences.

Notes

1 She is also said to have heard the term *Verfremdung* once in her time with the Berliner Ensemble. See Margaret Eddershaw (1994) 'Actors in Brecht', in

Thomson and Sacks (eds), *The Cambridge Companion to Brecht*, Cambridge: Cambridge University Press.

2 Jooss says this in the course of an interview with John Hodgson, issued on video by the Department of Drama, University of Hull.

3 See Graham Ley (1993) 'The Rhetoric of Theory: the Role of Metaphor in Brook's *The Empty Space*', *New Theatre Quarterly* 35 (August): 246.

4 The author of this chapter worked with Joan Littlewood, as stage-manager, technical director and actor, for various periods, adding up to between three and four years, from 1955 to 1973. When no formal teaching programme exists, it is easy to credit where the learning process began but very difficult to disentangle, after a period of years, the origins of your development from what you have learned since from your own experiences.

5 What has united Littlewood with Ewan MacColl, in my experience, has been a mixture of great generosity in playing down their own genius and an almost paranoiac resentment at not being given enough credit for it. Such blanket denials should be taken with a pinch of salt. Both sides of the dialectic can be seen in their autobiographies: *Joan's Story* (1994) London: Methuen and *Journeyman* (1990) London: Sidgwick and Jackson.

6 See H. Goorney (1981) *The Theatre Workshop Story*, London: Eyre Methuen, pp. 173–5. Most of what is expressed in this chapter is amplified greatly in this book.

7 Stated in BBC2 TV Programme on Littlewood, 1996.

8 Note dropped in conversation by Joan Littlewood.

9 Quoted in Charles Marowitz (1965) 'Littlewood Pays a Dividend', *The Encore Reader*, London: Methuen University Paperbacks, p.230. He gives no attribution for the original source.

10 The history of Theatre Workshop has three major sources: Joan Littlewood (1994) *Joan's Story*, London: Methuen; Howard Goorney's *The Theatre Workshop Story*, quoted earlier; Ewan MacColl (1990) *Journeyman*, London: Sidgwick and Jackson. The history of the earlier political theatre companies can be found in Goorney and MacColl (eds) (1986) *Agit-Prop to Theatre Workshop*, Manchester: Manchester University Press and Samuel, MacColl and Cosgrove (eds) (1985) *Theatres of the Left 1880–1935*, London: Routledge and Kegan Paul.

11 See Derek Paget (1995) 'Theatre Workshop, Moussinac and the European Connection', *New Theatre Quarterly* XI, Part 3 (43), August.

12 See quotation from Rosalie Williams in Goorney, *The Theatre Workshop Story*, p. 20.

13 See Goorney, p. 8.

14 See Rudolf Laban (1960) *The Mastery of Movement*, London: Macdonald and Evans; Rudolf Laban (1975) *Modern Educational Dance*, London: Macdonald and Evans; also Jean Newlove (1993) *Laban for Actors and Dancers*, London: Nick Hern Books.

15 See Goorney, pp. 41–2.

16 I am indebted to Albert Hunt, who first formulated this recognition of Theatre Workshop.

17 See Richard Findlater (1953) *The Unholy Trade*, London: Gollancz, p. 81.

18 The research for *The Dutch Courtesan* was an education in the nature of the Elizabethan underworld.

19 See Derek Paget (1990) 'Oh, What a Lovely War!: The Texts and Their Context', *New Theatre Quarterly* VI, Part 3 (23), August: 244.

20 Brian Murphy, in conversation, said he was thrown into panic when he left Theatre Workshop and went to work in repertory. He realised he would have to learn lines in isolation, which he had never done before.

21 During the rehearsals it was learned that Theatre 69 were planning to open the same play at an earlier date. The production was, therefore, cancelled, although there is a strong suspicion that no production was ever really intended and the work on the play was only ever intended as a training exercise.

22 It should be pointed out that the training of actors today is much more advanced than it was in the 1950s and 1960s, when actors tended to be more stereotypical, mannered and self-possessed. The irony is that around the time Littlewood gave up directing, actors were beginning to emerge who were much more adaptable to her way of working. Today, she would have no problems in finding the actors she would want.

23 In this she is in line with the process, stated as an aphorism, by the French director, Louis Jouvet: the text; the action; the emotions.

24 Keith Johnstone's (1981) book, *Impro*, London: Methuen, categorises the many means that actors employ to prevent themselves from being creative.

25 During the rehearsals for *The Hostage*, I was obviously pleased with myself and was becoming self-possessed. One day I arrived at the theatre earlier in the morning, passed Littlewood on the stairs and said, 'Good morning, Joan'. She stopped, glared at me and issued the damning judgement: 'You're nothing but a fucking broomstick, with fucking bananas for fucking fingers.' She moved on. I entered the rehearsal in a state of nervous shock but I was prepared to give her what she wanted.

26 In the video interview quoted in note 2, Jooss qualifies his statement, that Laban never discussed the theory behind his work, by describing a dance rehearsal in which Laban rejects every move made until – Jooss asserts – a 'space' exists inside the dancer. 'Whatever' fills that space will be 'authentic'. Only that human being can make that action. Whether Littlewood adopted this directly from Laban, whom she knew well, I cannot say – but something of this order characterised the Theatre Workshop rehearsals.

27 The use of this technique exists in many areas of popular comedy. See Morecambe and Wise prepare breakfast to the music of 'The Stripper'.

28 The texture of the performances achieved through counterpoint, contradiction and interwoven story lines was carried out by a group of actors, known collectively as 'the slag'. I am very happy to have spent several years as a member of that group.

29 see Goorney, p. 175.

Bibliography

Bradby, D. and Williams, D. (1988) *Directors' Theatre*, Basingstoke: Macmillan.

Goorney, Howard (1981) *The Theatre Workshop Story*, London: Eyre Methuen.

Goorney, H. and MacColl, E. (eds) (1986) *Agit-Prop to Theatre Workshop*, Manchester: Manchester University Press.

Laban, Rudolf (1960) *The Mastery of Movement*, London: Macdonald and Evans.

—— (1975) *Modern Educational Dance*, London: Macdonald and Evans, 3rd edn.

Littlewood, Joan (1994) *Joan's Story*, London: Methuen.

MacColl, Ewan (1990) *Journeyman*, London: Sidgwick and Jackson.

Marowitz, C., Milne, T. and Hale, O. (eds) (1965) *The Encore Reader*, London: Methuen.

Newlove, Jean (1993) *Laban for Actors and Dancers*, London: Nick Hern Books.

Paget, Derek (1990) 'Oh What a Lovely War!: The Texts and Their Context', *New Theatre Quarterly* VI, Part 3 (23), August.

—— (1993) 'The Rhetoric of Theory: The Role of Metaphor in Brook's *The Empty Space*', *New Theatre Quarterly*, 35 (August).

—— (1995)'Theatre Workshop, Moussinac and the European Connection', *New Theatre Quarterly* XI, part 3 (43), August.

Samuel, R., MacColl, E. and Cosgrove, S. (eds) (1985) *Theatres of the Left 1880–1935*, London: Routledge and Kegan Paul.

Thomson, P. and Sacks, G. (eds) (1994) *The Cambridge Companion to Brecht*, Cambridge: Cambridge University Press.

7 Strasberg, Adler and Meisner
Method acting

David Krasner

Method acting is one of the most popular and controversial approaches to acting in the United States. According to Harold Clurman, the 'Method', as it is commonly called, is 'an abbreviation of the term "Stanislavsky Method"'. The 'Method' itself, Clurman adds, is a 'means of training actors as well as a technique for the use of actors in their work on parts' (1994: 369). Like Stanislavsky's System, Method acting codifies acting exercises, rehearsal techniques and working procedures, with the intention of helping actors achieve greater persuasiveness, feeling and depth. The Method combines Stanislavsky's techniques and the work of his pupil Eugene Vakhtangov for the purpose of understanding and effectively performing a role.

Although there are many instructors, directors and actors who have contributed to its development, three Method acting teachers are recognised as having set the standard of its success: Lee Strasberg (1901–82), Stella Adler (1901–92), and Sanford Meisner (1905–97).[1] Whilst they collaborated together in the Group Theatre during the 1930s, each emphasised different aspects of the Method. My objective here will be first to present an overview of the Method, and then consider the theories, exercises and contributions of these three Method acting instructors. In addition, I will pay close attention to the differences of the three teachers – Strasberg's emphasis on the psychological, Adler's on the sociological, and Meisner's on the behavioural – demonstrating the diversity of Method training. Moreover, because the three teachers were interested in process rather than result – in teaching acting as a craft rather than promoting commercial productions – they tended to emphasise pedagogy over directing.[2] With this in mind, I will concentrate on theories and exercises of the Method, rather than particular productions.[3] First, a thumbnail sketch of the Method's history and theory.

Introduction to the Method

The American Method began in the United States at the American Laboratory Theatre, where from 1923 to 1926 acting classes taught by

Stanislavsky's émigré students Richard Boleslavsky and Maria Ouspenskaya introduced American actors to a new performing technique.[4] These classes, supplemented by the Moscow Art Theatre's visits to the United States in 1923 and 1924, introduced American actors to a new way of working that created a distinct 'Method'. The Method, like Stanislavsky's System, wanted to see both human beings as having depth, and the actor as a complex psychological being who generated layers of meaning in performance which lie beyond easy comprehension. Boleslavsky's and Ouspenskaya's students Harold Clurman and Lee Strasberg, along with Cheryl Crawford, met in 1925 at the Theatre Guild, where their association led to the Group Theatre (1931–40).[5] The Group consolidated around a collection of actors dedicated to producing new American plays, and performing them in a style derived from Stanislavsky's System. Moreover, the Group was committed to theatre that stressed social protest, moral and ethical concerns and political activism. Hence, 'Method acting' emerged as a technique that drew from Stanislavsky's emphasis on the craft of acting, and accentuated working on a role that called upon the actor to build from his or her personal life and political ideals.

Method acting was the Group's sole approach to rehearsals and plays. It evolved from the ensemble techniques and collective rehearsal procedures developed by Group actors, providing the company with a practical and theoretical grounding that differed considerably from the acting systems in the American theatre at the time. Stanislavsky's and Vakhtangov's work on the actor's 'inner life' was part of the Group's working procedures. Instead of the star system, ensemble work was emphasised; instead of relying on inspiration alone, Group actors were trained to evoke specific emotions and actions; instead of mannerisms, Group actors developed an unassuming natural stage presence; and instead of grandiose theatricality, Group actors stressed real behaviour in performance. Group actor and teacher Robert Lewis explains that real behaviour on stage must be 'really experienced, but artistically controlled, and correctly used for the particular character portrayed, the complete circumstances of the scene, and the chosen style of the author and play being performed' (1958: 99). For the Group, 'indicating' emotions and feelings were replaced by actual 'felt' experiences; inspiration and craft 'were not mutually exclusive' (Smith 1990: 38); and actors would experience their roles by observing and living the lives of their characters. As Stella Adler explained, the 'Group Theatre contributed a standard of acting that transformed the American theatre' (1976: 512).

Teachers of the Method were influenced by their collaboration at the American Laboratory Theatre, the Group Theatre and the Yiddish Theater.[6] During the 1950s and 1960s, Strasberg (at the Actors Studio),[7] Adler (at the Stella Adler Conservatory), and Meisner (at the Neighborhood Playhouse), advanced their own versions of the Method, each claiming to be the rightful descendants of Stanislavsky's System, and each using various stages of Stanislavsky's and Vakhtangov's work to underscore their approach. Whilst the three diverged on some matters of emphasis, they more or less agreed on ten principles essential to Method acting:

1   The actor must *justify* every word, action and relationship onstage. The actor moves and speaks spontaneously, but everything is thought out during rehearsals to ensure the maximum emphasis on *motivation*.

2   In finding the character's motivation, actors search for *objectives*, *actions* and *intentions*. Actors discover the character's *super-objective*, or '*spine*', that motivates all the actions on stage.

3   The character's super-objective must have *urgency*: every action and objective must have an immediacy ('how badly do you want the objective, and what consequences will occur if you do not attain it?'). This includes creating *obstacles* that prevent easy access to achieving the objective. The work on urgency must emerge from *relaxation*, *concentration* and the *creative selection* (choices) of objectives.

4   To support the objective, the actor creates *subtext*, or thought processes, that motivate the character's actions. Every word in a play has an underlying, non-verbal base which informs and supports the playwright's written word. The playwright's words serve as a surface blueprint; the subtext supplies the role's interior definition.

5   In finding the subtext of the role, the actor rejects generalisations, emphasising instead the specific *given circumstances* of the play, everything from period style and social fashion to the way a character behaves, lives and relates to other characters and situations.

6   In defining the given circumstances, actors behave *as if* they are living in the situation of the play. In doing so, the actor must bring his or her *imagination* into focus, *particularising* creative choices that will enhance the text and flesh out compelling ideas that lurk beneath the words.

7   An emphasis on *truthful behaviour*; feelings must never be 'indicated'. Rather, the actor works from his or her passions and emotions, which is often referred to in Method acting as working from the 'inside out'. Method acting director and former member of the Group Theatre, Elia Kazan, building on Vakhtangov's theories,[8] wrote that for Method actors, experience on the stage 'must be actual, not suggested by external imitation; the actor must be going through what the character he's playing is going through; the emotion must be real, not pretended; it must be happening, not indicated' (1988: 143).

8   To accomplish the experience of real feelings, the actor works *moment-to-moment* on *impulse*, talking and listening as if the events on stage are actually happening in the immediate present. In Method acting, characterisation is not fixed, but a fluid and spontaneous response to events on stage. Strasberg explains that

> the actor has to know what he is going to do when he goes on the stage, and yet has to permit himself to do it so that it seems to

happen for the first time. This means that the body, the voice, every facet of expression, must follow the natural changes in impulse; even though the actor repeats, the strength of the impulses may well change from day to day.

(1965: 167)

9 Rehearsals require *improvising* on the dramatic text – gibberish (Strasberg), paraphrasing (Adler), or repetition exercises (Meisner) – encouraging the actor's personal interpretation and investment, thereby freeing the actor from a dependency on words.
10 Finally, the actor *personalises* the role, i.e. draws from the self, from his or her emotional, psychological or imaginative reality, bringing into view aspects of one's memories, life experiences and observations that correlate with the role.

This final element has drawn criticism from Robert Brustein, who complains that the Method actor, reflecting their interest in the self, 'usually purveys a single character from role to role, one that is recognisably close to his own personality'. For Brustein, this 'subjective, autobiographical approach to performance is reflected in the most prominent American acting method, where the current jargon includes phrases like "personalisation" and "private moment", signifying techniques with which to investigate one's own psychic history' (1973: 1). What Brustein fails to realise is that the self is neither static nor fixed, but evolving – in other words, human beings reinvent themselves continuously. The self changes by entering into new relationships, and the actor must bring new ideas to each successive characterisation. Moreover, the self is never at the exclusion of the study of character; investing personal experiences with textual analysis and observations of life are not necessarily contradictory working procedures. Brustein's view of the Method is a common albeit misleading opinion present in much academic writing on the subject.[9] In what follows, I hope not only to avoid such errors, but define the three principal approaches to Method acting that illuminate its diversity and wide-ranging applicability. The three approaches described here were products of the Group Theatre experience, but each drew on specific facets.

Lee Strasberg

Truth and emotion: using the self in public

The human being who acts is the human being who lives.

(Strasberg 1965: 78)

Figure 7.1   Lee Strasberg

Source: Courtesy of the Billy Rose Theatre Collection, New York Public Library at Lincoln Centre

Lee Strasberg was the founding member of the Group Theatre. He later withdrew from the Group in 1937, continuing his career as a teacher and director. In 1949 he assumed the Directorship of the Actors Studio. Although not a founder of the Studio, he eventually became identified with the school. The term Method Acting itself is most closely associated with Strasberg and the Actors Studio.

Lee Strasberg developed a number of approaches to acting, but three aspects of his work stand out: relaxation, concentration and affective memory. For Strasberg, the fundamental effect of the actor must be directed towards the 'training of his internal skills' through a process of 'relaxation and concentration' (1987: 116). This dual process of relaxation and concentration leads performers to personalisation, what Strasberg student Kim Stanley explains as finding 'things in yourself that you can use' (quoted in Gussow 1982).

Strasberg's theory of the Method is predicated on 'procedure, not a series of rules to be applied specifically' (Hull 1985: 18). For Strasberg, there is no one way into a role; each presents its own problems to be studied and solved. But above all, Strasberg described an actor as one who 'can create out of himself' (1965: 81). To do this, the performer must 'appeal to the unconscious and the subconscious'. Arriving at the state of creativity requires the 'presence of something that stirs the actor subconsciously' (1965: 82). Strasberg defines the main feature of his teaching:

> Let's say the actor learns to relax and concentrate. He learns to arouse his imagination, which is his belief in the reality and logic of what he is doing; but then we find that the actor's expression of these things is weak. Often we see things going on inside that can't come out – the face contracts, the eyes contract – the emotion isn't let through. The actor feels at times like crying but he can't cry, he can't uncurl the muscles to permit the tears to flow. Such strong conditioning has been created against the expression of emotion. I would say that I have experimented with the whole problem of freeing the expression of the actor.
>
> (1964: 123)

For Strasberg, freeing the expression begins with relaxation and concentration. David Garfield observes that to facilitate relaxation, 'Strasberg has the actor sit in a chair and proceed to find a position in which, if he had to, he could fall asleep' (1980: 169). The actor must relax before an audience, something not easy to do. Of particular importance is the relaxation of the jaw, an area of much concern for Feldenkrais practitioners.[10] As feelings of relaxation increase and emotions stir, Garfield explains that the actor 'opens his throat and permits a sound from deep in the chest to come out, to make sure the emotion is not blocked' (1980: 168). The actor continues to emit sounds that help release tension and free creative expression.

In developing concentration, Strasberg emphasises a series of sense-memory exercises. Sense-memory is the stimulation of the senses (tactile, taste, olfactory, auditory and visual). The actor recalls important events in their life, and then tries to remember only the sensual facets: touch, taste, sight, etc. The ability to recall senses stimulates the body rather than the mind, giving the actor greater visceral awareness and experience.

In sense-memory exercises, the actor begins by handling imaginary objects. Actors recreate drinking coffee, shaving or other daily activities.[11] The point is not merely to mime the activity, but to find the psychological motivation underlying the experience. Garfield is clear on this: 'the ultimate range of imaginary objects that a performer must create on stage is enormous. It may include physical objects, overall sensations, mental or fantasy objects, situations, events, relationships, and other characters.' If the actor is to fulfil the obligations of the role, Garfield asserts, 'he must be well grounded in the simplest sense-memory work' (1980: 170). By 'grounded' Garfield means that the actor does not merely create an object, but invests in the object a personal history. For example, if an actor holds a glass, the glass is not merely an object, but a gift from a lover or friend. The actor recalls how the lover offered the glass as a gift, and in so doing, the actor remembers, through the senses, the time of day, the weather, the colour of the shoes of the lover, etc.

In Strasberg's private moment, the actor lives out their 'private moments' before a classroom audience. Private moment is the literal performance of an activity that one does in private. According to Doug Moston, it was developed by Strasberg in 1956 and 1957 'to aid actors in creating the ability to behave in a truly private fashion while being observed by an audience' (1993: 93). In being private in public, the actor frees inhibitions. Foster Hirsch explains that because private moment is an exercise rather than a performance, it 'releases the actor from any obligation to a text or...to an audience' (1984: 136). Working from private experience, the actor is free, as Strasberg puts it, 'to sit before us, to smell an aroma, and not to do anything physical, but to focus only on what you're doing with your concentration' (quoted in Hirsch 1984: 137). Private moments also allow the actor to experience feelings that, owing to inhibitions, they would otherwise not share. Strasberg uses an example of an actress whose voice was monotonous. In doing her private moment, he discovered that she enjoyed playing music when alone and would dance with 'abandon'. He then had the actress play the music she liked, and dance wildly on stage. He describes the experience:

> It would make your hair stand up. You would never have thought that this girl had this degree of response and expression. We made her do it, and it worked and from that moment on her voice and action changed. We got through some kind of block by making use of the Private Moment.
>
> (1964: 125)

Strasberg's most controversial exercise is affective memory, developed by combining Stanislavsky's early work on Pavlovian training,[12] Vakhtangov's work on performative emotions,[13] and the work of psychologist Théodule Ribot.[14] Its purpose is to release emotions on stage. Strasberg states:

The basic idea of affective memory is not emotional recall but that the actor's emotion on the stage should never be really real. It always should be only *remembered* emotion. An emotion that happens right now spontaneously is out of control – you don't know what's going to happen from it, and the actor can't always maintain and repeat it. Remembered emotion is something that the actor can create and repeat: without that the thing is hectic.

(1964: 132)

For Strasberg, affective memory 'is the basic element of the actor's reality' (1964: 131). In particular, it draws out the emotions from the past that are ingrained in one's mind and body, rather than what Strasberg identifies as the merely 'literal', or indicated, interpretation from the text (1964: 131; 1965: 112). Edward Easty explains that by

having a 'repertoire' of emotional experiences, the actor can call forth, at the proper time, the desire[s] one needed for the character. The broader his 'repertoire', the greater the resources for creativeness and the greater the number of roles he will be able to act.

(1981: 45–6)

Although it usually begins as an attempt to evoke emotions appropriate to the circumstances of the play, the emotion may appear in a somewhat different fashion, since, as Strasberg explains, 'the emotional value of the experience may have changed'. However, 'by attempting a lot of affective memories, the actor gradually obtains a stock of memories that are permanent and become easier to invoke as he continues to use them' (1965: 111). Robert Lewis maintains that in affective memory, emotions derived from the events you are calling up are 'likely to be different [i.e. they will change] in quality or quantity or both when you repeat the exercise' (1980: 126). This is not only to be expected but welcomed; since your feelings towards the event have evolved, your emotions will evolve accordingly. In fact, they will subtly change each time you perform the exercises. The significance lies in the fact that the actor becomes emotionally available, prepared to respond instantly and expressively with feelings and passions.

In affective memory, the actor is completely relaxed. Then, the performer tries to recall, as Lewis describes it, 'some event in your past which you think might stir up some feeling usable for the problem in your scene, preferably from your distant past' (1980: 126). The operative word here is 'problem', since the performer is having difficulty in coming to terms with feelings required for the scene. The actor is not trying to force emotions; rather, they recall the event by remembering all the sensations that occurred at the time: smells, taste, sights, sounds and tactile sensations. The actor relies on sense memory to trigger the emotion.

Wendy Smith provides a detailed explanation of affective memory. The actor concentrates on an incident from their own life that produced the desired emotion. However:

> The actor [does not] try to recall the feeling directly, but rather to re-experience the sensory impressions surrounding it; the size of the room it happened in, the colour of the walls, the fabric on the furniture, the time of day, how the people there were dressed, what they looked like, and so on. Then the actor went over the exact sequence of events, concentrating on re-creating as precisely as possible the physical reality of the moment. When done properly with a strong a situation, the exercise almost invariably brought the emotion flooding back to the present. The actor could then play the scene with the appropriate feeling.
>
> (1990: 38)

Strasberg explains that an 'actor who masters the technique of using the affective memory begins to be more alive in the present' (quoted in Hirsch 1984: 141)

Affective memory is simply one way of calling up the passions that help the actor play a role. It is not, as Colin Counsell would have it, effective merely for 'sad' or unhappy events (1996: 58). Rather, it is one way to evoke *all feelings* correlative to the events in the scene. Nor is it demanded that every Method actor perform an affective memory; in many instances, uninhibited actors at the Actors Studio were dissuaded from making use of it. Moreover, the feelings evoked during an episode of affective memory may surprise the actor (you may laugh when you thought you would cry), and that is significant – the performer has created a true, original and spontaneous sense or feeling in response to scenic events.

Strasberg insists that work on emotions must not be at the expense of actions or characterisation. Work on affective memory is not designed for film (though it can be used there), but for theatre, where the need to return to the emotion is required of the actor several times a week. As he says, in order to repeat a performance, 'you have to have emotional memory. If you don't, then you repeat only the externals of it' (1976: 549).

Strasberg pursued a stage reality that brought forth feelings from the actor. Critics of affective memory seldom understand its purpose: it is an exercise to be used in practice and rehearsal. In other words, it is a *rehearsal technique* that allows the actor to find the emotional triggers that set off appropriate feelings. Richard Hornby suggests that Method actors tend 'to lag behind the play, where quick, drastic ebb and flow of action is common' (1992: 183). But once the actor has incorporated the memory that evokes the emotion, feelings become part of the ebb and flow in a natural way. Like Diderot, Strasberg was interested in enabling the actor to repeat performances with uniform emotional intensity, and not 'dry up' after one or two rehearsals or shows. Strasberg sums up the exercise's purpose in the following:

Affective memory is the basic material for reliving on the stage, and therefore for the creation of a real experience on the stage. What the actor repeats in performance after performance is not just the words and movements he practiced in rehearsal, but the memory of emotion. He reaches this emotion through the memory of thought and sensation.

(1987: 113)

David Garfield asserts that affective memory 'is by no means an indulgence of Strasberg's. It is an absolute necessity to his concept of acting as the creation of real experience in response to imaginary stimuli' (1980: 175). Its purpose, Garfield adds, is 'to create whatever reality in whatever "style" the actor, the director, or the play calls for' (1980: 181). Along similar lines, Steve Vineberg enjoins us to consider that the 'aim of all Method teachers, whatever their means, is to produce genuine emotion on the stage, but Strasberg's actors have been accused of displaying emotionalism, as a result of his prodding and pushing at their feelings'. Whilst Strasberg's emphasis on feelings resulted in making his classroom appear more like group therapy than performance, Vineberg is correct to point out that he was no fanatic. Strasberg, Vineberg says, 'often took tension as a sign of emotional excessiveness, and his relaxation exercises fought against it' (1991: 109).[15]

Strasberg never denied the importance of voice, physicality or script analysis. But for him, the actor must purge the sense of 'performing' and find believability:

It is difficult to realise how much the sense of 'I'm doing, I'm acting' can commandeer the mind. It is difficult to realise how strong and animal-like the adherence to a verbal pattern or convention can be. It is difficult for the actor to perceive how ferociously the cliché holds on to him.

(1965: 212)

The emphasis on emotion and credible behaviour was, for Strasberg, a process of required actor training.

Stella Adler

Imagination, given circumstances and physical action

Your life is one millionth of what you know. Your talent is your imagination. The rest is lice.

(Hirsch 1984: 214)

Stella Adler was the youngest daughter of the Yiddish actors Jacob and Sarah Adler. As a child star on the Yiddish stage, she learned her craft from

Figure 7.2   Stella Adler

Source: Courtesy of the Billy Rose Theatre Collection, New York Public Library at Lincoln Center

the ground up. She was one of the original members of the Group Theatre, and in 1934 she and her then husband, Harold Clurman, went to Paris where they met Stanislavsky and probed deeply into his teaching. From 1934 onwards she broke with Strasberg on the fundamental precepts of the Method. Although she continued to appear on stage, by the 1950s she became one of America's leading acting teachers.

Adler emphasises a play's given circumstances, the actor's imagination and physical actions. She quotes Stanislavsky to the effect that the 'truth in art is the truth of your circumstances' (1988: 31). She acknowledges the importance of drawing on oneself in a role; but the source of inspiration is not purely psychology or past experiences (as in Strasberg), but the actors' imagination as they relate to the given circumstances of the play. Adler writes:

> The playwright gives you the play, the idea, the style, the conflict, the character, etc. The background life of the character will be made up of the social, cultural, political, historical, and geographical situation in which the author places him. The character must be understood within the framework of the character's own time and situation. Through the proper use of craft, the actor will see the differences of social, historical, and cultural environment between himself and the character. Through his craft he will be able to translate these difficulties and use them to arrive at the character.
>
> (1964: 149)

Imagination, Adler claims, can be touched upon 'as a source for the actor's craft' (1964: 143). For her, 99 per cent of events onstage derive at least in part from the imagination, because onstage

> you will never have your own name and personality or be in your own house. Every person you talk to will have been written imaginatively by the playwright. Every circumstance you find yourself in will be in an imaginary one. And so, every word, every action, must originate in the actor's imagination.
>
> (1988: 17)

Adler asks performers to concentrate on their creative imagination rather than their conscious past. By doing so, they would be optimally effective in creating a past in sympathy with the characters they portray. For Adler, the imagination is crucial to classical performances as well as plays that are stylistically non-realistic. In order for the actor to understand the life of a character within a period or stylised play, they must read, observe paintings, study architecture and listen to music, becoming what Paul Mann called an 'actor-anthropologist' (1964: 87).

Adler, however, rejects simplistic devices for finding character and inspiration. The most important thing for the actor is to choose images that *evoke an inner feeling*. Perfunctory choices may 'sound' correct analytically, but leave the actor devoid of feeling. The actor may feel they are making the 'right' choice intellectually, but the actual performance is dull and uninspired. The actor then may try to 'pump up' emotions rather than make decisions that effectively touch the heart. If the role and its context as written fail to inspire or move the actor emotionally, then the actor must look elsewhere. For example, if the play takes place at a lakeside resort in Switzerland, but the actor can find nothing moving or exciting about Swiss lakes, then, as Adler says, 'put your lake in Morocco'. In this way, the actor may 'get away from the real thing because the real thing will limit your acting and cripple you' (quoted in Flint 1992). In other words, if the actions, words or events of the play seem lifeless to the actor, then the actor must create another set of circumstances that correspond to the events of the play, but create excitement and passion internally.

Adler devises a number of exercises for developing the performer's personalisation of the role. For example, suppose an actor has to describe fruit in a grocery store. As Adler would have it, the actor's task is to personalise the experience:

> I saw fantastic pears that were big but looked too expensive to buy. Then I saw those wonderful Malaga grapes, long and very sweet. There were also some of those big, blue grapes, and the baby ones, the little

green ones. Those you can eat by the pound, and by the way, they're very cheap.

(1988: 21)

Adler wants to bring out the actor's feelings and passions towards the subject, revealing the performer's creativity relative to the circumstances. She is also convinced that paraphrasing the text is 'an essential feature of the actor's technique'. She explains that paraphrasing 'is taking the author's ideas and putting them into the actor's words, and thereby making them belong to the actor. Paraphrasing encourages you to use your mind and your voice and gives you some power that equals the author's power' (1988: 102). By paraphrasing, actors find in their imagination things that move them to react, speak and move. She goes on to say: 'Some actors hold back and do not react. Actors should consciously take things that will make them react. In your choice is your talent. Acting is in everything but the cold words' (1988: 26).

Whilst Strasberg emphasised the realisation of the character from the material of one's own personal life, Adler suggested that the actor's inspiration should come from the world of the play itself. Hirsch notes that Adler 'urges students to explore the given circumstances of the play rather than those of their private lives' (1984: 215). Still, Adler did not completely abandon the inner belief of the actor's performance; as she says, 'the whole aim of modern theatre is not to act, but to find the truth of the play within yourself, and to communicate that. If you play simply for the lines, you're dead' (quoted in Hirsch 1984: 216). The reality of place, where you are and why you are here, must contribute to the basic understanding of your motivation and justification as an actor.

Finding the correct physical actions for a scene also assists the actor in discovering the excitement of the role. For Adler, the 'actor must lose his dependency on the words and go to the actions of the play', because the actions 'come first and words second. Words come out of the actions' (1988: 115). The actor must find actions beneath words by developing the 'physicalisation of actions'. The method of physical action, which Adler borrowed from Stanislavsky's later work, draws from the active doing and performing of actual tasks. Moreover, the actor must build a repertoire consisting of a vocabulary of actions. As she claims, an action is something you do; it has an end; it is done within the given circumstances; and is justified (1988: 35). To find the right action, the actor looks for the play's 'ruling idea'. This ruling idea must appeal to the actor 'emotionally and intellectually'. Moreover, the actor 'must know how to make the [ruling idea] his own' (1988: 38). In other words, the actor must know how to personalise the material, playing the actions convincingly.

Adler also stressed justifying the things said and done on stage. She borrowed from Vakhtangov the idea of 'agitation from the essence', whereby the actor comes 'to realise the necessity of actions pointed out by the author

– they become organic' (Vakhtangov 1955: 145). The actor seeks justification of the author's perspective, what Vakhtangov called 'scenic faith' (1955: 146–7). Adler offers some elaboration on Vakhtangov's ideas:

> The justification is not in the lines; it is in you. What you should choose as your justification should agitate you. As a result of the agitation you will experience the action and the emotion. If you choose a justification and experience nothing, you'll have to select something else that will awaken you. Your talent consists of how well you are able to shop for your justification. In your choice lies your talent.
>
> (1988: 48)

Though Adler and Strasberg differ in emphasis, they shared the belief in truthful behaviour, self-exploration (whether psychological or sociological) and respect for acting as art. For Strasberg, the essence of acting is psychological; resources abound in the actor's memory. For Adler, the essence of acting is sociological; actors draw from the given circumstances of the play. However, Ellen Burstyn, who studied with both, remarked: 'Stella stresses imagination and Lee stresses reality. You use Stella's imagination to get to Lee's reality. They are finally talking about the same thing' (quoted in Flint 1992). For Adler, the building blocks of acting are discovered in the imagination and are arranged according to the play's given circumstances and the exigencies of physical actions.

Sanford Meisner

Behaviour, relationships and the reality of doing

> The foundation of acting is the reality of doing.
>
> (Meisner and Longwell 1987: 16)

Sanford Meisner was a member and principal actor of the Group Theatre. In the mid 1930s he became disillusioned with the Group and the direction in which it was heading. In 1935 he joined the Neighborhood Playhouse, and the following year became its Director. From 1936 until the time of his death Meisner spearheaded the Neighborhood Playhouse, developing it into a significant school of actor training.

Acting for Meisner is in the doing; from this all other facets of the role emerge. In his classroom were posted signs which read: 'Act Before You Think', and 'An Ounce of Behavior Is Worth a Pound of Words'. Active behaviour is the raw material of Meisner's theory. He states:

> Let there be no question about what I'm saying here. If you do something, you really do it! Did you walk up the steps to this classroom this

morning? You didn't jump up? You didn't skip up, right? You didn't ballet pirouette? You really walked up those steps.

(Meisner and Longwell 1987: 17)

Larry Silverberg elaborates on this theme, saying that for Meisner: 'if you read onstage, really read; if you eat, really eat; and if you want something (an objective), really want it, go after it, pursue it; don't stop until you have achieved it'. As Maria Ouspenskaya puts it, *'Really see*; instead of *acting*[,] seeing. Don't act, do' (1994: 3).

Meisner did not entirely reject use of emotional recall or substitution (replacing the play's events with your own), but he required that substitution must 'be done as *homework*' (1964: 145). Once inner feelings and physical tasks required by the director and the role are shaped during rehearsal, the actor plays spontaneously, all the while allowing subtle shifts in emphasis and focus. In other words, once the actor reaches the time to perform, what remains is the actual doing and reacting.

Figure 7.3   Sanford Meisner

Source: Courtesy of the Billy Rose Theatre Collection, New York Public Library at Lincoln Center

For Meisner, the play is merely a blueprint for the actor's interior life. He says:

> The text is like a canoe, and the river on which sits is the emotion. The text floats on the river. If the water of the river is turbulent, the words will come out like a canoe on a rough river. It all depends on the flow of the river which is your emotion. The text takes on the character of your emotion.
>
> (Meisner and Longwell 1987: 115)

Although for Meisner the point of doing resembled Adler's emphasis on physical actions, he departs from Adler in his introduction of the repetition exercise. As an exercise, repetition demands of actors that they verbalise what they perceive in another actor. In other words, one actor might begin by saying 'You're looking at me', and the other actor might reply, 'I'm looking at you'. The essence of the phrase ('looking at') is repeated about a dozen times, all the while each actor 'reads' the other actor's behaviour. Meisner explains that actors ought to observe behaviour, and in turn 'your instinct picks up the change in [the other actor's] behaviour and the [repetition] dialogue changes too' (Meisner and Longwell 1987: 29–30).

As actors gain confidence through repetition, their insight deepens with respect to the other member of the scene. In other words, rather than saying 'you're staring at me', they begin to address the feelings that lurk behind the stare. Such insight is then reflected in phrases such as 'you're angry with me', or 'you're laughing at me'. Actors no longer take 'inventory' of the other actor superficially, but observe the scene-partner's emotions, feelings and thoughts.

As actors gain more experience in the repetition exercises, they begin to improvise scenarios called 'The Knock on the Door'. The following is an example of a Meisner 'Knock on the Door' improvisation. Actor A is required to have an 'independent activity', which is a task that is real (no mime), urgent and particular. An independent activity is something that has a beginning, middle and end, and has to be done for compelling reasons. For instance, an independent activity can be stringing a guitar for an important audition. The actor is late; the guitar lacks strings. The actor intended to string the guitar, but his girlfriend was in an accident and he had to take her to the hospital. The element of urgency and lateness adds to his desperation and intensity.

Actor B enters the room ('knocking on the door') where actor A is completing his independent activity. Actor B has an 'objective' that relates to actor A. For instance, actor B imagines he is the father of actor A, and actor B does not want his son to leave medical school and be a musician. The father enters the room, and urgently tries to persuade the son to drop music and return to medical school.

In Meisner's version of this standard dramatic conflict, the actors do not discuss the given circumstances (though they must share an understanding of it). They do not talk about the story, but rather they use the repetition exercise only. In this way, the actors are compelled to deal with observed behaviour rather than dialogue and plot. This helps foster ensemble interplay, or communion, rather than words. Since the scenario/plot is artificial (it is an acted father–son relationship), Meisner wants actors to place their focus on subtextual dialogue – the 'chemistry' between the actors and the 'reality' of the situation (human behaviour). If an actor is yelling, that is tangible, something everyone can hear and observe. The other actor reads the behaviour of yelling and reacts to it instinctively. Reading behaviour compels actors to focus on scene-partners rather than the artifice of the plot. As a result, actors react spontaneously, play as an ensemble, and 'read' behaviour as it happens organically.

In the repetition exercises, Meisner found an exercise that refined impulse. For Meisner, impulse is a response to internal or external stimuli. As the actor receives the stimuli, they then feed it to the imagination and personal associations. The actor responds by acting on the stimuli, creating an 'impulsive' behaviour that emerges truthfully and spontaneously from reactions rather than from pre-planned behaviour. This procedure must be performed without intellectual interference, without 'thinking' or 'dwelling' on the reaction. As Meisner put it, the exercise eliminates 'all that "head" work'; it takes away 'all the mental manipulations and get[s] to where the impulses come from' (Meisner and Longwell 1987: 36). Larry Silverberg explains that in Meisner's repetition exercise, the actor must not use the work as a kind of trick, but rather as an attempt to commune with another actor, to enable the actor to move 'towards your fully *being with* another human being'. The aim of repetition, Silverberg goes on to say, is in 'becoming fully available to your partner, authentically responsive in each moment' (1994: 42–3).

Many commentators have misunderstood the purpose of the repetition exercise. Michael Quinn, for instance, has argued that in Meisner's version of the Method, the 'actor is the central subject, and the Other is the character – not the audience, the acting partner, or the director'. Quinn maintains that for Meisner 'the problem addressed in his class is teaching actors to project themselves into an Other [character] that is already there, written in terms which are fixed into the fiction' (1995: 14).

But this is mistaken, since the repetition exercise builds on the relationship of the actor with the acting partner; the 'Other' is the scene-partner, not the character. In other words, for Meisner the creation of character is fluid and spontaneous. Rather than a 'fixed' characterisation, the performance is based on relationships, either to scene-partners or the audience. Actors act on the relationship to the other actor, using the specifically observed behaviour of scene-partners, or, in the case of direct address to the audience, the spectators. If a scene-partner changes their behaviour, the actor must adjust their own behaviour to correspond to the different signals and stimuli. Meisner compels actors to work 'as if' they are the characters, but this does not imply fixity. Rather, the impulses received from the other actor, stimulated through repetition, take on a dynamic based on the continuing real life examination of human give-and-take. Reacting can therefore be said to be the foundation of Meisner's repetition technique.

Meisner believes that action is not in the character or the plot of the play but *in relationships*. To this end he stresses the repetition exercise, because the exercise compels the actor to 'work off the partner'. In this way the partner allows the actor to create the role from the given material present on stage and in the life of another person, rather than a mental preconception of character. More than Strasberg and Adler, Meisner emphasises ensemble behaviour, creating a spontaneous exchange in a jazz-like atmosphere of action and reaction. Performing the actions for Meisner is therefore not 'fixed into the fiction' as Quinn would have it, but relational, dialogic and alive to immediate and spontaneous human communication and interaction.

William Worthen also errs when he notes that in 'Meisner's well-known [repetition] exercise...the actors improvise a given situation using only a single word or phrase, repeated again and again' (1992: 61). Repetition does not emphasise a 'given situation' (as Adler would have it), but rather the *behaviour of the acting partner*, such as, *someone in a situation*. This is an important distinction, because Meisner's repetition exercise, as opposed to Adler's emphasis on circumstances, is intended to promote impulsive behaviour as a consequence of living relationships (the actual moment on stage), rather than merely the given situation.

In Meisner's work, 'an ounce of behaviour is worth a pound of words'. The repetition exercise is used to read behaviour either from the scene-partner or the spectators. In direct address, the actor's attention is not, as Worthen implies, 'diverted from the audience' (1992: 61); rather, the audience should be viewed as the scene-partner. In other words, in directly addressing the audience the actor uses the audience in much the same way as a stand-up comic does: gauging the laughter and responses of the spectators and responding according to the actor's impulses.

Meisner's repetition exercise helps to promote spontaneous reactions that became the trademark of his brand of the Method. As Richard Brestoff astutely observes: 'Meisner felt that the connection between actors was vital to the life of a scene, and that when that bond was broken, the acting lost its special quality and power' (1995: 129). Meisner's emphasis on truthful interaction between actors, Brestoff goes on to say, helps actors 'to respond genuinely to one another, and to live spontaneously, moment-to-moment, within imaginary circumstances' (1995: 137). Meisner's specific contribution to the Method is his emphasis on spontaneous communion between actors.

Conclusion: Method acting as a tool

Whether emphasising psychology (Strasberg), sociology (Adler) or spontaneous behaviour (Meisner), Method actors search for the reality that must underlie a quality performance. The Method is neither singular in its outlook, nor mutually exclusive; one facet of the Method does not cancel out another. Affective memory, the play's given circumstances and repetition may function together; voice, speech and movement are integrated; and textual analysis is integral to working on a role. Method acting, when properly used, is holistic, enabling the actor to perform on several levels with conviction and confidence.

At the end of the century, we can see how the American Method has evolved. Many of its main ideas are still actively employed. Founder and director of Chicago's Steppenwolf Theatre, Gary Sinise, elucidates what animates Method acting in a personal reflection:

> I try to keep them [the audience] leaning forward rather than leaning back because I feel those are the best experiences. The one that hits you in the guts will make you think about it, but a play that has you just thinking on an intellectual level won't necessarily hit you in the guts. The cardinal sin for me is boredom.
>
> (quoted in Smith 1996: 10, 14)

Method acting explores the range of actorial possibilities within a dynamic of emotion – what Sinise calls 'in the guts'. It transcends the artifice of staged contrivances, offering actors opportunities to explore roles by calling on them to investigate their personal experience, imagination and behaviour.

Notes

1 Other acting teachers have had significant impact on the American Method school of acting, as for example, Phoebe Brand, Uta Hagen, Robert Lewis, Paul Mann and Sonia Moore.

2 Strasberg's major directing works were *The House of Connelly*, *Men in White*, *Johnny Johnson*, and *The Case of Clyde Griffiths* in the 1930s, and *Three Sisters* in the 1960s. Meisner helped direct *Waiting for Lefty* in 1935. Still, Strasberg, Adler and Meisner, for the most part, did not stress directing, but teaching.

3 By and large, the teachers discussed here offered their schools as sanctuaries, places where actors could practise their craft, work on scenes and exercises, and perform in roles that they would not ordinarily be cast in. These safe harbours allowed actors a chance to escape the commercialism of show business. Method schools are not, as some have claimed, 'against' productions, but rather the Method offers places where actors can avoid the pressure of careerism and the business of selling their talent.

4 The American Laboratory Theatre was founded in June 1923 by Boleslavsky and several wealthy Americans who supplied the funds. Boleslavsky reached the United States in 1922, where he began a series of lectures at the Princess Theatre in New York that offered the philosophy of actor training from the Moscow Art Theatre (MAT). Miriam and Herbert Stockton, patrons of the arts,

offered Boleslavsky an opportunity to direct a training school based on the principles of the MAT, and Boleslavsky enlisted the aid of his friend and colleague, Maria Ouspenskaya. The Lab opened at 139 MacDougal Street in 1923. See W. Smith (1990), pp. 14–15, for details.

5 The Theatre Guild began in 1915 as the Washington Square Players in New York. They presented one-act plays that were considered modern and unconventional. In 1919, the playwright Lawrence Langner restructured the Players into the Theatre Guild. During the 1920s the Guild became known for producing the Expressionist dramas of Ernst Toller, as well as plays by George Bernard Shaw, Elmer Rice, John Howard Lawson, and Sidney Howard. By the 1930s the Guild's younger members joined the Group Theatre, and the Guild eventually dissolved.

6 Whilst a study of Yiddish Theater's influence on Strasberg, Adler and Meisner is outside the realm of this chapter, it is worth noting that all three were invested in the Yiddish Theatre. Yiddish Theater's emphasis on melodrama, emotion and social commentary left indelible impressions on Strasberg, Adler, Meisner and the Group Theatre in general, and its significance has often been overlooked.

7 The Actors Studio was co-founded by Elia Kazan, Robert Lewis and Cheryl Crawford in 1947.

8 Vakhtangov referred to this feeling as 'agitation from the essence'; for Vakhtangov, it is necessary for the actor 'to live your own temperament on the stage and not the supposed temperament of the character. You must proceed from yourself and not from a conceived image; you must place yourself in the position of the situation of the character' (1955: 146).

9 As a method of study and training, the American Method approach has had a history of controversy and strife. On the one hand, it has a cadre of loyal supporters, and an admirable roster of first-class actors who claim the technique as their own. On the other hand, the Method has had its programmatic attackers. Some claim it is too heavily invested in emotion (Counsell, Harrop); others see its emphasis on psychology as destructive (Hornby, Richardson); and as a violation of the true teachings of Stanislavsky (Brustein, Hornby). Other critics claim that the Method is narrow in its vision, encouraging sloppy speech habits, poor diction, and avoiding movement training. It is accused of being anti-intellectual (Brustein 1958), opposed to the reading and criticism of dramatic texts (Hornby), dogmatic in its approach (Richardson), and symbolic of mid-twentieth-century 'middlebrow culture' (Braudy, Conroy, Quinn).

10 See Feldenkrais (1972), pp. 68–9.

11 See Moston (1993), pp. 110–36, for an excellent discussion on sense memory.

12 Pavlov was the well-known turn-of-the-century behaviourist who experimented with canine response behaviour. After hearing a bell ring at feeding time, the dog in the experiment continued to salivate at the sound of a bell even after the food was removed. Pavlov thus concluded that all animals can condition their reactions based on physical cues.

13 Strasberg quotes Vakhtangov as saying that 'We never use real, that is, literal emotion in art, only affective memory emotion, only remembered emotion' (1965: 112).

14 Ribot was a French psychologist whose books, *La Psychologie des Sentiments* (1896) and *Problèmes de Psychologie Affective* (1910), influenced Stanislavsky.

15 Vineberg and Hornby offer two entirely different observations of Strasberg's portrayal of Hyman Roth in the film *The Godfather, Part II*. Vineberg finds the performance a superb and tightly controlled work where you 'can't find a moment of wasted emotion' (1991: 109), whilst Hornby finds Strasberg's performance 'unrevealing', lacking 'the emotional explosiveness of his finest students' (1992: 174).

Bibliography

Adler, S. (1964) 'Interview: The Reality of Doing', *Drama Review* 9(1), Fall: interview by P. Gray, 137–55.
—— (1976) 'Stella Adler', *Educational Theatre Journal* 28(4), December: 506–12.
—— (1988) *The Technique of Acting*, Toronto, Ont.: Bantam Books.
Boleslavski, R. (1933) *Acting: The First Six Lessons*, New York: Theatre Arts Books.
Braudy, L. (1996) 'No Body's Perfect: Method Acting and the 50s Culture', *Michigan Quarterly Review* 35(1), Winter: 191–215.
Brestoff, R. (1995) *The Great Acting Teachers and Their Methods*, Lyme, NH: Smith and Kraus.
Brustein, R. (1958) 'America's New Cultural Hero: Feelings Without Words', *Commentary* 25(January): 123–9.
—— (1962) 'The Keynes of Times Square', *The New Republic* (1 December): 28–30.
—— (1973) 'Are British Actors Better Than Ours?', *New York Times*, 15 April: 2.1, 30.
Clurman, H. (1950) *The Fervent Years*, New York: Alfred A. Knopf.
—— (1994) *The Collected Works of Harold Clurman*, M. Loggia and G. Young (eds), New York: Applause.
Conroy, M. (1993) 'Acting Out: Method Acting, the National Culture, and the Middlebrow Disposition in Cold War America', *Criticism* 35(2), Spring: 239–63.
Counsell, C. (1996) *Signs of Performance: An Introduction to Twentieth-Century Theatre*, London: Routledge.
Easty, E. (1981) *On Method Acting*, New York: Ivy Books.
Feldenkrais, M. (1972) *Awareness Through Movement*, New York: Harper and Row.
Flint, P. (1992) 'Obituary: Stella Adler', *New York Times*, 22 December: B10.
—— (1997) 'Obituary: Sanford Meisner', *New York Times*, 4 February: C25.
Garfield, D. (1980) *A Player's Passion: The Story of the Actors Studio*, New York: Macmillan.
Gussow, M. (1982) 'Obituary: Lee Strasberg', *New York Times*, 18 February: D20.
Harrop, J. (1992) *Acting*, London: Routledge.
Hirsch, F. (1984) *A Method to Their Madness: The History of the Actors Studio*, New York: W.W. Norton.
Hornby, R. (1992) *The End of Acting: A Radical View*, New York: Applause.
Hull, S. (1985) *Strasberg's Method*, Woodbridge, CT: Ox Bow.
Kazan, E. (1988) *A Life*, New York: Alfred A. Knopf.
Lewis, R. (1958) *Method – or Madness?*, New York: Samuel French.
—— (1980) *Advice to the Players*, New York: Theatre Communications Group.
Mann, P. (1964) 'Theory and Practice', *Drama Review* 9(2), Winter: interview by R. Schechner, 84–96.
Meisner, S. (1964) 'Interview: The Reality of Doing', *Drama Review* 9(1), Fall: interview by P. Gray, 136–55.
Meisner, S. and Longwell, D. (1987) *Meisner on Acting*, New York: Vintage.
Moston, D. (1993) *Coming to Terms with Acting*, New York: Drama Book.
Munk, E. (ed.) (1965) *Stanislavski and America*, New York: Hill and Wang.
Ouspenskaya, M. (1954) 'Notes on Acting', *American Repertory Theater* 2(2), November: 1–4.

Quinn, M. (1995) 'Self-Reliance and Ritual Renewal: Anti-theatrical Ideology in American Method Acting', *Journal of Dramatic Theory and Criticism* 10(1), Fall: 5–20.

Richardson, D. (1988) *Acting Without Agony: An Alternative to the Method*, Boston, MA: Allyn and Bacon.

Silverberg, L. (1994) *The Sanford Meisner Approach*, New York: Smith and Kraus.

Smith, S. (1996) 'Hooked for Life', *Playbill* 96(6), June: 10, 14.

Smith, W. (1990) *Real Life Drama: The Group Theatre and America, 1931–1940*, New York: Alfred A. Knopf.

Strasberg, L. (1964) 'Working with Live Material', *Drama Review* 9(1), Fall: interview by R. Schechner, 117–35.

—— (1965) *Strasberg at the Actors Studio: Tape-Recorded Sessions*, R. Hethmon (ed.), New York: Theatre Communications Group.

—— (1976) 'Lee Strasberg', *Educational Theatre Journal* 28(4), December: 544–52.

—— (1987) *A Dream of Passion: The Development of the Method*, New York: Plume.

Vakhtangov, E. (1955) 'Preparing for the Role', trans. B.E. Zakhava, *Acting: A Handbook of the Stanislavski Method*, T. Cole (ed.), New York: Crown Paperback, 141–51.

Vineberg, S. (1991) *Method Actors: Three Generations of an American Acting Style*, New York: Schirmer.

Worthen, W. (1992) *Modern Drama and the Rhetoric of Theater*, Berkeley, CA: University of California Press.

8 Joseph Chaikin and aspects of actor training

Possibilities rendered present

Dorinda Hulton

An actor should strive to be alive to all that he can imagine possible.[1] Such an actor is generated by an impulse toward an inner unity, as well as by the most intimate contacts he makes outside himself. When we as actors are performing, we as persons are also present and the performance is a testimony of ourselves. Each role, each work, each performance changes us as persons. The actor doesn't start out with answers about living – but with wordless questions about experience. Later, as the actor advances through the progress of the work, the person is transformed. Through the working process which he himself guides, the actor recreates himself.

Nothing less.

(Chaikin 1972: 5, 6)

Change and transformation are at the heart of Joseph Chaikin's life and work. He began his theatre career as an actor and has since worked as actor, director, teacher, workshop leader and writer. Despite suffering from an aphasic stroke in 1984 he continues to work. This chapter is primarily concerned with his investigations and explorations into actor training with the seminal American group the Open Theater between 1963 and 1973.

Context

Chaikin was born in 1935 of Russian-Jewish parents in Brooklyn, New York and grew up in Des Moines, Iowa, where he attended Drake University. He dropped out before completing his degree, but was awarded an honorary doctorate in 1972. Kent State University awarded him the same degree in 1990.[2]

In 1954, at the age of nineteen, Chaikin moved from Iowa to New York City, studied philosophy, and co-founded a small theatre company, The Harlequin Players, in which he worked as both actor and director. The company lasted for two years and performed plays by writers such as O'Casey and Pirandello.

In 1957, Chaikin managed to get his first professional acting job with a summer stock company in Pennsylvania. The experience encapsulated an antithesis to the collaborative approach. Recalling it, he remembers the excitement of getting the job, and then being asked, on the morning of his arrival, to come up with a full-blown 'characterisation' in one day. At the end of the morning, the director threatened to replace him if he had not come up with something funnier by the afternoon. He did not – and the director gave him till the following morning. After a sleepless night of 'funny walks' he finally came up with something the director *found* funnier. He kept the job. But the company of actors, he noted, 'were not friendly with one another', and in one week of rehearsal and two of performance, they played out various roles of 'betrayal and regret' (Kellman 1976: 18).

Between 1957 and 1959, Chaikin worked part-time in offices in New York, was regularly sacked, waited on tables, and took a number of minor jobs in the professional theatre. During this time he also studied with different acting teachers, most of whom adhered rigidly to a form of actor training which was based on a selection of Stanislavsky's earlier perceptions and exercises. The approach was firmly rooted in the past, and although it was one which was to contribute significantly to the future development of acting in the cinema, the assertion that it was applicable by any actor, to any play, written in any period, within any style, was regarded with some scepticism by Chaikin. He rejected the dogmatism of the 'Method', and with it, the notion of working within pre-defined boundaries, preferring to believe that, had Stanislavsky been alive, he would 'still be exploring' (Chaikin 1972: 57, 58).

In 1959 Chaikin joined the Living Theatre, led by Judith Malina and Julian Beck. At the time the company was producing plays such as Pirandello's *Tonight We Improvise* and Paul Goodman's *The Young Disciple* which included pre-verbal elements as part of its language.[3] Chaikin's first role with the Living Theatre was a small part in Goodman's *The Cave*, but he hoped it would lead to 'better' ones.

By 1962 he was playing the lead in Jack Gelber's *The Connection* on a European tour which made him feel, he says, 'very swelled, like a minor star', and whilst they were in Europe, the Becks asked him to play Galy Gay in Brecht's *Man is Man*. The play, written in 1924, presents the transformation of an Irish labourer into a human fighting machine. Back in New York, Chaikin remembers:

> it sounds like a fairy story, but it was in the playing of Galy Gay that I began to change. There I was, night after night, giving all my attention to pleasing, seducing, and getting applause from the audience, which is the very process wherein Galy Gay allows himself to be transformed from an innocent and good man into a thing, a machine – all because of flattery, one flattery after another.
>
> (Pasolli 1970: xiv)

In playing the role, Chaikin found himself moving towards a different kind of understanding of the possible relationships between actor, character, audience and play, and emerging out of this, a sense of theatre's power to effect change and transformation: transformation in the person of the actor within the process of acting, as well as Brecht's agenda for social change in the audience:

> it came mostly from considering the lines of the play, night after night after night. And saying them. … the responsibility of coming out to the audience and talking directly to them – something I had never had to do before – knowing that what I said to the audience I didn't believe, and then coming to believe what I was saying.
>
> (Chaikin 1972: 50, 51)

Figure 8.1   Joseph Chaikin with the Living Theatre in Brecht's *Man is Man*
Source: Photo, Karl Bissenger, 1962

A related change was also occurring for Chaikin around this time. In the autumn of 1961 Russia had resumed nuclear testing and the United States was 'considering the resumption' of testing. Early in 1962 President Kennedy announced resumption, and with other members of the company Chaikin became involved in the Women's Strike for Peace. The rally took place in Times Square and Chaikin, with other demonstrators, was attacked by police with night-sticks, arrested and jailed. Rehearsals for *Man is Man* took place amid preparations for the second General Strike for Peace, and a month after the play opened the Cold War heated to melt-down when an American spy plane flying over Cuba was hit by a surface-to-air missile. Chaikin, who had considered himself to be apolitical, recognised that the political aspect of the Living Theatre, which he had previously thought of as being ridiculous, was, in fact, very necessary (Tytell 1997: 176). He also had a 'real craving' to investigate the processes of collaboration with, or between, actors, directors and writers – the ensemble experience.

Nola Chilton, an acting teacher in New York at the time, had been experimenting with ways of preparing actors to engage with the non-naturalistic imagery of the absurdist playwrights. Chaikin was a member of this group, and when Chilton left for Israel, in 1962, he and the others who had been working with her decided to continue.

In 1963, with these seventeen other young actors and four writers, Chaikin co-founded the Open Theater. People came and went but the company functioned for over ten years, in New York City, as a forum in which actors, writers, teachers, directors, musicians, visual artists and intellectuals gathered and exchanged ideas and practices of theatre, and its relationship to society. R.D. Laing, the phenomenological psychologist, for example, talked with the company; and various critics – Gordon Rogoff, Richard Gilman and Susan Sontag – also attended sessions and talked with the group about different relationships between theatre theory, painting and the company's own experiments.[4] These experiments and investigations were part of a vigorous avant-garde movement which flourished in New York throughout the sixties, at a time of political and social upheaval in the country, as well as a redefinition of American identity – fractured and polarised by the war in Vietnam.[5]

The Open Theater was the first well-known American group to explore collaborative creation, and four major projects were undertaken in which the actor played a central role in generating and researching material for performance, with the writer or dramaturg contributing, shaping and editing material – rather than in the interpretation of already existing scripts. Chaikin was the director for each of these projects, and each was performed widely in varying contexts.

The group, however, began as a workshop – that is a laboratory or research theatre rather than a production company – and central to its identity from the outset was a collective commitment towards exploring a new language for performance: one which was *not* based on naturalism or psycho-

Figure 8.2   (Left to right) Cynthia Harris, Shami Chaikin, Tina Shepard, Jim Barbosa, Ron Faber, Ralph Lee and Peter Maloney in *The Serpent* developed by the Open Theater between 1967 and 1969

Source: Photo, Freddie Tornberg

logical motivation, but which was eclectic, inclusive and innovative, based on questions rather than answers, on imagined possibilities rather than given formulae.

Chaikin's book *The Presence of the Actor* was published in 1972. In it he questions a number of assumptions about acting, and actor training, but gives no easy answers and certainly no formulae. It is a book full of dreams, hopes, wishes, challenges and provocations towards creativity.

The Presence of the Actor is a singular book: not chronologically arranged, with a non-linear structure and non-prescriptive tone which invites the reader to make connections between its disparate parts and to allow contradiction. It consists, Chaikin says, of notes written from several 'levels' of himself, and within it and in other writing he reaches often for metaphors or images, of 'space' and 'place', in order to communicate his ideas and perceptions. He speaks, for example, of territories, zones, spheres, abandonment, exile, occupation and habitation.

A key image is that of 'a house on fire'. Addressing the actor he suggests:

Imagine a burning house:

1   You live in the house which is on fire. Even your clothes are charred as you run from the burning house.
2   You are a neighbour whose house might also have caught fire.
3   You are a passer-by who witnessed the fire by seeing someone who ran from a building while his clothes were still burning.
4   You are a journalist sent to gather information on the house which is burning.
5   You are listening to a report on the radio, which is an account given by the journalist who covered the story of the burning house.

(Chaikin 1972: 9, 10)

Chaikin reaches for the image of a 'house', in my understanding, as a means of suggesting to the actor the different perspectives from which it is possible to respond within the processes of acting.[6] Inside the house is the 'living room', where each thing must confirm and validate each other thing; the 'attic', a place to store memories; and the 'cellar', a private place, a place to which no one else knows the passage. Outside the house are the witnesses to the 'fire', and outside it also, are the 'sky' and the 'stars'.[7]

Chaikin developed a number of exercises, with innumerable variations upon them, which provide a means of 'inhabiting' and journeying within and between such 'spaces' – and it is in the relationship between the 'inside' and the 'outside', as I understand it, that the 'wordless questions about experience' begin.

In *The Presence of the Actor*, however, Chaikin expresses a resistance towards describing exercises, and a resistance to 'recipe-books' that document exercises. His argument that they cannot be documented is based on a distinction between 'content' and 'structure'. The exercise is 'an agreed-upon structure', and whilst the structure can be explained, the content, which is associated with 'internal territory', is untranslatable. It is untranslatable because it is irretrievably located within particular people, at a particular time, in a particular place within a particular socio-political climate.

Chaikin's assertion here reads as a direct rejection of his own training with teachers of 'Method' acting, and the idea of its universal application. This approach, in which Chaikin had been a sceptical participant, was based on a number of Stanislavsky's earlier exercises, and transformed into a dogmatic code. Chaikin's perceptions of the main features of this code are listed here, as a means of indicating the kind of actor training that he was reacting *against*:

1   The principle of objectives, actions, and obstacles. This technique helps the actor draw from his character and circumstances (a) what his over-all objective in the play is, (b) what his dramatic action

must be in order to achieve this objective, and (c) what obstacles stand in his way. That is, he learns to find the dramatic collision which is at the centre of every scene...

2   Sensory attention and emotional recall. Here concentration and relaxation are emphasised. The text is disregarded and the actor is urged to show only what he is feeling at the moment. Improvisations, that seem like psychotherapy are freely used...

3   Logical analysis of the text. Every moment of the play is analyzed and scored in terms of the character, the situation, etc. And once the score is finished, it remains fixed, regardless of the actor you are playing with, the director, the audience, etc.

4   Inspiration. This [*sic*] teacher does not use direct criticism but 'inspires' the actor by giving him a kind of spiritual blood transfusion.

(Chaikin 1972: 43, 44)

None of these features addressed the idea of the creative actor who would collaborate with writers and directors in the making of 'theatre events'. All (with the exception of the fourth) assumed a text written by a playwright which was to be interpreted by the actor.

As an actor with the Living Theatre, Chaikin had become interested in Brecht's idea of *verfremdungseffekt*, and his own perception of a confusion amongst American actors at the time, between the notion of 'detachment' and that of 'not caring'. Like Brecht, Chaikin cared. And he was interested, in his work with the Open Theater, not only in the idea of actors who were able to collaborate in the making of 'theatre events', but also actors who cared about the whole theatre event they were engaged in (Chaikin 1972: 38). 'My intention is to make images into theater events, beginning simply with those which have meaning for myself and my collaborators; and at the same time renouncing the theater of critics, box office, real estate, and the conditioned public' (Chaikin 1972: 3).

Chaikin and his collaborators had no system to realise this intention, and located as their investigations were in personal and cultural histories, he was wary of the application of external structures (in the form of exercises) within other contexts.

All prepared systems fail. They fail when they are applied, except as a process which was significant, at some time, for some one or some group. Process is dynamic: it's the evolution that takes place during work. Systems are recorded as ground plans, not to be followed any more than rules of courtship can be followed. We can get clues from others, but our own culture and sensibility and aesthetic will lead us to a totally new kind of expression, unless we imitate both the process and the findings of another. The aesthetic remakes the system.[8]

(Chaikin 1972: 21)

Some of the exercises explored by the Open Theater were brought to the company by other workshop members or visiting teachers, and many, as noted earlier, with innumerable variations upon them, were developed by Chaikin. In the following section of this chapter it is the intention to search for clues within three of these structures, which may be seen as interrelated and which will, I hope, offer glimpses of the training as a whole. This search will be guided by questions of inheritance, innovation and development, as well as my own understanding as a practitioner of certain key ideas and dynamics within each exercise.[9]

Exercises

Inheritance – the colours exercise

At the outset of their investigations, as noted earlier, the company engaged in exercises which attempted to explore 'non-naturalistic' approaches to character. As an example, a brief outline of one of these exercises, brought to the company from Nola Chilton's workshop, follows:

> *The actors respond immediately – physically and/or vocally – to the naming of certain colours, or other imagistic words, or phrases. This response is instant, impulsive and made without thinking.*[10]

Two key ideas inherent in this exercise – and others like it – were developed by Chaikin and became of central importance in further explorations. The first is the possibility that actor training might incorporate practice in non-cerebral, impulsive action and reaction to (sometimes quite abstract) images phrased in words. The terms 'non-cerebral' and 'impulsive', however, need to be qualified. Although both terms imply instant rather than planned response, neither is intended to suggest that such a response is unconnected to imagined, or remembered, associations located within 'internal territory' – and in Chaikin's thinking, this 'internal territory' is not bound by notions of a 'naturalistic' approach to acting.

In *The Presence of the Actor* Chaikin lists three possible sources of an actor's 'impulse': the first is 'reasoned association' – in which the actor, for example, moves towards a window in order to see what is outside; the second has to do with the perception of 'external demands' – in which the actor, for example, makes a sound in order to 'do what is good for her'; and the third possible source – the one which, my understanding, is most relevant to many of the exercises developed by Chaikin – is that the actor responds to 'inner promptings' and 'associations' in order to give form to a sound and/or movement. And in relation to such 'inner promptings' and 'associations', Chaikin asks:

From what part of himself is he [the actor] drawing these associations as he performs? Does he draw from information and ideas of the character, the audience, and his self-image? Does he draw from a 'body memory'? Does he draw his impulse from a liberated consciousness or from the same consciousness which he believes to be necessary for his daily personal safety? Does he draw from a common human source or from a contemporary bourgeois ego?

(Chaikin 1972: 8, 9)

The second key idea inherent in the 'colours' exercise is the possibility that training might engage the actor in the 'characterisation' of abstractions, objects, parts of people, projections of people. Chaikin's 'questions of character' give some indication of this second possibility:

Whom do you see when you look at me?
Whom do you think I see when I look at you?
Who or what is it that you think cannot be seen by anyone – is it still
   you?
What bits of information would be used to publicly describe you?
Does each piece of information have a value attached to it?
What system of perceiving and assessing determines that value?
Would you say that there are parts of yourself which have not lived yet?
What would bring forth the life of those parts?

(Chaikin 1972: 16, 17)

These questions stand in ironic contrast to those of Stanislavsky whose 'given circumstances' questions are lodged within naturalism and an already existing text. Chaikin's questions are very often to do with what is *not* given, and *not* known – the invisible as much as the visible. Rather than the sense of coherence deriving from a 'super-objective', they are essentially generative of a number of contradictory perspectives on character, ones which might be perceived as being either 'inside' or 'outside' a person. They suggest division and fragmentation, and underlying them there is a sense of absence in relation to a single, separate notion of 'character'.

Innovation – the sound and movement exercise

Chaikin was interested, then, not only in the possibilities of collaborative creation with actors who cared about the whole theatre event they were engaged in, but also in ways of generating a new language of performance. This language would not be one confined to models of social behaviour appropriate to given naturalistic texts, but one which might reflect a sense of 'the divided self' within society.[11]

He was interested also in including within such a language a means of giving voice to the forbidden, forgotten, hidden areas of what it means to be human, and speaking to those same areas in an audience. In this attempt, sound and movement imagery became a potential means by which this 'untranslatable' inner territory might be communicated, and Chaikin innovated a key set of exercises which had the potential to develop its vocabulary. The 'sound and movement exercise' was one of these.[12]

> *The actors might begin, for example, sitting in a circle – each actor making a sound, before altering it, and passing it on to the next person. The same might be done with a movement, that is, by passing around, again in a circle, a gesture with each person repeating the gesture and altering it before passing it on to the next person. Sound arising from the gesture might then be added, and with the development of related skills, the predictable 'one–two' rhythm of the sound and movement might become more lively and complex.*

> *In a development of this structure, the actors begin by standing in a circle, or in two lines facing each other, and the sound and movement is passed across the circle, or between the two lines – each actor taking a sound and movement out into the space, and allowing its form to alter. The process of change and transformation continues until the actor recognises, or discovers, some kind of associative connection with it. This invites further alterations to the form until, finally, the sound and movement can be repeated with clarity, and without alteration. An 'internal' image, or associative connection, recognised or discovered by the actor has, in effect, translated itself into abstract, dynamic, 'external' form – an image in sound and movement.*

> *The actor, sustaining both the 'internal' image, and its 'external' form in sound and movement, moves towards another actor standing within the circle, or in the opposite line. For a few seconds both actors repeat the sound and movement, simultaneously – the first actor 'giving' the image and the second actor 'receiving' it. The second actor then moves out into the space and the process continues: the form of the sound and movement is allowed to alter – a new association surfaces in relation to the changing form – which in turn shapes the rhythm and dynamic of another sound and movement image – which in turn is given to another actor – received by that actor – and so on through the whole group – the last image potentially carrying traces of all previous forms.*

The exercise may be further developed using a theme, which will feed a series of associations for the actors to work with. Within this development there is the complicating factor of the actor having to deal with a constantly changing set of 'internal' associations, at the same time as dealing with a different set of 'external' associations which have been given by another actor. Where stimulus and reaction begin and end is unclear, and whether stimulus or reaction is located within the 'inside' or the 'outside' of the actor is also unclear. This is an important point: within the process of change and transformation, there is essentially a flow or dialogue between the two.

'Don't let anyone tell you to go from the inside out – or the outside in. It's a circle' (Blumenthal 1981: 56).

A second important dialogue occurs within the 'sound and movement exercise'. This second dialogue, between body and mind, can be seen most clearly at the heart of the exercise – that is, within the process of change and transformation. During this process, when an actor takes the sound and movement out into the space, and allows it to alter, it is very clear when the actor 'pre-judges', mentally or physically, in one moment what will happen in the next. In such a case, the alignment between the person and the, as yet, inchoate image, within the process of transformation, is sensed *not* to be alive, moment to moment.

It is equally clear, however, when the actor allows a particular kind of shifting balance, or dialogue, between body and mind, in listening to and watching for the emerging form, the emerging image, and is able, moment to moment, to come into alignment with it. In such a case, there is a perceptible quality of 'presence', moment to moment within the process of change and transformation, this quality of 'presence' having more to do with the actor in operation with imagery rather than uniquely with the actor's 'self'. The image, in fact, becomes a 'possibility' rendered present.

> An exercise is a form usually repeated in order to develop one thing or another. … Some exercises are for bringing suppleness to the body or range to the voice. … Most exercises are practices in order to develop something other than the exercise itself. What then remains insufficiently exercised in many workshop situations is the doing of the act itself – that of performing in the present – the act of being itself.
>
> (Joseph Chaikin archives)

There are, therefore, two interrelated dialogues which occur within the 'sound and movement exercise': the first between the 'inside' and the 'outside', and the second between the body and the mind. Both these dialogues inform the content and the structure of the training as a whole.

I should note in passing that there is sometimes a polarity created between exercises which invite somatic exploration and those which have their starting point in 'thinking' or 'feeling'. In my understanding, within the 'sound and movement exercise' it is not so much one dynamic, or the other, which is being exercised, but a flow between the two. There is sometimes, also, an association made between exercises which invite somatic exploration with a state of ignorance in the actor, and a corresponding state of knowledge in the director. It is, of course, perfectly possible for an actor to understand the reasoning behind 'an agreed-upon structure' which, paradoxically, also invites somatic exploration. And certainly Chaikin, working within a 'research theatre', understood conscious 'ignorance' to be an inspirational point of departure for both actor and director.

Finally two further factors mark Chaikin's innovatory structure. Both factors are also connected centrally to the training as a whole, and Chaikin identifies them as being the underlying principles of ensemble work: empathy and rhythm (Chaikin 1972: 59).

These two factors can be seen most clearly during the stage in the exercise when the two actors are sharing the same sound and movement simultaneously. Apart from the shared *gestalt*, within the sound and movement form, which is held between them at this time, there is both an empathetic and a rhythmic relationship. Thus, the intention within those moments is not simply to imitate the outward form of the other actor's sound and movement but to share the same inner rhythms and energy, that is the same kinetic and psychic space.

Development – the chord exercise

The exploration of these principles of rhythm and empathy underwrote the development of innumerable variations of this exercise and others by Chaikin. As an example, I would like to include a brief outline of the 'chord' exercise.[13]

> *The actors might begin standing in a circle, or lying on their backs with their heads inwards, a communal sound being gradually shared amongst them, beginning with the sounds of the breath – transforming into a hum – and then into a sung chord in which harmonies and counter-rhythms might develop. Movement might then be included, with each actor adjusting to the shape of the whole group.*

This exercise, and others like it, invite the 'exiled emotions' of gentleness and sharing to determine the course of an improvisation, rather than a spirit of competition. The rhythms explored within it, their patterns, dynamic and intensity, are not imposed technically in order to shape the sound and/or movement. Rather, it is the intention that the actors listen carefully to the communal sound, or watch carefully the composite form which is being made, and allow their own energies both to feed and to respond to the contribution of others. The sounds and movements become more than the sum of their parts.

Both the 'sound and movement exercise' and the 'chord' have been included in training programmes by generations of companies interested in developing ensemble practices. They were also included in early programmes by the Open Theater (*as* performance), and in 1964 in *Mysteries and Smaller Pieces* by the Living Theatre. The performance quality of the two exercises, and others like them, however, is highly dependent on the relative skills of the participants, and an understanding of their dynamics and purpose. The 'chord' was adopted by demonstrators against the war in Vietnam, and became, in a way, a pacifist statement, a kind of emblem for the Open Theater itself.

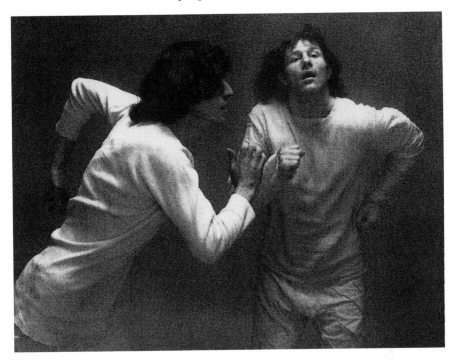

Figure 8.3   (Left to right) Paul Zimet and Raymond Barry in *Terminal* developed by the Open Theater between 1969 and 1971

Source: Photo, Max Waldman

Performance

The programme note for the first performance by the Open Theater in 1963 contained the following:

> What you will see tonight is a phase of work of the Open Theater. This group of actors, musicians, playwrights and directors has come together out of a dissatisfaction with the established trend of the contemporary theatre. It is seeking a theatre for today. It is now exploring specific aspects of the stage, not as a production group, but as a group trying to find its own voice. Statable tenets of this workshop: (1) to create a situation in which the actors can play together with a sensitivity to one another required of an ensemble, (2) to explore the specific powers that only the live theatre possesses, (3) to concentrate on a theatre of abstraction and illusion (as opposed to a theatre of behavioural or psychological motivation), (4) to discover ways in which the artist can find his expression without money as the determining factor.
>
> (Open Theater archives 1963)

This performance and other early performances by the Open Theater consisted of collections of exercises, playlets, political sketches and improvisations in which, for example, sound and movement work, representative of 'inner' experience, was juxtaposed or elided with situational work indicating 'outer' behaviour. They were, in fact, mixed programmes whose structure and content questioned the distinction between process and product, acting and actuality.

Between 1963 and 1973, and subsequently in later collaborative projects, Chaikin continued to develop ways in which improvisatory exercises could be used both *as* performance, and as a means of generating material for performance. Much of this exploration continued to be cross-fertilised by ideas, practices and skills which were brought to the company by other workshop members, directors and visiting teachers. Grotowski's visit in 1967, for example, resulted in the incorporation of an exercise known as the 'cat' – a sequence of movements adapted from Hatha Yoga which was used as a basis for physical and vocal improvisation. Moments uncovered within non-verbal exercises such as the 'cat', or the 'sound and movement exercise', were then selected, pared down and rhythmically scored, juxtaposed in relation to pieces of found text, and often further developed, edited and shaped by a writer, or dramaturg, with Chaikin as director.[14]

Jean-Claude van Itallie, a writer with the company between 1963 and 1973, noted that 'There was an emphasis in the work upon dream, myth, fantasy, poetry, ritual, and the confrontation of social issues'. The company was 'in short: a theatre committed to the imagination, the deep life of the time, and the true resources of the stage...' (Fundamentals of Open Theater, Open Theater archives).

I would like now to consider the process of generating material for performance, and to offer glimpses in relation to 'content', by outlining two further exercises developed by Chaikin. These exercises might be seen as developments of the sound and movement exercise, incorporating words.

Generating material for performance – emblems

Each actor took it in turn to tell a story, which might be either autobiographical or one discovered through research. The actors, as storytellers, could be as subjective as they wished in the telling of the stories and it was their aim to engage the workshop audience with the same points of contact as they, themselves, discovered. The tellings were made up of 'words, sounds, movements and silences', and once each story had been told, both the storyteller and the workshop audience tried to identify moments within it which might be chosen as 'emblems' for the story (Chaikin 1972: 116).

'Emblems', in fact, by nature of their economy – through a process of selection and reduction – provided a means by which imagery generated for performance could transcend its particular or autobiographical source.

Figure 8.4   (Left to right) Tina Shepard, Paul Zimet and Joe Ann Schmidman in *The Mutation Show* developed by the Open Theater in 1971

Source: Photo, Howard Gans and Claude Furones

In his notes from the summer of 1970 Chaikin gives an example of this process in relation to a story told by the actress, Tina Shepard. At the time the company was beginning work on generating material for its new piece *Terminal*, which took as one of its starting points the actors' responses to the themes of death and dying, and the way in which they perceived society to have constructed different ways of disguising these experiences. Shepard's story was about her mother, who was dying from cancer, and about the difficulty she felt in saying all the things she was expected to say – 'you look very well' or 'you look better'. Somewhere in the story was the line 'I see you' (said to her mother) 'but I don't see you dying' (said to the workshop audience). The story was much longer in the telling, but these two phrases and the particular gesture the actress used of 'hiding and revealing' were combined and selected as an 'emblem' for the story. This 'emblem' was not so much a symbol which represented the whole story, as an image which was both expressive, and indicative, of an essential part within it (Chaikin 1972: 108, 109).

This same distinction would be applicable to the notion of an 'emblem' for a character, action or place. For example, a further means of generating 'character' developed by Chaikin was to discover the 'emblem' of a character in breath. In this process, the actor might start with a breathed sound into which is fed the sense of the energy, or inner rhythm, of the character at a particular moment within a story. This energy and rhythm would, then, be taken into the body, transforming itself into a gesture, a way of moving.

Chaikin's inspiration for the notion of 'emblems' derived from the ideograms of Chinese classical theatre, in which, through the use of specific gestures, characters are immediately recognisable to an audience familiar with the language of that form. The character of Death, for example, waves his arm each time he enters a scene – the wave of the arm not being, of course, in this instance, representative of 'character', in the way in which the term might be understood within naturalistic theatre (Pasolli 1970: 90, 91).

In defining an 'emblem' Chaikin said:

> The crown is emblematic of the king. The bars are emblematic of the prison. If an emblematic part of an action is played out, with the actor living *in* the action, there is a resonance beyond what there would be if the entire action were played out. The spectator completes the action from the part of it which is being performed. The emblem becomes a meeting point for the actor and the spectator.
>
> (Chaikin 1972: 113)

Generating material for performance – jamming

A related means of generating material for performance was explored through a development of the work on 'emblems', which came to be known as 'jamming'. As Chaikin noted in *The Presence of the Actor*, the term came from jazz, from the jam session.

In 'jamming', the actor improvised physically, vocally and verbally using the content, meaning and intention of an 'emblem' as a basis to work from and return to, 'travelling within the rhythms, going through and out of the phrasing, sometimes just using the gesture, sometimes reducing the whole thing to pure sound' (Chaikin 1972: 116).

Chaikin gives an example of 'jamming' by the actress, Joyce Aaron, whilst the company was working on *The Serpent*, a piece developed between 1967 and 1969. Exploration for this piece engaged the actors in addressing and questioning assumptions of innocence, guilt and responsibility, which were perceived as being part of a cultural inheritance from the book of Genesis. The words within the 'emblem' used by the actress were: 'What was given to me was impossible to work with.' In jamming, they became something like: 'What was – what was given – was given – what was given? – given to – was what? – to me? – what was given to me was given to me – was – was impo – was impossible...'

Chaikin described 'jamming' as a kind of 'contemplation' or 'extended study' of different associative senses within an 'emblem'. Certainly within the exploration the actor would sometimes need to 'rest and let the image move itself' in the mind. Within such a process, there is a dialogue between allowing the meanings within an 'emblem' to determine the development of

Figure 8.5 (Left to right) Tina Shepard, Shami Chaikin and Tom Lillard in *Nightwalk* developed by the Open Theater between 1972 and 1973

Source: Photo, Donald Cooper

the exploration, and consciously recognising and shaping that development (Chaikin 1972: 116, 117).

Process and production

The four major collaborative projects undertaken by the Open Theater directed by Chaikin were *The Serpent*, developed between 1967 and 1969 (with the writer Jean-Claude van Itallie); *Terminal* between 1969 and 1971 (with the writer Susan Yankowitz and co-director Roberta Sklar); *The Mutation Show* in 1971 (without a writer);[15] and *Nightwalk* between 1972 and 1973 (with dramaturg Mira Rafalowicz and contributing writers Jean-Claude van Itallie, Sam Shepard and Megan Terry).

All four 'theatre events' were performed widely in Europe, the Middle East, North Africa and America – in theatre spaces, colleges and prisons. Each was non-linear in structure and interwoven with musicality and humour. Each essentially explored a central theme from a number of different perspectives, and also, implicitly, invited a recognition between actors and audience of the need for personal, social and political change.

Dialogue with an audience within these 'theatre events' might be understood as a series of translations: associative connections or 'internal' images discovered by the actor, translated into dynamic 'external' forms – as images in sound movement and words – 'read' by an audience, and translated, by them, back into associative connections or 'internal' imagery. Dialogue between characters as it might be understood within naturalistic theatre was virtually non-existent, and often replaced by direct address.

The last performance of *Nightwalk*, which was also the last performance by the Open Theater, was in December 1973, at the University of California, Santa Barbara. The piece was concerned with the perception of disconnection within society, and a longing for wholeness. In its last image, the actor, Raymond Barry, facing the audience, gestured with his right arm in a vibrating movement suggesting, simultaneously, both dividing and connecting energies. The sense of both presence and absence is implicit in the words, and the silences between them:

> There was himself and herself and herself and himself
> and between us
> there was himself and herself and herself and himself
> and between us
> there was each self and each other self, each self and each other self
> and between us
>
> (Malpede 1974: 150)

All four projects attempted to remain true to the integrity of the aims of the Open Theater as stated in the programme note of their first performance. The original impetus for the company, however, had been to 'explore things', to be a research theatre, and Chaikin felt that, although the group had found a common language within the context of the forum which was the Open Theater, they had taken things as far as they could – without becoming a production company.

In 1973, the Open Theater disbanded. A year before it ended, it became clear to Chaikin that this had to happen for a further reason. In 1974 he went into hospital for open heart surgery and it was uncertain whether he would recover. Since that time – despite further heart surgery and the aphasic stroke in 1984 – Chaikin has moved back and forth between interpretative work on 'inherited' plays, and experiments within further investigative and collaborative projects.[16]

His need to re-discover words has engaged him in working with the disabled, and in making, with others, a number of pieces about aphasia. His own disability, he recognises, places him in another 'place', another 'space', 'yet another SPHERE'.

> Now, that I am Aphasic, –
> I am, – 'The Other'.
> I under-stand more – about vul-ner-a-bi-li-ty...
> What is normal?
> Who sets the standard?[17]

Chaikin continues to ask questions and continues to 'strive to be alive to all that he can imagine possible'. In reaching for words to tell the story of his stroke he said 'I am thinking about the stars – not down – but up'.[18] At the time of writing in the summer of 1998, Chaikin is teaching a master class in New York for twelve actors and four directors, entitled *From Shaw to Shepard*. In the new year he will be directing Samuel Beckett's *Endgame* in New York.

Chaikin has directed Beckett's texts for a number of years and shortly before he died in 1989, Beckett dedicated his last poem to Chaikin (Knowlson 1997: 703).

Entitled 'what is the word', it ends:

> glimpse –
> seem to glimpse –
> need to seem to glimpse –
> afaint afar away over there what –
> folly for to need to seem to glimpse afaint afar away over there what –
> what –
> what –
> what is the word –
> what is the word
>
> (Joseph Chaikin archives)

In *The Presence of the Actor*, Chaikin observed that whilst Stanislavsky had directed other people's plays, Brecht had directed his own. Perhaps he might concede that in searching for a new language for performance, and in exploring different possible relationships between 'the word' and sound and movement imagery, Chaikin challenged the twentieth century's ideas and practices of play 'wrighting' itself.

Moreover, his collaborative investigations and explorations into actor training – although never aspiring to be a system – placed the actor at the heart of the creative process, and at the heart of transformation and change within that process. Ideas and practices of theatre making which, at the end of the century, seem familiar, would be less so, had it not been for his influence.

Notes

1 In his Foreword to *The Presence of the Actor*, Chaikin formally states that, despite using the term 'he', in speaking of 'the actor', he means both women and men (Chaikin 1972: x).

2 Chaikin has been awarded six Obies, including an Obie for lifetime achievement in the theatre. His other awards include the Drama Desk Award, the Vernon Rice Award, the Brandeis University Award for Distinguished Actors, the New England Theatre Conference Award, the Edwin Booth Award, as well as two Guggenheim fellowships and grants (inventory prepared by Christine McBurney-Coen, Joseph Chaikin archives, Kent State University).

3 Influenced by the theories of Antonin Artaud the Living Theatre was to become by the late 1960s one of the best known, and one of the most attacked, cultural experiments of that decade.

4 Members of the ensemble, at different times, included Joyce Aaron, actress; James Barbosa, actor; Shami Chaikin, actress; John Dillon, production manager; Brenda Dixon, actress; Ron Faber, actor; Gwen Fabricant, designer; Peter Feldman, director; Rhea Gaisner, workshop director and assistant director; Jayne Haynes, actress; Jean-Claude van Itallie, playwright; Ralph Lee, actor; Tom Lillard, actor; Ellen Maddow, actress and musician; Peter Maloney, actor; Howard Meyer, electrician; Richard Peaslee, actor; Marianne de Pury, composer, musician and administrator; Mira Rafalowicz, dramaturg; Mark Samuels, actor; Jo Ann Schmidman, actress; Sidney Schubert Walter, actress; Tina Shepard, actress; Roberta Sklar, co-director; Megan Terry, playwright and director; Barbara Vann, actress; Stan Walden, actor; Lee Worley, actress and workshop director; Susan Yankowitz, playwright; and Paul Zimet, actor.

5 This movement was paralleled in Europe with experiments led by Peter Brook and Jerzy Grotowski, and to an extent there was a certain amount of transatlantic cross-fertilisation between their ideas and practices.
   Chaikin collaborated with Brook on *US* in 1966; and in 1967, Grotowski came to work with the Open Theater (Pasolli 1970: 97, 114). In 1968, Chaikin was invited to work with Brook's company in Paris (Mitter 1992: 30, 31).

6 Chaikin also invented a number of exercises to explore different possible relationships or ways of 'connecting' with an audience. 'The first step, that of dedicating, is choosing, closing in on a place of contact between you and another…' (Chaikin 1972: 143).

7 This image has been pieced together from a number of scattered fragments (Chaikin 1972).

8 Chaikin recommends that an acting company invents its own exercises, especially in looking for alternative ways to represent character (Chaikin 1972: 17).

9 Descriptions of the exercises contained within this chapter and analyses of the dynamics within them are derived from personal practice, contact with other practitioners, and the application of Chaikin's thinking to the structure of the exercises. Published sources are cited in the bibliography; unpublished sources are housed in the Joseph Chaikin and Open Theater archives at Kent State University.

  Brief descriptions of many other exercises may be found in *A Book on the Open Theatre* by Robert Pasolli. Eileen Blumenthal's *Joseph Chaikin* places the workshop investigations more substantially within their context.

10 The outline of the 'colours' exercise is based on an undated, unsigned manuscript in the Open Theater archives, Kent State University.

11 This term refers to the title of R.D. Laing's book, *The Divided Self*. It is beyond the scope of this chapter to discuss, in any detail, the intriguing parallels which may be drawn between Chaikin's thinking and practice and those of R.D. Laing.

12 The outline of this exercise, in its beginning stages, is based on Peter Feldman's account in 'The Sound-and-Movement Exercise as Developed by the Open Theatre'. In this paper, Feldman (co-founder, and director with the Open Theater between 1963 and 1970) discusses the connections between this exercise and Stanislavsky's 'as if'.

13 In this outline, the way in which the 'chord' exercise might be developed to include movement is noted by Eileen Blumenthal (Blumenthal 1981: 74).

14 The process of development, editing and shaping was a complex and often problematic one, which varied from project to project. Eileen Blumenthal's *Joseph Chaikin* vividly documents examples of this process.

15 *The Mutation Show* was not credited with a writer. However, two successive writers in residence, W.E.R. La Farge and John Stoltenberg, contributed to the exploratory work for the piece.

16 Chaikin's collaborative ventures have included *Tongues* and *Savage/Love* with Sam Shepard (Daniels 1994); an adaptation, with the director Steve Kent, of Samuel Beckett's *Texts for Nothing* (Chaikin 1981); *Imagining the Other*, a project with Arab and Israeli actors (Joseph Chaikin archives); and *The Winter Project* with dramaturgs Mira Rafalowicz and Bill Hart. This latter group met for a few months each year between 1976 and 1983, and five 'works-in-progress' were generated by them. Eileen Blumenthal's *Joseph Chaikin* documents examples of these investigations, and Chaikin's other work, until 1981.

17 This is part of a speech Chaikin made in 1989, for the Aphasic Society, at City Hall, New York (Joseph Chaikin archives).

18 In conversation, summer 1998.

Bibliography

Context

Chaikin, J. (1977) 'Joseph Chaikin' (interview by Andrzej Bonarski), in B. Marranca and G. Dasgupta (eds), *Performing Arts Journal* 1, no. 3: 117–23.

—— (1974) 'Notes on Acting Time and Repetition', in K. Malpede (ed.), *Three Works by the Open Theater*, New York: Drama Book Specialists/Publishers.

—— (1972) *The Presence of the Actor*, New York: Atheneum.

—— (1970) 'The Context of Performance', in T. Cole and H. K. Chinoy (eds), *Actors on Acting*, New York: Crown.

—— (1969) 'Chaikin Fragments', in R. Schechner (ed.), *The Drama Review* 13(3): 145–7.

—— (1968) 'The Actor's Involvement: Notes on Brecht' (interview by Erika Munk), in R. Schechner (ed.), *The Drama Review* 12(2): 147–51.

—— (1964) 'The Open Theatre' (interview by Schechner), in R. Schechner (ed.), *Tulane Drama Review* 9(2): 191–7.

Coco, W. (ed.) (1983) 'The Open Theatre (1963–1973) Looking Back', in B. Marranca and G. Dasgupta (eds), *Performing Arts Journal* VII(3): 25–48.

Kellman, A. (1976) 'Joseph Chaikin the Actor', in M. Kirby (ed.), *The Drama Review* 20(3): 17–26.

Mitter, S. (1992) *Systems of Rehearsal*, London: Routledge.

Schechner, R. (1969) 'An Interview with Joseph Chaikin', in R. Schechner (ed.), *The Drama Review* 13(3): 141–4.

Shank, T. (1982) *American Alternative Theatre*, London: Macmillan.

Tytell, J. (1997) *The Living Theatre*, London: Methuen.

Exercises

Blumenthal, E. (1981) *Joseph Chaikin*, Cambridge: Cambridge University Press.

Feldman, P. (1977) 'The Sound and Movement Exercise as Developed by the Open Theatre' (interview by Peter Hulton), in P. Hulton (ed.),*Theatre Papers*, Dartington College of Arts, Devon.

Hulton, P. (1977) 'From Action to Theatre Image', in P. Hulton (ed.), *Theatre Papers*.

James, W. (1977) 'What is an Emotion?', in P. Hulton (ed.), *Theatre Papers*.

Laing, R.D. (1959) *The Divided Self*, London: Tavistock Publications.

Meckler, N. (1994/95) *Ways of Physicalising Thoughts, Feelings and Text*, Exeter: Arts Documentation Unit.

Pasolli, R. (1970) *A Book on the Open Theatre,* New York: Avon Books.

Performance

Beckett, S. (1974) *Texts for Nothing*, London: Calder and Boyars.

Chaikin, J. (1981) 'Continuing Work' (interview by Peter Hulton), in P. Hulton (ed.),*Theatre Papers*.

Daniels, B. (ed.) (1994) *Joseph Chaikin and Sam Shepard: Letters and Texts, 1972–1984*, New York: Theatre Communications Group.

Dillon, J. (1972) 'The Development of Performance Material in the Open Theatre', manuscript, Open Theater archives.

Itallie, J-C. van (1966) 'Playwright at Work: Off Off-Broadway', in R. Schechner (ed.), *Tulane Drama Review* 10: 154–8.

Knowlson, J. (1997) *Damned to Fame*, London: Bloomsbury.

Malpede, K. (ed.) (1974) *Three Works by the Open Theater*, New York: Drama Book Specialists/Publishers.

The Open Theater (1969) *The Serpent*, New York: Atheneum.

Yankowitz, S. (1997) '1969 Terminal 1996: an Ensemble Work', in B. Marranca and G. Dasgupta (eds), *Performing Arts Journal* XIX(3): 80–106.

Videotapes of performances referred to in this chapter may be viewed in the Theatre on Film and Tape Archive, at the New York Public Library for the Performing Arts, New York.

The Joseph Chaikin archives and the Open Theater archives are housed in the University Libraries Department of Special Collections and Archives at Kent State University, Ohio.

9 Peter Brook

Transparency and the invisible network

Lorna Marshall and David Williams

Our primary concern in this chapter is to outline the evolution of Peter Brook's ideas on the preparation of actors. Our particular focus is the development of two interrelated qualities that are prerequisites for performers in his own company: a state of openness and immediacy he calls 'transparency'; and a state of connectedness and responsiveness he calls 'the invisible network'. As we shall see, both of these qualities are conceived and explored on internal and external levels. Indeed, like self and other, actor and character, performers and audience, for Brook inner movement and external action must always be in a dynamic relationship of exchange.

Context

Peter Brook's extraordinarily productive career as a director spans the half-century since the end of the Second World War, and includes over seventy theatre and opera productions and a dozen films. It will be useful in this context to divide his extensive body of work into three periods, despite the fact that such historiographic 'dismemberings' will inevitably be simplifications.

The first phase (1945–63) covers the years of Brook's professional apprenticeship in a wide range of performance contexts, forms and styles. At the age of twenty-two, he was already a director at the Royal Opera House, Covent Garden; and by 1963, when Brook was thirty-eight, he had directed over forty productions, including nine Shakespeare plays and seven major operas. Landmark productions included a luminous *Love's Labour's Lost* for the Royal Shakespeare Company (1946), an explosive reworking of Strauss's *Salomé* (1949) designed by Salvador Dali, a startling *Titus Andronicus* (1955) with Laurence Olivier and Vivien Leigh, and an elemental, absurdist *King Lear* (1962) with Paul Scofield.

Although he was known primarily as a director of classical theatre, Brook also juggled productions of major twentieth-century European playwrights (Cocteau, Sartre, Anouilh, Genet, Dürenmatt) and works by seminal modernists (including Eliot and Miller), plus overtly commercial projects – boulevard comedies, musicals and television drama. Brook's trajectory reflects his deliberate immersion in a contradictory array of experiences, seeking to find a complex, composite reality through the exploration of opposites. In retrospect, he has referred to this period as 'a theatre of images', informed by an escapist aesthetic of illusionist decoration and artifice – a theatre in which the world of the stage was wholly separated from that of spectators, and where the director's 'vision' was omnipotent.

The second phase (1964–70) constituted a period of reappraisal, maturation and proactive research. Brook was becoming increasingly disaffected with the existing processes and forms of much contemporary theatre – a short-sighted, convention-bound theatre he stigmatised as 'deadly' (Brook 1968: 11–46). In his search for theatre languages that could more accurately reflect contemporary reality, he questioned the theatrical *status quo* at every level. Rejecting ossified ('deadly') processes, he returned to core constitutive questions:

> Theatres, actors, critics and public are interlocked in a machine that creaks but never stops. There is always a new season in hand and we are too busy to ask the only vital question which measures the whole structure. Why theatre at all? What for? Is it an anachronism, a superannuated oddity, surviving like an old monument or a quaint custom? Why do we applaud, and what? Has the stage a real place in our lives? What function can it have? What could it serve? What could it explore? What are its special qualities?
>
> (Brook 1968: 44)

This period of work reached fruition in a remarkable series of productions Brook has characterised as a 'theatre of disturbance' (see, for example, Trewin 1971: 199). An explicit shift in his concerns and processes became evident in an experimental project conducted under the aegis of the Royal Shakespeare Company, with a group co-directed with Charles Marowitz. Public 'work-in-progress' showings of this early, tentative research in 1964 were entitled the 'Theatre of Cruelty' in homage to Antonin Artaud. The culmination of this research occurred with the celebrated production of Peter Weiss's *Marat/Sade* (1964), a collectively devised response to the Vietnam War ambiguously entitled *US* (1966), and a choral, ritualised *Oedipus* (1968) in an abrasive new version by the poet Ted Hughes.

This transitional phase was also characterised by a growing awareness of the importance of the actor within an ensemble. The creativity of actors would be instrumental in challenging the complacency of prevalent practices and creative hierarchies, as well as finding theatrical forms as multifaceted as Shakespeare's. Brook took Elizabethan dramaturgy as his model; he particularly admired its shifts of gear in the mix of comedy and tragedy, its vivid language, and the directness of its forms. Shakespeare was his prototype for a conflation of the 'rough' and the 'holy' into a textured totality he called the 'immediate'.[1] This area of Brook's research reached its apogee with his swansong with the RSC, a joyously airborne production of *A Midsummer Night's Dream* (1970), which radically dismantled received ideas of the play. In this work, Brook and his group of actor-acrobats created a counter-image to the harrowing, confrontational tenor of the earlier work of this period with a bright circus-inflected celebration reuniting stage and auditorium.

In retrospect, the 1960s marked a period of significant development for Brook in terms of his conception of the training of actors. He used detailed exploration of improvisatory techniques to dislodge actors from reductive psychological behaviourism, and, as they began to tap other energies, Brook was able to recognise their creative primacy: 'It takes a long while for a director to cease thinking in terms of the result he desires and instead concentrate on discovering the source of energy in the actor from which true impulses can arise' (Brook 1998: 83).

Brook's goal, to amplify actors' capacities as instruments responsive to all the sources of the creative process, has been pursued and refined by him to the present day. Eventually, it took him from the restrictive working conditions in commercial theatre in England, and led him to a new base in France.

The third phase comprises Brook's work since 1970 with his international group in Paris, the International Centre for Theatre Research (CIRT). Its focus has ranged from private research behind closed doors, to explorations of theatrical communication in the field (on journeys to Iran, Africa and the USA), to recent forays into the fantastic inner landscapes of neurological disorders for the production of *The Man Who* (1993). Core projects have included *Orghast* (1971) in the tombs of Persepolis, Iran; *Timon of Athens* (1974); adaptations of Colin Turnbull's anthropological study of the demise of a Ugandan tribe *The Ik* (1975–6); a presentation of a twelfth-century Sufi poem *Conference of the Birds* (1979); *La Tragédie de Carmen* (1981); a nine-hour version of the Hindu epic *The Mahabharata* (1985–8); and a spartan staging of Shakespeare's *The Tempest* (1990) with the African actor Sotigui Kouyaté as Prospero.[2]

So, after almost three decades with his own company, what are the qualities Brook most admires and requires in his actor-collaborators? And what are the recurrent impulses and characteristics of the performances they have made together?

Briefly, all of Brook's work with the CIRT has been marked by continuing attention to the following ideals:

1   The development of actors with a capacity to articulate the trajectories of inner impulses, conveying these impulses in external forms with clarity and immediacy – '*transparency*' (Brook 1998: 224) – and the search for a charged simplicity and economy in those forms, a '*distillation*' (ibid.).

2   The actor as a primary creative source in an ensemble conceived as a 'storyteller with many heads' (ibid.: 197) – a team of players. Therefore actors need to be open, complicitous and responsive to the requirements of an embodied transform-ability Brook has called 'lightness'.[3]

3   The extreme pragmatism of improvisation as the key to the preparation of performers. Related to this, the importance of direct experiences of differing performance conditions and audiences. Work-in-progress is often presented in unconventional spaces to unfamiliar audiences (in schools, hospitals, prisons etc.). Such experiences aim to unsettle actors' habitual responses and open them up to different energies and qualities of exchange.

4   The absolute necessity for structure, and the conviction that forms can engender freedom for actors. Structure and play are seen as counterbalancing elements, interwoven supports for each other.

5   Research as 'self-research'; a process of evolution and individual development in which theatre serves as potent site and means, but rarely as the exclusive end. In other words, theatre as a means to go beyond theatre – theatre-making as the site for what James Hillman has called 'soul-making'.

6   The act of theatre as affirmative 're-membering' (Brook 1998: 225), in which a mythical narrative or fable is actualised here and now: 'reuniting the community, in all its diversity, within the same shared experience' (Brook 1978: 7).

Ultimately, all of Brook's work with the Centre at its base at the Bouffes du Nord theatre in Paris has been driven by the desire to discover what makes theatre 'immediate' (or 'un-deadly'). His diverse training exercises and rehearsal methods have been developed and endlessly reinvented to support and realise this desire. When examining Brook's work, it is essential to understand its open-endedness; he has no single form or style in mind, no pre-conceived vision of a desirable end product. Moreover, he has often reiterated the instability of the relationship between surface forms and the underlying processes and impulses that 'in-form' them: in other words, between 'means' and 'meanings'.

He suggests that all of his theatre productions possess two distinct, if closely interrelated, aspects. First, the external *mise-en-scène* is comprised of contextually determined forms emerging from the performance's physical conditions. Second, beneath these specific patterns of images, no more than tips of invisible icebergs, lies what he terms 'the hidden production': 'an *invisible network* of relationships' that can give rise to other forms and patterns without forfeiting a work's 'essential meaning' (Brook 1998: 151–2). In this context, it may be fruitful to view Brook's preparation of actors through the lens of this metaphor – as a collaborative 'weaving' of an 'invisible network' that feeds, generates and energises all aspects of theatrical communication.

Exercises

Preparation

Given the importance of actors' processes in Brook's work, appropriate training is evidently essential. However, 'preparation' is a more useful term than 'training' when considering the Centre's approach. Brook is not engaged in developing the skills of the actor from the ground up, of 'forming' actors for his own particular style of work. In general, Brook's actors come to the company with a distinguished track record. Most have had years of training within a particular theatre culture – in Japanese Noh, Balinese Topeng, African storytelling and dance, English or Polish classical theatre, and so on; and all have performed extensively in a variety of contexts. By most standards, they are already 'fully trained'. Their bodies, emotions and voices have already learned how to respond to the demands of different kinds of theatre-making.

At the same time, all of the CIRT's projects include an element of physical and vocal work geared towards further extending the actors' technical skills. Sometimes this takes the form of training in particular styles of physical or vocal work (for example, Tai Chi). At other times the approach is less familiar. During the Centre's early research, Brook often arranged contact with groups with particular perceptual abilities – for example, deaf practitioners (such as the American Theatre of the Deaf) and deaf audiences, who were usually children. Interaction with their amplified tactile and visual sensibilities was perceived to be as informative as any other more conventional 'specialist' training – perhaps even more so. In addition, performers in particular projects are exposed to appropriate training regimes under the direction of specialists within the group. For example, the CIRT performer Alain Maratrat passed on his extensive knowledge of south-east Asian martial arts to the *Mahabharata* company, as did practitioners of certain South Indian forms (such as Kathakali and Kalarippayattu).

However, the main thrust of Brook's 'training' lies in another direction. Through the preparatory work, the actors encounter the absolute imperative for responsiveness, openness, and the ability to operate as team-players within the group. Their earlier training is useful in terms of the depth of theatrical experience it can afford, and of the self-discipline required for a profession that is an ongoing process of learning to learn. But with Brook they are invited to work beyond or beneath enculturated theatrical conventions, whether it be the 'psychological truths' of Western naturalism or the codified gestures of Asian forms. Brook's processes resemble the *via negativa* of Grotowski; they necessitate an un-learning, a peeling away of habit and the known in favour of the potential and the 'essential'.

Brook's ideal actor has moved beyond ego-driven virtuosity to a kind of psycho-somatic integration that he calls 'transparency'. Alive and present in every molecule of their being, they have 'the capacity to listen through the body to codes and impulses that are hidden all the time at the root of cultural forms' (1998: 167). At the moment of transparency, as in certain kinds of possession in which consciousness does not disappear, actors become a site or conduit for the manifestation of the 'spirit' or 'life' of words, song, dance – a 'life' that Brook believes exists beneath theatrical forms. At the point of transparency, *it* speaks/sings/dances them. Thus, actors need to become

> instruments that transmit truths which otherwise would remain out of sight. These truths can appear from sources deep within ourselves or far outside ourselves. Any preparation we do is only part of the complete preparation. The body must be ready and sensitive, but that isn't all. The voice has to be open and free. The emotions have to be open and free. The intelligence has to be quick. All of these have to be prepared. There are crude vibrations that can come through very easily and fine ones that come through only with difficulty. In each case the life we are looking for means breaking open a series of habits. A habit of speaking; maybe a habit made by an entire language.
>
> (Brook 1987: 107)

It is with such a goal in mind that, for example, Brook invited the internationally renowned Feldenkrais teacher Monika Pagneux to prepare the young cast of his *Don Giovanni* in Aix-en-Provence (1998) – to unsettle received *bel canto* habits, to stimulate individual and collective dexterity and economy and to encourage a fluid openness and integration.

The starting point for Brook's training is responsiveness: the ability to sense and play with, and off, material in a simple, direct way. This 'material' can be impulses arising within the actor or suggested externally, in the relationship with another performer or performers, or in elements of the text itself. Performers are encouraged to develop and exercise a tripartite attentiveness: to inner impulses, to fellow performers and to the space. For Brook, initially such 'respons-ability' is developed physically through the body and its intuitive intelligence, rather than intellectually through analysis or discussion. His preparation of actors realigns the assumed relationship of mind and body in Western cultures, reversing the conventional Cartesian hierarchy and traditional point of access to 'meaning':

> It is always a mistake for actors to begin their work with intellectual discussion, as the rational mind is not nearly as potent an instrument of discovery as the more secret faculties of intuition. The possibility of intuitive understanding through the body is stimulated and developed in many different ways. If this happens, within the same day there can be moments of repose when the mind can peacefully play its true role. Only then will analysis and discussion of the text find their natural place.
>
> (Brook 1993: 108)

Although the body is initially privileged as mediator of experience and storehouse of knowledges, the ultimate ideal is an actor who has developed to the point where all available channels – those of the body, the intellect, and the emotional faculties – are open, interconnected and active (Brook 1987: 232). Research and training thus constitute a 'clearing of paths' (Brook 1973). As in Gurdjieff's system of 'harmonious development', to which Brook's work is indebted, personal evolution stems from simultaneous work on the three core centres of body, thought and feelings. Once this internal network of relationships is active, it permits openings and connections to others, the wider 'network of relationships' that Brook refers to above.

In *There Are No Secrets*, Brook describes the preparatory process for *The Tempest*. The group began by withdrawing from its familiar base in Paris, and moving to a secluded rehearsal space in the cloisters of a former monastery in Avignon. Scripts of the play were ignored completely for the

Figure 9.1   Stick exercise with the American Theater of the Deaf, Paris, 1971

Source: Photo, CICT

Note: The sticks externalise and amplify personal impulses which harmonise as a collective impulse when individuals 'listen' to the group. At such moments, transparency and connection intersect.

first ten days, as the actors prepared their bodies and voices through group games and improvisations whose sole purpose was 'to develop quick responsiveness, a hand, ear and eye contact, a shared awareness that is easily lost and has to be constantly renewed, to bring together the separate individuals into a sensitive, vibrant team' (Brook 1993: 107).

Such activities are not warm-ups before performers turn to the 'real' task of acting, as is often the case in contemporary theatre. Instead, they are oriented towards amplifying spontaneity, responsiveness and complicity, whilst exercising the 'muscles' of intuition and the imagination.

In practice, these activities take many different forms: leader/led 'conversations' between actors involving physical and/or vocal exchange; collective exercises in rhythm, polyrhythm and counterpoint, of both auditory and spatial kinds; choral work in which individual actions feed and sustain collective images; and improvisatory play focused around simple objects – balls, cloths, doors, boxes, sticks. Brook compares this kind of preparatory work to the training of a sports team: 'only an acting team must go farther; not only the bodies, but the thoughts and feelings must all come into play and stay in tune' (ibid.).

'Tuning' here is a musical or orchestral metaphor. It represents a quality of listening and interaction in which the personal (individual instruments) needs to serve the supra-personal (the orchestral collective). Paradoxically the recognition of the primacy of the whole over its individual parts – the team over the player – can enable a deeper 'individuality' and sense of self to flourish in 'the projection of a collective imagination far richer than our own' (Brook 1998: 183).

In *The Invisible Actor*, Yoshi Oida describes one of the many exercises that invite heightened attention to the circulation of energies underpinning the 'invisible networks of relationships'. Two people exchange a conversation using only the actions of one hand. Each person 'listens' to physical impulses offered by the other, and responds to them, in a direct and immediate way using their own hand. Oida is at pains to point out that these puppeted hand languages should not be referential, like a code to be deciphered 'like sign language or a game of charades':

> Instead, you try to concentrate your whole existence into that one hand. It is a kind of strange animal, communicating to another equally strange animal. When you find the genuine life of this creature, and it is able to develop a real and varied relationship with the other animal, it is fascinating to watch.
>
> (Oida 1997: 75–6)

The aim is to condense the full sensitivity and expressivity of the body into one isolated part. Oida suggests that the quality of deep attention brought to bear in such seemingly banal interactions is crucial. When a connection is established, the space between the two hands is animated in a kind of small, energised dance of relatedness. Here 'drama' is generated via the combustion of contact between two 'life forms', their particular qualities amplified because they are reduced and distilled:

> What is interesting is the exchange. The 'acting' doesn't reside in the hand of each actor; it exists in the air between the two hands. This kind of acting is not narrative, not psychology, not emotion, but something else, something more basic. It is very difficult to describe exactly what it is.
>
> (Oida 1997: 76)

On a micro level, therefore, this exercise represents a provocation to concentration (inward towards one's own hand) and openness (outward towards the other's hand). At the same time, it reflects the quality of exchange desired on a macro level within the company as a whole, and ultimately with those present as spectators. The network links the actor to self, to partner, to ensemble, to audience.

It is important to note that all such exercises can, and should, be re-made for particular contexts. The exchange could be exclusively vocal, such as improvised responses to the sounds of an existing text; or it could involve any parts of the body, with or without voice. There is no stable vocabulary of exercises, no immutable 'box of tricks'. What is central here is the *exchange* and its subtle repercussions – the pleasure of the changes it instigates:

> You have to work at a level deeper than that of the intellect. As a result, each time you 'exchange', something inside you changes in reaction. From moment to moment you alter and respond. In this way, as the sounds and movements are exchanged, your inner being constantly shifts.
>
> (Oida 1997: 78–9)

Responding to text

Once the sense of an ensemble has begun to be established, and individual 'instruments' are 'tuned' and able to 'play' in relation to each other, then the group turns to language. Often tied to habitual responses, words can enforce the 'deadly' and impede an immediacy of communication. Brook's preparation of actors includes a re-examination of all aspects of their use of language.

Like other external stimuli employed to provoke internal responses, texts are initially treated as materials to be explored and 'understood' physically and emotionally, rather than intellectually in terms of their surface content and meaning. In this context, the kind of responsiveness Brook seeks in his actors has little to do with intellectual understanding *per se*, or even with the ability to establish personal emotional identification with the words in question. It is something more fundamental, like glimpsing the particular topography of a world or landscape. Brook's discourse in this context often describes patient and sensitive physiological discovery. He has talked, for example, of the voice as a mountain with many caves that the actor needs to explore, or of the imperative to treat a new word like a blind man finding a butterfly (Smith 1972: 76, 130).

As with any existing cultural formation or expression, Brook wants his actors to disinter elements underlying language through a sensitisation to its deeper resonances. The actors are invited to taste the textures and qualities of energy – the 'music' – underpinning its particular forms and to listen to the ways in which this 'music' impacts on their inner landscapes. To return to Brook's description of preparation for *The Tempest*:

> After a few days our study included words, single words, then clusters of words and then eventually isolated phrases in English and French to try and make real for everyone, including the translator, the special nature of Shakespearean writing.
>
> (Brook 1993: 108)

Indeed Brook believes that it is possible to respond with integrity to a given text even when the actor cannot understand the referential meanings of the words. In the early 1970s, this belief was the axis of the language work which culminated in the performance of *Orghast* at Persepolis. Brook describes his multicultural group's imperative to side-step the assumed consensus of an existing shared language:

> The theme of the first year's work of the International Centre of Theatre Research was to be a study of the structures of sounds. Our aim was to discover more fully what constitutes living expression. To do this, we needed to work outside the basic system of communication of theatres, we had to lay aside the principle of communication through shared words, shared signs, shared references, shared languages, shared slang, shared cultural or subcultural imagery.
>
> (Brook 1987: 108)

In preparation for *Orghast*, the actors initially experimented with the sound qualities of swear words, but soon moved on to the creation of their own language constructed from an accumulation of simple sounds. Oida explains:

> We took words from various languages and jumbled them up together to create interesting sounds, e.g. 'Bashta hondo stoflock madai zutto'. We had to create a meaning for this phrase according to the situation that was being improvised. Working with a partner (who obviously didn't know the literal sense of your words), you had to communicate

what you wanted to say through your uses of intonations and clarity of intention. We worked a great deal in this created language…

(Oida 1992: 47)

Subsequently, they experimented with 'dead' languages that had once communicated specific meanings through words and grammar, but that were unknown to all of the actors in the group. One exercise involved Ancient Greek, a language in which the meanings of words are known to scholars, whilst their precise articulation in speech still remains the subject of conjecture. Brook describes how a passage of Ancient Greek was given to the actors as a single unbroken unit, without any of its usual verbal or compositional divisions. Like any newly encountered word, this 'nugget of "unknowingness"' (Brook 1998: 168) had to be explored for its musical potential: 'It was not divided into verses, nor even into separate words; it was just a long series of letters, as in the earliest manuscripts. The actor was confronted with a fragment: ELELEUELELEUUPOMAUSFAKELOSKAIFREE-NOPLEGEIS' (Brook 1987: 108).

The actors were invited to approach this fragment 'like an archaeologist, stumbling over an unknown object in the sand' (Brook 1987: 108), deciphering its deeper layers by means of their own intuitive sensitivities and 'knowledges':

> The actor's truly scientific tool is an inordinately developed emotional faculty with which he learns to apprehend certain truths, to discriminate between real and false. It was this capacity that the actor brought into play, tasting the Greek letters on the tongue, scanning them with his sensibility. Gradually the rhythms hidden in the flow of letters began to reveal themselves, gradually the latent tides of emotion swelled up and shaped the phrases until the actor found himself speaking them with increasing force and conviction. Eventually every actor found it possible to play the words with a deeper and richer sense of meaning than if he had known what they were meant to say.
>
> (1987: 108)

Once again, Brook's linguistic model is musical: a communicative medium of the senses in which means and meaning are indissolubly interwoven. For Brook, such music represents an untranslatable language sufficient unto itself: pre-intellectual, emotional, physically rooted, and potentially trans-cultural.

Inside/outside

Brook has endeavoured to illustrate key elements of his perspectives on acting processes with reference to a familiar shorthand: acting as from the 'inside-out', and from the 'outside-in'. Although these two terms are often used to describe two mutually exclusive approaches to creativity in acting, for Brook they are complementary and inseparable.

In the early 1990s, during a public forum on the Centre's work, he invited those present to enact and experience these different, but inter-related, approaches in a simple and direct manner. First of all, they were asked to respond to their own internal impulses in an external action:

> Make a movement with your right arm, allow it to go anywhere, really anywhere, without thinking. When I give the signal, let it go, then stop the movement. Go! Now hold the gesture just where it is, don't change or improve it, only try to feel what it is that you are expressing. Recognise that some sort of impression cannot fail to emanate from the attitude of your body. I look at all of you, and although you did not attempt to 'tell' anything, to try to 'say' anything, you just let your arm go where it wished, yet each of you is expressing something.
>
> (Brook 1993: 68)

A movement is triggered without conscious intellectual volition or composi-tional shaping; although it is of course in some sense 'chosen' by the individual participants, for they are its origin and site. Once this movement has been arrested at an externally determined point, participants are encour-aged to explore this attitude; they are invited to 'taste' its expressive particularity and informational resonances and associations, as if it were a film still they temporarily inhabit. No gesture will be neutral or void, Brook suggests, for each one represents an 'attitude' in both senses of the word – a 'dis-position'. Each can be read in many different ways from both the inside and externally.

Brook then proposes something slightly different using exactly the same starting point, an unpremeditated arm movement stopped at a particular moment:

> Now hold the attitude just where it happens to be and try, without modifying your position, to feel a relationship between the hand, the arm, the shoulder, up to the muscles of the eye. Feel that it all has a meaning. Now allow the gesture to develop, to become more complete through a minimal movement, just a small adjustment. Feel in this minute change, something transformed itself in the totality of your body, and the complete attitude becomes more unified and expressive.
>
> (Brook 1993: 68)

Here the emphasis is on sensing relations between the parts and a whole, physically and then cognitively. The endeavour to transform an accidental attitude into a form that has 'meaning', through minimal adjustment, engages the will and imagination. The perspective used in this compositional refining is sensory and internal; at the moment 'meaning' comes into being, 'inside' modifies 'outside'.

At this point, Brook returns to the beginning of the exercise, once again shifting its parameters:

> Instead of making a movement that is your own, take a movement that I give you; place your hand, open, in front of you, the palm facing the outside. You do not do this because you feel you want to, but because I'm asking you to, and you are prepared to go along with me without yet knowing where this will lead. So welcome to the opposite of improvisation: earlier you made a gesture of your own choice, now you are doing one that is imposed. Accept doing this gesture without asking yourselves 'What does it mean?' in an intellectual and analytical manner, otherwise you will remain on the outside. Try to feel what it provokes in you.
>
> (Brook 1993: 69)

Here the physical attitude is defined from the outside, then projected inwards. Participants are invited to 'listen' and experience the inner associations thus triggered, without trying to decipher or impose conceptual signification; so 'outside' refashions 'inside'. However, once it has been allowed to resonate, and is both 'heard' and accepted, a fresh imaginal response arises within the actor, which in turn informs the external physical attitude. As Brook explains, this bridging of inner and outer constitutes a moment of openness in which energy circulates freely – in other words, a moment of transparency:

> Something is given to you from the exterior, which is different from the free movement you made previously, and yet if you assume it totally, it is the same thing, it has become yours and you have become its. ... The true actor recognises that real freedom occurs at the moment when what comes from the outside and what is brought from within make a perfect blending.
>
> (Brook 1993: 69)

Perception and reception now become active and creative, rather than passive. Inner/outer, subject/object and structure/freedom are now in dynamic coexistence, rather than being mutually exclusive (as they are so often assumed to be). Whereas a great deal of conventional acting is constituted by adding gesture to feeling, or vice versa, Brook looks for a state of responsive connectedness where feeling and gesture are indivisible and synonymous. If acting comprises the process of making the 'invisible' visible, the exchange between inside and outside needs to be two-way and continuous.

Production

The desired confusion of inner and outer, invisible and visible, is one of the cornerstones of Brook's preparation of actors from the *Marat/Sade* to *The Man Who*. For example, during an intensive study period in the preparation of *The Ik*, members of the group copied the postures of members of the Ik tribe, as recorded in documentary photographs. These postures were re-created in painstaking detail, with the actor 'listening' to information provided by the physical form. Whilst others observed and corrected, the actor would then improvise the action or movement immediately preceding or following the instant captured in the photograph. Through this highly disciplined form of 'outside-in' improvisation, where the precise still-point of a photograph would be passed through as if it were one frame in a continuum, actors were able to access internal responses and echoes outside the limitations of personal biographical experience. As Brook remarks:

> This was a far cry from what is usually understood by 'free improvisation'. We found it enabled European, American, Japanese, African actors to understand something quite directly about playing starving people, a physical condition none of us has ever experienced and therefore cannot reach by imagination or memory.
>
> (Brook 1987: 135)

For the production of *Conference of the Birds*, on the other hand, the group worked with Balinese Topeng masks to facilitate a storytelling transformability that reflected the fable's rapid shifts in reality. Brook viewed these particular masks as objective, archetypal manifestations of essential types which would help actors clarify and crystallise their own impulses. Extending their earlier study of the physiological attitudes of the Ik, the actors scrutinised and manipulated the masks at arm's length (like Balinese performers); then, at the moment of putting masks on, they would modify their own facial expression in the direction of the mask's physiognomy. In this way, actors aimed to make intimate skin contact with 'the face of a very strong, essential type' (Brook 1981: 63). Paradoxically Brook conceives of such masks as 'anti'-masks that *uncover*, offering 'a soul-portrait, a photo of what you rarely see...an outer casing that is a complete and sensitive reflection of the inner life' (1987: 62). Potentially these masks – like all such external stimuli employed to provoke internal movement – are both transformative agents of understanding for their wearers and 'lie-detectors' amplifying dissonances in circuits and flows:

> A mask is two-way traffic all the time; it sends a message in, and projects a message out. It operates by the law of echoes; if the echo-chamber is perfect, the sound going in and the one going out are

reflections; there is a perfect relation between the echo-chamber and the sound; but if it isn't, it's like a distorted mirror.

(1987: 63)

Similar processes were employed in preparing the production of *The Man Who*. Through first-hand observation of, and contact with, patients in a Parisian hospital, the small, collaborative team involved in the project evolved detailed physiological impressions of the symptoms of particular neurological conditions. By imitating in detail the external forms of internal states, the actors' imaginations were activated. Recently, Brook has described a moment in the production's first public run-through that seems an apt summation of our discussion of certain core components in Brook's practice: inside/outside, transparency, distillation, immediacy, the invisible network:

> There came a moment when I felt we had found a link with what we had attempted in Africa when we had first put a pair of shoes on the carpet in front of the audience to establish a common ground. In *The Man Who*, the pair of shoes was replaced by a table, a candle and a box of matches. Yoshi Oida came to the table, lit the candle with special concentration and then for a long time gazed intently at the flame. Then he blew it out, took another match, lit the candle and blew it out again. As he started once more, I could feel the tension in the audience increasing. The audience could read into the simple actions far more than they apparently expressed;...it understood directly what was going on.
>
> (Brook 1998: 223–4)

Finally, let us return to the notion of the actor as 'team-player'. We have already seen how part of the actor's preparation focuses on amplifying sensitivity towards fellow actors. This 'tuning' in turn supports their ability to meet what is required of them in an ensemble of storytellers. Yoshi Oida uses Brook's sporting metaphor to describe collectivist ethics and practices of storytelling in *The Mahabharata*:

> As in *Conference of the Birds*, we were a team of storytellers...[Brook] used the image of football to help us understand what he wanted. As if the play were a game of football, there were twenty-two team members and one ball, the ball being the story. Since we were all on the same team, it didn't matter who played which part, or if you changed characters in the middle. Together we told one story, keeping one ball in play. In order to continue telling the story, you had to be ready to pick up the ball when your scenes arrived.
>
> (Oida 1992: 172)[4]

Figure 9.2   Le Mahabharata at the Bouffes du Nord, Paris, 1985

Source: Photo, Michel Dieuzaide

Note: An archery contest. Bamboo sticks are used to suggest weapons and to construct a dynamically layered space. The actor-storytellers aim to produce an energised depth of field, rather than an absolute uniformity.

However, the imperative to 'pick up the ball' goes beyond training, rehearsal and even onstage performance. Oida has also described how actors did not stay in their dressing rooms during performances of the *Mahabharata*. Instead, they would stand in the wings, watching and listening to the way in which a sequence was unfolding prior to their entrance. In this way, they could sense how to adapt their entrance and performance in order to keep the 'ball' in play (Oida 1992: 173). So the necessity for connection to the 'invisible network' even affected actors' behaviour offstage.

Therefore, one can see how the notion of a dynamic relationship between the inside and the outside ('transparency') manifests itself at many different levels of the creative process – from a sensitising of the individual actors to their own impulses and those of others, to methodologies for revealing hidden layers of texts, and for enabling character transformation that is not merely reduced to personal biography. It also influences particular choices of tools and artistic forms, both in rehearsal and in performance. The masks, for example, precisely *enact* Brook's propositions concerning 'transparency' and the 'invisible network'. The way in which such concepts permeate all aspects of his company's performances is characteristic of Brook's pragmatism. Concepts are only ever sanctioned in terms of usefulness; and more often than not with Brook, they arise from working processes, rather than being imposed upon them.

Notes

1 For a detailed discussion of the characteristics of 'rough theatre' and 'holy theatre', and their conjunction in a prismatic totality Brook calls 'immediate theatre', see Brook (1968).

2 For details of all of the CIRT's work since 1970, with extensive bibliographies, see Banu (1991), Hunt and Reeves (1995), and Williams (1992).

3 In conversation in 1986, Brook described the quality he most admired in one of his actors, Maurice Bénichou, in terms of 'lightness'. This quality can be understood through Paul Valéry's suggestion that 'one should be light as a bird, not light as a feather'. In other words, one must recognise and bear the substantive weight of what it is one enacts, its gravity; one must remain present, engaged and embodied in the doing that takes us into the world – but with a lightness of touch that is buoyant and playful, that enables one not to be encumbered or consumed, but to take off, to move on, to be 'free'.

4 For an analysis of the workings of this storytelling model in performance, see David Williams (1991), in particular pp. 117–92.

Bibliography

Banu, Georges (1991) *Peter Brook, de Timon d'Athènes à La Tempête*, Paris: Flammarion.

Brook, Peter (1998) *Threads of Time: A Memoir*, London: Methuen.

—— (1993) *There Are No Secrets: Thoughts on Acting and Theatre*, London: Methuen.

—— (1987) *The Shifting Point*, London: Methuen.

—— (1981) 'Lie and Glorious Adjective', *Parabola* 6, 3 (August).

—— (1978) 'Lettre à une étudiante anglaise', in Shakespeare, *Timon d'Athènes* (adapted by Jean-Claude Carrière, 1974), Paris: CICT.

—— (1973) Brook at the Brooklyn Academy of Music (workshop sessions transcribed by Sally Gardner), September–October. Unpublished, unpaginated; held in the CICT archives.

—— (1968) *The Empty Space*, Harmondsworth: Penguin.

Hunt, Albert and Reeves, Geoffrey (1995) *Peter Brook*, Cambridge: Cambridge University Press.

Oida, Yoshi, with Marshall, Lorna (1992) *An Actor Adrift*, London: Methuen.

—— (1997) *The Invisible Actor*, London: Methuen.

Smith, A.C.H. (1972) *Orghast at Persepolis*, London: Eyre Methuen.

Trewin, John C. (1971) *Peter Brook: A Biography*, London: Macdonald.

Williams, David (ed.) (1992) *Peter Brook: A Theatrical Casebook*, London: Methuen.

—— (ed.) (1991) *Peter Brook and the Mahabharata: Critical Perspectives*, London and New York: Routledge.

10 Grotowski's vision of the actor

The search for contact

Lisa Wolford

Jerzy Grotowski is arguably one of the most influential figures in the development of experimental theatre and actor training techniques over the past thirty years. Whilst only a relatively small number of people had the opportunity to witness the productions of the Laboratory Theatre or to undergo extended apprenticeship with Grotowski or the actors of his company, the techniques of performance training that these artists helped to develop have been widely disseminated through print sources as well as through workshops, productions and classroom teaching. 'Unfortunately', as Peter Brook observes, 'this ultra-rapid diffusion has not always gone through qualified people, and around the name of Grotowski – like a rolling stone – have come to attach themselves, to graft themselves, all kinds of confusions, excrescences and misunderstandings' (in Schechner and Wolford 1997: 379). In a somewhat more acerbic tone, Thomas Richards relates that he is

> aware that many people have experienced 'Grotowski workshops' conducted by someone who studied with Grotowski in a session of five days, for example, twenty-five years ago. Such 'instructors', of course, often pass on grave errors and misunderstandings. Grotowski's research might be mistakenly construed as something wild and structureless, where people throw themselves on the floor, scream a lot, and have pseudo-cathartic experiences. Grotowski's connection to tradition, and his link to Stanislavski, run the risk of being completely forgotten or not taken into account.
>
> (1995: 4)

The phenomenon to which both Brook and Richards allude has serious implications, and I would not argue against their assertions that misrepresentations of Grotowski's work are magnified by dubious modes of dissemination.

A tendency to emphasise the experimental aspects of Grotowski's work with the Laboratory Theatre or to focus on selected elements of the company's aesthetic (e.g. the extreme physicality of the actor's work, the non-naturalistic style of presentation, or the ritualistic aspects of the group's

Figure 10.1   Jerzy Grotowski, Chicago, April 1995
Source: Photo, Pancho Colladetti

productions) has indeed, as Richards argues, had the effect of downplaying the indebtedness of Grotowski's practice to the work of Stanislavsky. 'For many people', Grotowski observed, 'it is difficult to differentiate between techniques and aesthetics' (1980: 121).

A generation in rebellion against the tenets of naturalistic theatre created a false polarisation between Grotowski's approach and that of the Russian master, failing to recognise that both directors' work was underpinned by concrete principles of craft that could be applied in a range of theatrical styles and aesthetic circumstances. Indeed, throughout his life, Grotowski always acknowledged Stanislavsky as a primary influence on his work, emphasising points of continuity and confluence in their respective projects over aesthetic differences. He recounts that as a young student, he was 'possessed' by Stanislavsky, convinced that Stanislavsky's teachings provided 'a key that opens all the doors of creativity' (Grotowski 1980: 193). A central element of Grotowski's approach to actor training, like Stanislavsky's, was the effort to help the actor *live more truthfully* on stage; the difference between the directors' styles arises in their respective perceptions of how that 'truth' might best be expressed within an aesthetic framework.

Grotowski, who was also influenced by the work of Vsevolod Meyerhold, shared Meyerhold's belief that a naturalistic emphasis on simulating the surface aspects of daily social existence often obscured a more profound level of Truth. Yet whilst Grotowski's incorporation of codified physical training methods might owe more to Meyerhold's practice than Stanislavsky's, his emphasis on the 'total act' and on guiding the actor to develop the most subtle nuances of inner life within the framework of the role had little to do with the principles of constructivist theatre.

Privately, Grotowski would sometimes recount that when he studied directing at the State Institute of Theatre Art in Moscow, his teacher, Yuri Zavadsky, often remarked on the uncanny similarity between the young Grotowski's way of working with actors and that which he remembered as characteristic of Stanislavsky. Grotowski also voiced a strong conviction that Stanislavsky's work in the domain of physical actions was the most vital and enduring discovery of his remarkable research into the foundational tenets of the actor's craft. Had Stanislavsky lived longer, Grotowski observed, he would have continued even beyond this vital discovery. In a sense, Grotowski implied that his own research could be seen to mark the continuation of Stanislavsky's investigation, taken up from the point to which it had evolved at the time it was interrupted by Stanislavsky's death.[1]

How can the influence of Stanislavsky be traced in Grotowski's theatrical and post-theatrical work, despite the apparent dissimilarities of their respective projects? What are the essential characteristics of Grotowski's approach to actor training? What elements can be seen as consistent throughout the various phases of his work?[2] Is it possible, as Jan Kott queries, to apply Grotowski's methods in a theatre with different aesthetic and ideological aims? (in Schechner and Wolford 1997: 135). To what extent can the methodologies of actor training developed by Grotowski and his collaborators be incorporated in naturalistic theatre or other types of performance that differ radically from the aesthetics of the Laboratory Theatre? These are some of the questions this chapter sets out to address.

Rather than focusing primarily on detailed descriptions of selected physical and vocal training techniques, I will examine certain basic elements and underlying principles of Grotowski's approach to performance that I would argue are fundamental to understanding his theatrical practice. I take this approach for several reasons. First, because descriptions of physical and vocal training techniques are already available in Grotowski's own writings, particularly in *Towards a Poor Theatre*. Furthermore, in the years since publishing his book, Grotowski became increasingly wary about providing descriptions of specific physical and vocal exercises, as he observed a tendency to fetishise such techniques as if they provided a 'recipe for creativity'. Exercises, he warned, serve only as the preparation for genuine creativity. He cautions against a tendency to believe that physical training techniques have value in themselves, noting that it is tempting for actors to use exercises as a type of 'absolution' for not giving themselves fully in the context of the role. Physical exercises can prove useful in helping to prepare the author's body as instrument, and especially in allowing the actor to address specific limitations (e.g. a lack of stamina or strength or flexibility), but are not in themselves sufficient to enable the actor to accomplish the task of revealing him/herself in performance. 'In the training of the actor', Grotowski warns, 'in exercises, it is always possible to find a false satisfaction that permits one to avoid the act of personal sincerity' (1980: 196). In order to avoid unintentionally providing more 'recipes', I will refrain from speaking of the precise elements of Laboratory Theatre training in any way that might be interpreted as an indication of 'how to do' these exercises.

Throughout the course of his creative work, Grotowski warned actors to be wary of 'methods ready-made for each occasion', which he asserted were creatively inhibiting and could only lead to stereotyped portrayals (Grotowski 1975: 185). Grotowski was dubious of not only the efficacy of such methods, but also the impulse behind the desire for recipes and easy solutions.

> We want to learn means: how to play? How best to pretend to be something or someone?... But if one learns how to do, one does not reveal oneself; one only reveals the skill for doing. And if someone looks for means resulting from our alleged method, or some other method, he does it not to disarm himself, but to find asylum, a safe haven, where he could avoid the act which would be the answer.
>
> (Schechner and Wolford 1997: 218)

Grotowski consistently denied that any such thing as a 'method' associated with his work could be said to exist, arguing that only a handful of theatre practitioners – most notably Stanislavsky – have ever developed an approach to performance training that is sufficiently detailed and systematic to be accurately described as a method (Grotowski 1975: 174).

> When I came to the conclusion that the problem of building my own system was illusory and that there exists no ideal system which could be a key to creativity, then the word 'method' changed its meaning for me. There exists a challenge, to which each must give his own answer. ... The experience of life is the question, and the response is simply through true creation. It begins from the effort not to hide oneself and not to lie. Then the method – in the sense of a system – doesn't exist. It cannot exist except as a challenge or as a call.
>
> (Grotowski 1980: 193)

In a discussion of the Laboratory Theatre's training techniques, Jennifer Kumiega suggests that if 'the only method that deserves the name of the Grotowski method is that of having no fixed and universal method at all', then what remains are techniques and ethics. 'Techniques we can understand as the minutiae of method', she elaborates, 'the practicable directives which, in certain combinations, produce the verifiable results which are usually classed as method. Ethics are what inform the use of technique...' (1985: 111). Kumiega concludes that it is 'the ethic, the attitude with which [these techniques] are discovered, researched and performed, that is of primary significance' in understanding Grotowski's approach to performance (1985: 112).

My own experience of working with Grotowski and a number of his close collaborators confirms the wisdom of Kumiega's directive. I am firmly convinced that it is more productive for artists interested in developing their own independent practice to look for inspiration in the *ethos* and funda-mental tenets of Grotowski's work than through importing codified exercises. Whilst my discussion of Grotowski's vision of the performer and his approach to actor training will focus primarily on his work with the Laboratory Theatre, my analysis will also be informed by my experience as an actor in Grotowski's Objective Drama programme at the University of California-Irvine, in which I participated for several years (1989–92), and on my observations of the research conducted at the Workcenter of Jerzy Grotowski and Thomas Richards in Pontedera, Italy (1986–present).[3] I have chosen to concentrate on certain basic principles of physical training as developed by Grotowski and his collaborators. Whilst Grotowski's approach to vocal work is also profoundly significant, this is a complex matter better dealt with in its own right than subsumed in a discussion of physical training; also, the importance of song in the latter phases of Grotowski's research makes it difficult to speak of voice work solely in relation to the 'Theatre of Productions' phase of his creative activity.[4]

Poor theatre: the art of the actor

Although the nature of Grotowski's creative practice underwent many changes over the course of his lifetime, one element that remained consistent was his emphasis on sustained and methodical research involving the fundamental principles of the actor's craft. In *Towards a Poor Theatre*, Grotowski articulated the need for a type of performance laboratory modelled after the Bohr Institute (1975: 95–9), a forum for investigation of the principles governing artistic creativity. Whilst he rejected any possibility of discovering formulae for creation, which he asserted would inevitably be sterile, Grotowski voiced a desire to demystify the creative process, seeking to define a methodology of performance training that would free the actor to accomplish his or her work without obstruction and also without waiting for random inspiration.

The Teatr Laboratorium, the group Grotowski founded in Opole, Poland, in 1959, became known for a distinctive performance style that emphasised the encounter between actor and spectator as the core of the theatrical exchange. Reacting against what he foresaw as the encroachment on to theatre of film and other new technologies, Grotowski asserted that rather than trying to compete with new media, the theatre could best survive by emphasising that which set it apart from other forms of representation: the living presence of the actor, 'the closeness of the living organism' (Grotowski 1975: 41). Rejecting what he described as a 'kleptomaniac theatre', a theatre 'rich in flaws' that promiscuously combined elements from a range of plastic and performing arts in order to create engaging spectacle, Grotowski and his collaborators developed an aesthetic that minimised reliance on autonomous costume, make-up, scenery and lighting (Grotowski 1975: 15–53).

> Elimination of plastic elements which have a life of their own (i.e. represent something independent of the actor's activities) led to the creation by the actor of the most elementary and obvious objects. By his controlled use of gesture, the actor transforms the floor into a sea, a table into a confessional, a piece of iron into an animate partner, etc. Elimination of music (live or recorded) not produced by the actors enables the performance itself to become music through the orchestration of voices and clashing objects.
>
> (1975: 21)[5]

Because Grotowski's theatre positioned the actor at the centre of the theatrical event, performers were expected to be capable of extraordinary acts beyond the reach of the spectator. Grotowski was not interested in a theatre that concerned itself only with the banalities of daily life, nor with an actor whose work consisted of representing mundane behaviour. Ninety per cent of what goes on in daily life, he said, is not the material from which great art can be made; likewise, the ability to speak naturalistic text in a relatively believable manner or to mimic social behaviour was never, for Grotowski, a measure of the actor's skill. 'If [the actor's] body restricts itself to demonstrating what it is – something that any average person can do – then it is not an obedient instrument capable of performing a spiritual act' (Grotowski 1975: 33).[6]

The actor as envisioned in Grotowski's theatre was a holy figure, a type of 'secular saint' whose extraordinary discipline and ability allowed him or her to cast aside daily life masks in order to accomplish an act of self-penetration and disarmament. Poor Theatre made extreme psychic and physical demands on the actor without offering the prospect of material success or widespread public recognition; consequently, those who were drawn to this type of work were motivated by other needs. Central to Grotowski's conception of performance was the notion of the 'total act', a culminating moment in the actor's role in which s/he is able to transcend the performance score and the technical demands of the part, revealing a truth that is paradoxically both personal and universal. It is an act of self-sacrifice, requiring that the actor reveal in the presence of the spectator that which is most secret and essential, an impossible truth that transgresses the barriers of the admissible. In speaking of the 'total act', Grotowski's language was highly metaphoric; he described it as a giving of oneself in totality, 'in one's deepest intimacy, with confidence, as when one gives oneself in love' (1975: 38). Such an act cannot be willed, cannot be achieved by means of technical skill, but can arrive only in a moment of grace to one who is in a state of passive readiness.[7]

Actors in the Laboratory Theatre were not concerned with questions of character in the recognised sense or with placing themselves in the given circumstances of the fictional role. As Philip Auslander observes: 'Grotowski privileges the self over the role in that the role is primarily a tool for self-exposure' (1997: 64). Rather than concerning themselves with portraying the character as delineated in the dramatic text, actors in the Laboratory Theatre constructed a form of testimony that drew on the deepest and most secret experiences of their own lives, articulated in such a way that this act of revelation could serve as a provocation for the spectator:

> If the actor, by setting himself a challenge publicly challenges others, and through excess, profanation and outrageous sacrilege reveals himself by casting off his everyday mask, he makes it possible for the spectator to undertake a similar process of self-penetration. If he does not exhibit his body, but annihilates it, burns it, frees it from every resistance to any psychic impulse, then he does not sell his body but sacrifices it. He repeats the atonement; he is close to holiness.
>
> (Grotowski 1975: 34)

Auslander notes that the 'object of their performance was not to communicate an image of an affective state but to produce a state of self-contemplation in the spectator by example' (1997: 25). By accomplishing an act of transgression and self-sacrifice, a 'magical act' which the audience was 'incapable of reproducing', the actor served as a type of proxy, inviting the spectator to measure him/herself against the truth revealed in the performance (Grotowski 1975: 41). This was the essence of the communion that Grotowski viewed as one of the unique possibilities of live performance, inducing a type of cathartic process not dissimilar to that attributed to the theatre of ancient Greece.[8]

Despite his concern for creating communion between actor and spectator, Grotowski discouraged actors from 'publicotropism': catering to the whims of the public. He claimed that such 'flirtation' inevitably reduces the actor's revelation to coquetry and prostitution. He insisted that the actor must not take the audience as his or her point of orientation, but neither could he or she ignore their presence, as this would inject a degree of falsehood into the very basis of his work (1975: 181). Thomas Richards suggests that in the productions of the Laboratory Theatre, character functioned as a type of 'public screen' protecting the actors, behind which they could explore an intimate process in relative security (1995: 108). The actor's testimony, his or her total act, is offered to the spectators' view, accomplished in their presence, but never *for their sake*. The communion Grotowski speaks of as central to the theatrical exchange is thus inherently paradoxical, based on a complex dialectic of presence and absence, since both actor and spectator perceive one another obliquely, through a mediating veil.

Psychophysical training

Grotowski asserted that a primary aspect of Stanislavsky's legacy, his great service to the profession, was his emphasis on the need for the actor to commit to daily training and ongoing professional education in addition to his/her work on performances (Kumiega 1985: 110). Grotowski consistently upheld this mandate, requiring the actors under his direction to engage in regular physical and vocal training. Rather than contributing to the development of a particular role (e.g. as an actor might practise juggling or dance in order to accomplish a particular fragment of stage business), the daily commitment of performing these training structures functioned as a type of 'work on oneself' in the sense articulated by Stanislavsky, serving to develop the foundational level of the actor's capacities. Physical and vocal training as practised under Grotowski's direction were not concerned with teaching the actor *how to do* – how to perform virtuosic physical feats, for example – but rather contributed to what Eugenio Barba describes as the pre-expressive level of the actor's work. As Barba observes, 'before representing anything at all the performer must *be*, as a performer' (1995: 105). Training not only serves to strengthen the actor's physical and receptive capacities, but also has value as a discipline, an embodied commitment to constantly struggling to supersede the limits of one's abilities.

Grotowski adamantly rejected any form of training that sought to develop in the actor a collection of skills or 'bag of tricks':

> I don't agree with the kind of training in which it is believed that various disciplines, applied to the actor, can develop his totality; that an actor should, on one hand, take diction lessons, and on the other hand voice lessons and acrobatics or gymnastics, fencing, classical and modern dance, and also elements of pantomime, and all of that put together will give him an abundance of expression. This philosophy of training is very popular. Almost everywhere they believe this is how to prepare actors to be creative and they are absolutely wrong. ... An actor can dance, it's true. He can do modern or classical dance, meaning he can make fairly disciplined dance movement. So if he must dance on stage, he'll be able to dance; he won't create his own dance, he'll be able to repeat a dance dictated by someone else. Afterwards...he does some elements of pantomime, he learns to walk in place, how to make the signs of pantomime. So if there are some bits of pantomime in the production, he can use this. But observe that, in this way, he always uses things which are not a result of the creative process, which are not personal, which come from another domain.
>
> (Grotowski 1979: 7)

Grotowski argued that whilst actors trained in this manner might display virtuosity or technical skill, their performances almost always lack any line of living impulses. Impulse, in Grotowski's terminology, refers to a seed of a living action born inside the actor's body which extends itself outward to the periphery, making itself visible as physical action. ' "In/pulse" – push from inside. Impulses precede physical actions, always. The impulses: it is as if the physical action, still almost invisible, was already born in the body' (quoted in Richards 1995: 94).

Grotowski maintained that one of the most profound and persistent misunderstandings about the work of the Laboratory Theatre has been the tendency to think of the group's training in terms of a collection of exercises, something that pertained solely or even primarily to the corporeal aspect of the actor's work. He suggested that it would be more apt to speak of *psychophysical* training, since the work conducted under his direction had the aim of developing the actor's imaginative and associative capacities, his or her ability to respond to stimuli, whether tangibly present in the space (e.g. arising from the actor's connection to his/her partner) or emanating from the actor's memory. Whilst the training of Laboratory Theatre actors indeed served to develop important physical capacities such as strength, agility, stamina, flexibility and gestural articulation, the goals of the training were also directed towards more subtle ends. Grotowski described his methodology of training as a *via negativa*, a process of elimination. In contrast to training programmes that aim to give the actor a set of skills, the objective of Grotowski's methodology was to take away from the actor all that obstructed him or her in regard to movement, breathing, and, most importantly, human contact (Grotowski 1975: 177). Like Stanislavsky, Grotowski emphasised contact with the acting partner as a primary route to discovering truth and organicity on stage. 'Don't do anything for [the audience]', Stanislavsky advised, 'do everything only for your partner. Check, through your partner's reaction, if you are acting well' (Toporkov 1979: 86).

Although numerous elements of the exercises practised by actors in the Laboratory Theatre were physically demanding and could be interpreted as athletic or even acrobatic, the primary goal of the work was 'not a muscular development or physical perfectionism, but a process of research leading to the annihilation of one's body's resistances' (Grotowski 1975: 114). Rather than focusing primarily on the external level of the actor's physical capacity – e.g. the ability to perform acrobatics or execute codified movements – the types of training developed by the Laboratory Theatre were intended to enhance the actor's receptivity to impulse and to eradicate blockages, both physical and psychological, so that no obstruction might interfere between the germination of a living impulse and its manifestation through physical action.

> The actor who undertakes an act of self-penetration, who reveals himself and sacrifices the innermost part of himself...must be able to manifest the least impulse. He must be able to express, through sound and movement, those impulses which waver on the borderline between dream and reality.
>
> (Grotowski 1975: 35)

Corporal exercises

In developing the training structures that came to be regarded as characteristic of their work, Grotowski and his collaborators drew from a number of existing psychophysical disciplines and methods of actor training. Grotowski cited Stanislavsky's work with physical actions, Meyerhold's biomechanics and the Delsarte system as particularly fruitful in the development of his own practice, along with the work of Vakhtangov and Dullin. He acknowledged having been inspired by the training methods of Kathakali, Peking Opera and Noh Theatre, but eventually came to the conclusion that Western actors were better served by looking to Asian theatre practices as a model for a rigorous work ethic than by attempting to appropriate codified exercises. The actors of the Laboratory Theatre also experimented with Hatha Yoga as an element of their training structure, but found that work with yoga positions resulted in an introspective state unsuitable for the work of the actor. They discovered, however, that 'certain yoga' positions help very much the natural reactions of the spinal column; they lead to a sureness of one's body, a natural adaptation to space. So why get rid of them? Just change all their currents' (Grotowski 1975: 208).[9]

By instructing actors to remain attentive to external stimuli and receptive to interaction with colleagues whilst practising elements derived from Hatha Yoga, Grotowski shifted the practitioners' attention from the internal focus characteristic of traditional yoga practice to an outward-directed and dynamically shifting focus better suited to the actor's craft. Using the yoga positions as a point of departure, Grotowski and his collaborators developed a series of exercises that came to be known as the *corporels*. These corporal exercises included a range of headstands, shoulderstands, rolls, somersaults and leaps that developed the flexibility of the spinal column and allowed the actor to test the range of the body's equilibrium. Grotowski suggested that a primary purpose of the corporal exercises was to help the actor regain a sense of trust in his/her own organism:

> There is something to be accomplished and it is beyond you. Don't prevent yourself from doing it. Even a simple roll in the corporal exercises – risky, within a limited sphere, certainly, but still risky, with the possibility of pain – all that's needed is to not prevent yourself from taking the risk. The corporal exercises are the groundwork for a kind of challenge to surpass ourselves. For the participant, they should be nearly impossible, but even so, he should be able to do them. He should be able to do them. I say this with a double meaning. On one hand, they should appear impossible to do and even so, he should not prevent himself from doing them; on the other hand, he should be capable of doing them in an objective sense; in spite of appearances, they should be possible to do. Here begins the discovery of trust in your own self.
>
> (Grotowski 1979: 16)

The corporal exercises were an important element in training not only for the Laboratory Theatre, but also in latter phases of Grotowski's research. Participants in Objective Drama worked with a range of somersaults, headstands and shoulderstands similar to those described in *Towards a Poor Theatre*. Initially, we worked with each of the headstands and shoulderstands in a technical way, learning to execute the positions correctly. Once we were able to find the positions, we were encouraged to play with displacing balance and moving the spinal column in such a way as to test the limits of the body's equilibrium. As a further step in the process of working with the corporal exercises, we were encouraged to create sequences of improvised, non-verbal 'dialogue' with other participants, using selected elements of the corporal exercises as a point of departure and trying to find a type of organicity and flow in the sequence, whilst still maintaining the precision of the positions. Our daily training structure concluded with these sequences.

When I observed the training of the research team led by Thomas Richards at the Pontedera Workcenter in 1992, I witnessed a more physically demanding sequence structured around the corporal exercises; in this instance as well, the positions were incorporated into a type of improvised dialogue amongst the members of the research team.

The emphasis on maintaining contact with a partner outside the self, whether physically present in the space (e.g. an acting partner) or summoned from the actor's memory, was a consistent focus of the psychophysical techniques developed by Grotowski and his collaborators. The training structure employed during the Objective Drama phase of Grotowski's work required that participants develop a number of individual exercises designed to address each actor's specific limitations.[10] The exercises were initially set on a technical level under the supervision of the workleader, with each participant working separately. Once participants were able to execute the basic structure of the exercises, we were instructed to develop a score of associations in conjunction with each segment of the training, and to explore these associations each time we performed the training. Such associations might involve relation to a person or object in the room, an image, or a specific memory. Even during exercises, Grotowski counselled that it was necessary for the actor to 'justify every detail of his or her training with a precise image, whether real or imaginary' (1975: 103).

For example, a segment of my own training structure involved sit-ups, with the basic intention of improving abdominal strength. So as not to perform the exercise in an absent-mindedly repetitive or mechanical way, I was instructed that I should be aware each time I rose from the floor of why I was doing so, what motivated the movement, for example, what I might be reaching for. I was instructed that the association should be as specific as possible, never something 'in general'. Whilst the external structure of the exercises used in the training structure was supposed to remain unchanged, improvisation was encouraged in relation to the flow of associations, as was interaction amongst the members of the group. Characteristically, participants would adjust their way of performing a particular exercise, allowing the tone or tempo-rhythm of their movement to be influenced by contact with another actor in the space, allowing improvised 'dialogues' to emerge. Under all circumstances, however, participants were expected to maintain the score of their personalised training structure and to perform each exercise with full effort and attention.

As someone who struggled with balance and other aspects of the physical work, requiring days of effort before I could manage even a simple head-stand with reasonable control, I discovered that working in connection with a partner was the most effective means of 'not preventing myself' from accomplishing something beyond my preconceived notions of what I could and could not do. If my attention shifted from preoccupation with a difficult task that I felt was beyond me to interacting with a partner in the space, I often found that obstacles disappeared. 'You won't fall', Grotowski observed, 'if it is truly your nature which guides you' (1979: 17). Connection with the other was what was necessary to allow me to tap into the directive of my nature instead of following the dictates of my discursive mind.

A similar process can occur if one enters into dialogue with a non-human partner (an animal, a natural force), so long as one remains truly responsive to the actions and reactions of the other. At least in relation to my own process, I have observed that the temptation to follow the discursive voice becomes stronger when interacting with a memory or imaginary stimulus – there is always the possibility of allowing the conscious mind to manipulate the image/memory, playing it back as one would play a film, or elaborating it with the deliberation of an author writing a fictional scenario. The purpose of the work with memories and images was not to play them out in this way, as a type of internal projection, but rather to arrive to a state in which one does not anticipate or prescribe what details will emerge.

Plastiques

The emphasis on spontaneity within a structure that characterised the training of the Laboratory Theatre is epitomised by the sequence of exercises known as *plastiques*. The *plastiques* are in a sense less physically demanding than the corporal exercises, focusing more on precise detail and on the articulation of movements emanating from the spine and tracing their way outward towards the periphery of the body. Influenced by Dalcroze, Delsarte and other European systems of actor training, the sequence involved a number of relatively codified movements which the actors learned to perform with careful precision – e.g. an impulse emanating from the spine and manifesting through an abrupt movement of the trunk, or a particular way of rotating the wrist and hand.

Once the external details of the plastic elements were mastered, actors were encouraged to improvise in relation to the sequence, combining the individual elements in spontaneous dialogue or contact with the acting partner or responding to other external stimuli. Grotowski elaborated that the process of working with these elements required that the actor begin by fixing and memorising precise details, then look for the way to transform these details – to make them alive, so that they would become spontaneous and organic, rather than mechanical or calculated – by rediscovering personal impulses within the frame of the codified forms. It was necessary for the actor to be able to combine the elements in different sequences, to change the order and the rhythm, not in a premeditated way, but with the flow dictated by his or her own 'body life'. 'It is thought that the memory is something independent from the rest of the body', Grotowski asserted. 'In truth, at least for actors – it's something different. The body does not *have* memory, it *is* memory. What you must do is unblock the *body-memory*' (Grotowski 1979: 13). He explained that if the actor performs the *plastiques* by directing himself with the conscious mind, treating the body like a puppet guided by a puppet master, then it is impossible for the actor to engage the body-memory. If, however, the actor begins to work in such a way that s/he maintains the precise details but does not consciously manipulate sequence or rhythm of the plastic elements, 'almost like taking the details from the air', then it is possible to awaken the body-life.

> That's how the *body-memory/body-life* reveals itself. The details exist, but they are surpassed, reaching the level of impulses, of the *body-life*. ... The rhythm changes and the order. And one after the other, the *body-life* 'eats' the details – this happens by itself – which still exist in the exterior precision, but it's as if they explode from the inside, from the vital impulse. ... We have freed the seed: between the banks of the details now flows the 'river of our life'. Both spontaneity and discipline at the same time. This is decisive.
>
> (Grotowski 1979: 13–14)

The notion that spontaneity and discipline, rather than being mutually contradictory, actually reinforce one another was a central principle of Grotowski's work which can be seen not only in relation to training but also in the actor's work on the role in performance. Grotowski articulated this principle as *conjunctio oppositorum*, a conjunction of opposites, asserting that the actor's mastery of an established structure – his or her ability to accomplish something, whether a performance score or a sequence of codified movements, that is fixed in its details – paradoxically allows for a kind of freedom. Without the presence of some type of established structure, Grotowski warned, the actor's work quickly descends into chaos; it is impossible for the actor to be truly creative if he lacks discipline and the capacity for precision. Training both tests and develops these capacities within the actor, specifically in regard to his/her ability to maintain the precise details and exterior structure of the plastic exercises. Once the individual elements of the plastic exercises were fully mastered – sufficiently absorbed by the actor that they become, in a sense, unconscious – then the actor was instructed to shift the emphasis of her attention to exploring contact with something outside the self, to the flow of life that can emerge within the frame of the set details.

An analogous dynamic operates in the actor's work in performance. Vasily Toporkov notes that the 'secret' discovered by Stanislavsky in the final period of his work was that 'through the correct execution of physical actions, through their logic and their sequence, one penetrates into the deepest, most complicated feelings and emotional experiences' (1979: 87). Grotowski emphasised the necessity for the actor to develop an established score – precisely fixed, *not* at the level of blocking or gesture, but at the level of physical actions. 'It is easy to confuse physical actions with movements', he explained.

If I am walking toward the door, it is not an action but a movement. But if I am walking toward the door to contest 'your stupid questions', to threaten you that I will break up the conference, there will be a cycle of little actions and not just a movement. This cycle of little actions will be related to my contact with you, my way of perceiving your reactions; when walking toward the door, I will still keep some 'controlling look' toward you (or I will listen) to know if my threat is working. So it will not be a walk as movement, but something much more complex around the fact of walking. *The mistake of many directors and actors is to fix the movement instead of the whole cycle of little actions (actions, reactions, points of contact) which simply appears in the situation of the movement.*

(quoted in Richards 1995: 76, emphasis mine)

Physical action consists not of the bare fact of walking, which in itself is only an activity, but in the actors' awareness of *why* and/or *for whom* they are walking; the movement itself is only a pretext or a means. In constructing her work on a role in performance, the actor must fix the structure not as a sequence of movements – i.e. blocking – but in regard to the points of contact with the partner. This score must be precisely elaborated and absorbed to such a degree that it becomes fully memorised; once fixed, it should not be abandoned or altered (except by conscious choice, e.g. through the intervention of the director). Yet within this structure, the actor should discover an ever-changing flow of life that arises from contact with his or her partners. Grotowski often compared the actor's score to the banks of a river which guides and contains the flow of life: the cycle of living impulses.

Conclusion

On a profound level, the demands of the training structures developed by Grotowski and his collaborators served to prepare the actor not only by enhancing their physical abilities (such as strength, flexibility, agility and gestural articulation), but more importantly by engaging the associative and imaginative faculties, calling upon the actor to participate in training with the whole of his or her being. In a very tangible sense, the types of psychophysical work developed under Grotowski's direction allowed the actor to exercise not only his or her body, but also responsiveness and receptivity to contact. This quality of receptivity, both in the sense of permeability to the subtle impulses that emerge from within the body – the ability to manifest these impulses without obstruction – and in the sense of being able to maintain a living, organic contact with one's acting partners, comprised a central aspect of Grotowski's vision of the actor's craft.

'Performer', Grotowski wrote in a text pertaining to the final period of his work, 'must develop not an organism-mass, an organism of muscles, athletic, but an organism-channel through which the energies circulate, the energies transform, the subtle is touched' (in Schechner and Wolford 1997:

376). In a more pragmatic tone, he often said that acting is *re*acting, that the most fundamental actions are watching and listening. *Really* listening – actively, honestly, fully – not 'showing' listening. The fact that such a statement is not particularly revolutionary or unique, that it is thoroughly familiar to those who know the teachings of Stanislavsky or Vakhtangov, does not make it any less essential or any less true. It is a basic principle, the efficacy of which is not confined to any particular aesthetic or style of theatre. If I were asked to convey in a few words the most fundamental aspect of what I learned as Grotowski's student in California or as an observer of the research team in residence at his Italian Workcenter, this would be one of the first things that would come to my mind: the indispensable necessity for the actor to live in relation to something or someone outside the self.

Rather than trying to disseminate his ideas broadly, making his techniques and approaches to acting craft available to as wide an audience as possible through short-term workshops and descriptive publications, Grotowski preferred to work in a deeper, more intimate way with select individuals, striving to transmit essential lessons about artistic (and extra-artistic) matters in a format of extended apprenticeship and exchange. Richards, whom Grotowski described as his 'essential collaborator' in Art as vehicle, worked with Grotowski intimately and systematically from 1985 until Grotowski's death on 14 January 1999. Mario Biagini, who emerged as an important workleader in the final phase of Grotowski's practice, studied with him for nearly as long, beginning with the founding of the Pontedera Workcenter in 1986. The body of work to which Grotowski devoted his life continues to be developed under their auspices. Whilst the research conducted by Richards and Biagini at the Workcenter cannot easily be contained within the category of 'theatre', at least as the term is understood in contemporary Western parlance, I am confident that their ongoing work will continue to yield insights about performance craft that will prove valuable for a new generation of theatre artists and performance practitioners, even if the source of that influence remains almost invisible from the vantage of more conventional forms of theatre.

Grotowski often made reference to 'The Well' hexagram of the *I Ching* in describing his conception of the relationship between the work of a relatively secluded laboratory such as the Workcenter to the more recognisable practice of what he called Art as presentation. '[T]he well can be well dug and the water inside of it pure, but if no one draws water from this well, the fish will come to live there and the water will spoil' (in Richards 1995: 134). Grotowski was an artist and a teacher of extraordinary wisdom and accomplishment, a master of a calibre that is seen only rarely in a given generation, but the living water in the well of which he spoke existed for countless generations before his birth, and will survive his passing.

Notes

1 In addition to Grotowski's essay, 'Reply to Stanislavski', Thomas Richards' 1995 book, *At Work with Grotowski on Physical Actions*, provides an extremely valuable and detailed exploration of the connections between Grotowski's practice and Stanislavsky's.

2 For a comprehensive analysis of the various stages of Grotowski's work (Poor Theatre, Paratheatre, Theatre of Sources, Objective Drama and Art as Vehicle) see Schechner and Wolford 1997.

3 Although the activities of the Workcenter do not include publicly accessible performance, the final phase of Grotowski's practice was characterised by a renewed emphasis on the actor's craft; the results of this research are by no means insignificant for practitioners involved in more conventional forms of theatre practice. For further details about the culminating stage of Grotowski's investigation, see Schechner and Wolford 1997: 365–453.

4 For a discussion of the more complex and subtle aspects of vocal work in Art as vehicle, see especially the full-length version of *The Edge-Point of Performance* (Richards 1997).

5 Rather than serving a decorative or mood-establishing function, sceneography in Laboratory Theatre productions was used in such a way as to suggest a specific relationship between the viewer and the performance event; each of Grotowski's well-known productions created a different spatial relationship between the actor and the audience, metaphorically 'casting' the spectator by suggesting a perspective and point of view from which they should approach each perfor- mance. Spectators at the Laboratory Theatre's production of Marlowe's *Doctor Faustus*, for example, were metaphorically positioned as guests at Faust's last supper, seated around a table on which the major actions of the performance took place. The stage design for Grotowski's production of *The Constant Prince* was meant to suggest a type of operating theatre, in which spectators viewed the action from an elevated space. See *Towards a Poor Theatre* for further details of architectural arrangement in these and other Laboratory Theatre productions.

6 It is perhaps useful to historicise Grotowski's early work within the context of a theatre system dominated by Soviet realism and naturalistic performance styles. At the time that Stanislavsky began to articulate his approach to actor training, the idea that an actor's body might be able to convincingly recreate 'ordinary life' on stage was in itself somewhat revolutionary.

7 In an essay printed in appendix to Richards 1995, Grotowski discusses the work of Ryszard Cieslak in the role of the Constant Prince, critically recognised as one of the most extraordinary performances in the history of the Laboratory Theatre and a quintessential example of the actor's 'total act'. See Richards 1995: 122–4. For critical responses to Cieslak's performance in this role, see Schechner and Wolford 1997: 116–68 *passim*.

8 Auslander's essay '"Holy Theatre" and Catharsis' (reprinted in a collected volume *From Acting to Performance* 1997) provides an insightful exploration of the approach of the dynamics of the cathartic process in the relation between actor and spectator both in Grotowski's 'Poor Theatre' period and in his post- theatrical work.

9 The cat exercise described in *Towards a Poor Theatre* (Grotowski 1975: 103) provides a quintessential example of a corporal exercise, and is perhaps the best- known and most frequently copied of the exercises developed by actors of the Laboratory Theatre.

10 During the time I participated in the programme, the structure of the training consisted of six individual exercises and a number of activities performed collec- tively by the group as a whole (running and walking sequences, along with the

corporal exercises); the training structure varied during earlier phases of the programme.

Bibliography

Auslander, Philip (1997) *From Acting to Performance*, London and New York: Routledge.

Barba, Eugenio (1995) *The Paper Canoe*, London and New York: Routledge.

Grotowski, Jerzy (1980) 'Risposta a Stanislavskij', trans. Carla Pollastrelli, in Fabrizio Cruciani and Celia Falletti (eds), *Stanislavskij: L'attore creativo*, Florence: La casa Usher.

—— (1979) 'Exercises', originally published in *Dialog* (unpublished translation from French and Italian by James Slowiak).

—— (1975) *Towards a Poor Theatre*, London: Methuen. First published Denmark 1968 by Odin Teatrets Forlag.

Kumiega, Jennifer (1985) *The Theatre of Grotowski*, London: Methuen.

Richards, Thomas (1997) *The Edge-Point of Performance*, Pontedera, Italy: Documentation Series of the Workcenter of Jerzy Grotowski.

—— (1995) *At Work with Grotowski on Physical Actions*, New York and London: Routledge.

Schechner, Richard and Wolford, Lisa (1997) *The Grotowski Sourcebook*, New York and London: Routledge.

Toporkov, Vasily (1979) *Stanislavski in Rehearsal: The Final Years*, trans. Christine Edwards, New York: Theatre Arts Books.

11 Training with Eugenio Barba

Acting principles, the pre-expressive and 'personal temperature'

Ian Watson

A context

Eugenio Barba, the director of the Odin Teatret, is one of those rare theatre people who combines the creativity of an artist with the more reflective skills of a researcher, theorist and teacher. Since 1964, when he founded the Odin, he has created over twenty original works, ranging from intimate theatre pieces to large-scale outdoor spectacles. He has established one of Western Europe's only government-funded theatre laboratories, the Nordisk Teaterlaboratorium (NTL), which, apart from researching performance, incorporates a publishing house, a film and video archive, and production facility. He also heads the International School of Theatre Anthropology (ISTA), which he founded in 1979 to investigate the connections between traditional Eastern and contemporary Western performance. In addition to his practical successes, Barba has produced many articles as well as books, which together encompass important writings on actor training, dramaturgy, performance and theatre sociology. Besides this published material, Barba has also lectured and taught on both the practical and theoretical aspects of his work in Europe, North and Latin America, as well as in Asia. He is an advisory or consultant editor to journals such as *TDR, The Drama Review* and *New Theatre Quarterly*. And his intellectual work has been officially recognised by both Denmark's Aarhus University and La Universidad Nacional de San Cristóbal de Huamanga in Peru who have both presented him with honorary doctorates (Aarhus in 1988 and La Universidad Nacional de San Cristóbal de Huamanga in 1998).

Barba's personal history in many ways mirrors the cultural pluralism of his professional development. He is an Italian who, as a young man, settled in Norway. He is also a former member of the Norwegian Merchant Marine whose journeys took him to various parts of Asia. He studied theatre for the first time in Poland in the early 1960s with Jerzy Grotowski, following which he founded the Odin Teatret in Olso – only to move his theatre to Holstebro, Denmark, within two years. One of the original models for his company and its work methods was the Kathakali school in Cheruthuruthy, India, that he had visited whilst still living in Poland. The Odin has consisted of actors from many different countries over the years, most of whom do not share a common native language, leading to a creole of sorts both in the rehearsal room and in its productions; whilst the company is rarely at home since it and Barba tour extensively, especially in Europe and Latin America. Barba also spends an appreciable amount of time in Bali, Japan, India and Brazil, working with the artists who attend the various ISTA gatherings. It is hardly surprising that several years ago he charac-terised his sense of place as corporeal rather than one contained within national boundaries: 'My body is my country' (1988a: 293). But, even though his life challenges the very idea of national identity, Barba views his professional heritage in familial terms, seeing himself as a descendant of Stanislavksy, the 'father' of modern Western theatre (1988a: 292).

Barba's contention aside, his theatrical lineage is much closer to Meyerhold than it is to Stanislavsky. Granted, Stanislavsky conducted the major study of the actor's art in the early years of the century, but Barba has rejected the very basis of Stanislavsky's system (psychological realism), embracing instead a theatre that explores a language of its own rather than one that simulates daily life on stage. He has developed a theatre in which the *mise-en-scène* takes precedence over interpreting the author's vision, in which causal connections between scenes has been rejected in favour of an episodic montage, and in which the actor/audience relationship and the performance space is adjusted for each production. All of these are ideas more often associated with Meyerhold than Stanislavsky.

Despite his European heritage and what he has termed his 'period of [theatrical] apprenticeship' (1986: 239) with Grotowski, Barba has always been fascinated by the East. This fascination began with an interest in the Asian religions in his youth, and gradually moved to its theatre after his exposure to Kathakali. Barba maintains that the root of this fascination lies in understanding presence. Why is it that if you are watching two actors on stage, even if you are unfamiliar with their theatrical form and cannot understand what they are saying, you are unable to take your eyes off one of them whilst the other is of no interest at all? (1985a: 12). His search for an answer to this question lies at the root of most of his performance research, even today. In keeping with his denial of borders, his research encompasses not only the icons of contemporary European theatre such as Stanislavsky, Meyerhold, Eisenstein, Decroux and his mentor Grotowski, but also Asian performers and theoretical treatises such as Kathakali, Noh, the onnogata, Barong, Rukmani Devi, Mei Lanfang, Zeami, and the Natyashastra (1988b: 126; 1995: 42). Barba's professional identity is that of the theatrical poly-glot.

The breadth of Barba's professional identity is nowhere more obvious than in his approach to training. The latter is central to Barba's vision of the theatre. It is the foundation of his entire aesthetic: training provides the basis for his unique dramaturgical and rehearsal processes; it is the origin of his major production styles – the studio/theatre performance and the open-air street spectacle; and the research orientation of the Odin's current training continues to inform Barba's creation of new theatre pieces.

Training has been a major factor in Barba's approach to theatre since the Odin was formed. The group's initial working sessions were devoted entirely to it, and the actors have continued to train ever since. This training usually consists of separate physical and vocal sessions because Barba believes it is necessary to explore physical and vocal rhythms independently to ensure that neither one dominates the other.

Barba's initial ideas on training were influenced by several factors. The single most important of these was his role as Grotowski's assistant immediately prior to forming the Odin. During Barba's years in Poland, Grotowski initiated his now famous 'poor theatre' performer training programme, which introduced Barba to a theatre that touched a personal chord. His formative education was in a military school in Naples where discipline and authority were all important. Barba rebelled against this approach to education at the time, but he saw it reflected in Grotowski's research with his actors, and in the Kathakali academy he visited in India. Barba was well aware of his lack of formal theatre training when he formed his fledgling company in Norway; he was equally cognisant of his young actors' limitations. Unlike Grotowski's performers, who were all trained professionals, his actors were high-school students who had been rejected by the national theatre school in Oslo. They needed training. He lacked the background to provide it. But he had seen what authority and discipline could achieve. So, with the models of Poland and India filtered through his experience in Naples, he established an intensive training regimen when he formed his new company. This regimen focused on the acquisition of skills and later evolved into using training as a research tool.

Unfortunately, Barba and his actors not only lacked basic theatre skills, they also wanted for the funds to pay teachers. This latter disadvantage, like so many in Barba's history, proved to be instrumental in establishing his future course. Due to the fact that he could not afford teachers, the actors taught themselves. Members of the company with skills, no matter how rudimentary, taught them to the others. Thus, gradually, the original members of the group developed a body of skills that formed the basis of their subsequent training and which they were able to teach new actors as they joined the company.

Yet the group's training was not as hermetic as this description may imply, since several external factors contributed to its development. A series of workshops Barba organised when the group first moved to Holstebro exposed the Odin actors to Western performers and directors such as Grotowski, Ryszard Cieslak, Etienne Decroux, Jean-Louis Barrault and Dario Fo, as well as Oriental masters that included the Noh actors Hisao and Hideo Kanze, the Kyogen performer Mannojo Namura, and the Odissi dancer Sanjukta Panigrahi. In addition to these contacts, the actors attended workshops conducted by Asian performers of Kathakali, Noh and Topeng at the Third Theatre gatherings in Belgrade (1976) and Bergamo (1977); and at these same gatherings other groups similar to the Odin demonstrated and discussed their approaches to training. Except for a few obvious examples, such as the influence of Grotowski, it is difficult to establish a direct connection between these experiences and developments in Barba's training methods. But, given the correlation between the Odin's present training and Oriental theatre, it is clear that at least this early exposure to Eastern masters has influenced the evolution of Barba's and his group's training considerably.

The most important feature of this evolution has been the gradual shift in emphasis from skill-oriented training to the use of training as a form of performance research. In the Odin's early years in Holstebro, there was a large turnover of new actors joining and leaving the group. But, as the company stabilised and ceased to take in new actors, the need to teach and learn basic skills became less of a necessity. In the best tradition of the auto-didact, the actors, under Barba's guidance, turned their attention to developing their own training programmes. The performers no longer concerned themselves with accumulating skills but rather with testing and exploring their potentials and limitations. Training for Barba became something created and shaped by each of the actors individually.

Training[1]

Training according to Barba is

> a process of self-definition, a process of self-discipline which manifests itself indissolubly through physical reactions. It is not the exercise in itself that counts – for example, bending or somersaulting – but the individual's justification for his own work, a justification which although perhaps banal or difficult to explain through words, is physiologically perceptible, evident to the observer.
>
> (1986: 56)

Since the exercises are less important than how the actor chooses to use them in training for Barba, he has not developed a prescriptive body of exercises or systematic hierarchy of information that a neophyte actor has to master in order to perform. For this reason, the only way to understand his training methods is to consider how they have developed over the past thirty-plus years at the Odin Teatret. It is with the Odin actors that he has formulated his understanding of training, it is with them that he has realised a rehearsal methodology that is rooted in his approach to training, and it is with them that he has created and directed all of his major theatre pieces.

When Barba began working with his Odin actors in the early 1960s, his training was collective. The actors trained together and everyone learned the same basic acrobatics, gymnastics, pantomime skills and vocal techniques.

Figure 11.1   Barba: Training at the Odin Teatret in the early 1970s
Source: Odin Teatret Foto

Even during this early collective training phase, however, Barba had already established what was to become the hallmark of his training methodology; he rarely taught anything in the conventional sense of the word – the actors taught what they knew to each other whilst he remained witness and guide to their endeavours.[2]

It was during this period that Barba first came to realise the importance of individual rhythm in the training process. This realisation led to a gradual change of focus in the exercises, from an emphasis on skill to an emphasis on the individual actor's pace and rhythm (Barba 1979: 65). At the same time as this shift was taking place in Barba's thinking, his actors began to explore material that Barba eventually shaped into what he terms composition exercises.

Composition, which owes something of a debt to Barba's mentor Grotowski, does not consist of specific exercises like body-rolls or headstands. In fact, it can involve virtually any series of movements because the focus is on the physical ideograms created by the composition of body elements during the movements, instead of on the movements themselves. These ideograms can have their source at a purely technical level, as in dividing the body so that one half moves rapidly whilst the other half moves slowly in order to express an inner physiological tension, or they can involve physical expression of a mental association, such as using the image of a flower's growth from germination to maturity and death to influence how one moves through space. As one of Barba's Odin actors, Torgeir Wethal, describes it:

> You allowed an inner action sequence to live within these exercises. You were in a completely personal situation in a particular place at the same time as you were doing the exercise, precisely and concretely. Your inner movie has a great influence on the details of an exercise, the rhythm, the tempo.
>
> (Christoffersen 1993: 49)

In a composition exercise the actor concentrates on the balance of muscular tensions and/or psychophysical association, rather than on executing a task correctly. These concerns emphasise process over product, that is, doing the exercise rather than learning a specific skill.

The shift towards process in Barba's thinking about training was accompanied by an increased use of improvisation. Barba has employed improvisation to develop performances during rehearsals since his first production, *Ornitofilene*, in 1965. But until his production of *Min Fars Hus* in 1972, almost ten years after the company was formed, these improvisations were based on texts written prior to rehearsal. *Min Fars Hus* was the first production developed entirely, from its inception through to the *mise-en-scène*, by Barba and his actors during rehearsals. This development included the creation of a fabricated language as well as explorations of biographical and literary material related to Dostoevsky, whose life and works were the inspiration for the piece. Drawing upon their vocal training, Barba and his company developed a language loosely based on the phonetic quality of Russian for the production. In conjunction with these linguistic explorations, the company created a physical score from improvisations based on the actors' reactions to and associations with events in Dostoevsky's life.

Influenced by the emphasis on composition in the group's training at the time, the *mise-en-scène* was the combination of a dynamic physicality and an operatic-like vocal score. This score consisted of incantations, singing and dialogue, all in a language that required the audience to focus on its musicality rather than its semantic content. The work, rooted in parallels between the performers' lives and Dostoevsky's experiences, was deeply personal and, in keeping with the Odin's earlier productions, far removed from realism.

The increased emphasis on improvisation in *Min Fars Hus* placed the creative responsibility entirely upon the performers and the director, since they no longer had a single, cohesive literary source to guide their rehearsals. This change in the use of improvisation fed back into the training and, combined with the focus on process in composition and the emphasis on individuality in rhythm, led to the creation of a new type of training altogether.

In the latter stages of rehearsals for *Min Fars Hus* one of the actresses, Iben Nagel Rasmussen, began to develop her own training. This training consisted of an improvised series of physical and vocal exercises that she felt best challenged her own abilities and weaknesses. Despite the fact that the collective training continued during this period, her experiments did not go unnoticed and there was a great deal of discussion between her, Barba, and her fellow actors. Barba encouraged others to develop their own training and eventually collective training was abandoned altogether. Each actor now explored what they felt was important for them, but within the supportive environment of a single room where others were engaged in similar research.

Barba, whilst following these changes in the Odin's training, began a systematic study of Oriental theatre with the express aims of discovering the source of the performer's presence in traditional Asian forms and exploring its possible relevance for Western actors (1986: 115). From these comparative studies he concluded that the two fundamental elements of Oriental forms that contribute to the actor's commanding stage presence are the use of learned body techniques designed to break the performer's automatic daily responses and the codification of principles which dictate the use of energy during performance.

In daily life, much of our physical action is automatic due to constant repetition. Our body 'knows' how to accomplish relatively complex tasks, like walking and climbing stairs, without having to think through the various muscular adjustments involved, because we have done them so often.

Figure 11.2   Barba: An Odin training session
Source: Photo, Christoph Falke

In Eastern traditional forms such as Kathakali and Noh, on the other hand, the body is intentionally distorted, particularly through the positioning of the feet and legs. In Kathakali the performers stand on the outer edges of their feet with their legs in an open position, and in Noh the actors lock their hips and bend their knees, altering the line of the spine and the distribution of weight. These 'distortions' constitute what Barba refers to as extra-daily technique, that is, learned technique which establishes a pattern of performance behaviour which is different from daily behaviour. According to Barba, this extra-daily technique is a major source of actor presence during performance, since it establishes a pre-expressive mode in which the actor's energies are engaged prior to personal expression (1986: 119–20).

Personal expression in traditional Eastern performance is rigidly codified and can vary greatly from one form to another. Barba's studies revealed, however, that, despite these differences, the codes incorporate similar principles that dictate the body's use of energy. Principles such as the use of opposing body tensions to create a dynamic on stage, a balance between energy expended through space (i.e. motion) and energy expended through time (i.e. dynamic inertia), and the use of distorted equilibrium to alter muscular tensions during performance. An example of distorted equilibrium may help clarify Barba's point. In Noh, Odissi dance and Balinese dance drama the performers use precarious balance to engage their performance energies. The locked hips, bent knees and the way the actor walks by sliding his/her feet across the stage without lifting them in Noh changes the normal position of the spine, alters the centre of balance and engages the trunk as a single unit. All of which creates opposing tensions in the upper and lower parts of the body that require the performer to find a new point of equilibrium. In Odissi dance the 'tribangi', which is a major component of the form, requires the dancer to manipulate his/her body as if the letter 'S' were passing through the hips, trunk and neck. This position, which distorts the line of the spinal column, affects the performer's balance and thereby alters the normal relationship between body weight, centre of gravity and the feet. Similarly, in many Balinese forms of dance drama the performer pushes down on the soles of the feet whilst at the same time lifting the toes, thus reducing contact with the ground. To compensate, the dancer widens his/her gait and bends his/her knees, which alters the centre of gravity and the normal position of the spine. These adjustments increase the level of muscular activity, which, as in similar distortions in Odissi dance and Noh, produce a dynamic, rather than static, physical state.

Through his knowledge of the few similarly codified Western forms, such as mime and ballet, Barba realised that many of the principles in Eastern performance are shared by their Western counterparts. The principle of opposing body tensions, for example, is a major component of mime, and the alteration of normal equilibrium is a fundamental element of ballet. More importantly for the evolution of his own idea on training, he further realised that his Odin actors were employing similar principles (1995: 6).

Barba began to publish the results of his research, which, combined with the influence his discoveries had on his work and on his discussions with his actors, led to a further development in his individualised training method. There was a gradual shift in emphasis from composition, with its focus on physical expression, to an exploration of the principles underlying performative action, that is, to the source of the pre-expressive. Training for Barba today is, as one of his Odin actresses described it, 'improvisation structured by the application of principles' (Carreri 1985). A simple example, quoted by another company member, clarifies what she meant:

> To stand on one's head involves mastering particular technical skills such as placement of the hands, legs, and head, and the adjustment of body weight and balance. It also involves the principle of shifting the body's weight quickly so that one is off-balance, finding a point of equilibrium which is held for a period, and returning to the normal body position. Standing on one's head is a skill that has to be learned, the principle underlying it, meanwhile, can be applied to many situations including walking, sitting, and working with a requisite [hand prop].
>
> (Wethal 1985)

Barba's system of training focuses on exploring this and similar principles, rather than mastering skills. Consider a typical training session I observed at the Odin in the mid 1980s:

> There are five actors in the room, three women and two men, all working separately. Following a brief warm up consisting of simple stretch exercises, the actors begin to work on their individual activities. Actress 1 is sitting in a deck chair. She moves her right arm across her body, then her left arm. She moves her head from right to left, then up and down. All actions are slow, precise, and punctuated with a brief pause. She sits up in the deck chair, she sits back, she sits up again, then repeats this up and down action several more times. During these actions her trunk appears to move as one unit, with no curve in the spine or separation between chest and waist.
>
> Meanwhile, Actor 1 moves to the back of the room and begins to do a tap dance type shuffle. He raises his arms in the classical ballet position and spins around several times. He lowers his arms and begins what appears to be a simple dance. The top half of his body does not seem to be engaged in the dance. He stops suddenly and does several shoulder stands, returning to the upright position each time. He lunges into the shoulder stands, but has great control and executes them precisely. He returns once more to a simple dance and moves around the room, occasionally breaking into the tap dance shuffle he began with.

There are no clearly identifiable skills being learned, the actors are not doing scenes from a play, nor do they seem to be exploring ways of creating a character and, despite the fact that people are together in a room, each is concerned with their own work. The focus is elsewhere, as the actress working with the deck chair told me following the session. She explained that she had been working with several principles that day including moving with one part of the body at a time, leading all movement with the eyes and segmenting various sections of the body. What appeared to be haphazard movements were, in fact, actions strictly monitored by adherence to consciously chosen principles.

Training and performance

The fact that the majority of Barba's Odin actors continue to train today, even though most of them have worked with him for more than twenty years, suggests a great deal about the connections between training and performance in Barba's understanding of theatre.

One aspect of training for Barba is its parallel to physical exercise. Just as aerobics are an ongoing process which maintain one's fitness without continually having to learn new skills, training for Barba is a daily workout that exercises the actor's means of expression in preparation for performance.

But this is a long way short of the entire story, because the daily regimen of training has ramifications beyond merely tuning one's physical instrument. Even though Barba rejects training as a means of learning techniques, it continues to be an indirect way of developing new skills. Similarly, it plays an important part in maintaining the actors' physical and mental disciplines, as well as providing a means of honing the skills they have already learned. It also prepares the Odin actors for Barba's somewhat unusual way of creating productions, and is a source of personal development as well as social cohesion within the group.

The secondary role of skill acquisition in today's training at the Odin stems from Barba's emphasis on acting principles. The performers may no longer be concerned with learning new gymnastic exercises or perfecting the high-pitch singing technique of Beijing opera, but they are continually exploring ways of mastering the principles of acting. These explorations include devising solutions for physical and vocal problems (how to control a particular fall, for example, or how best to use one's voice in street performances) whilst remaining faithful to the principles they are working with. This problem-solving often expands the actors' skills because their solutions frequently demand an ever-increasing repertoire of physical and vocal techniques, even if this expansion is not the primary focus of their research.

Discipline has always been an important factor in training for Barba. In the Odin's and Barba's formative years, this discipline was imposed by Barba himself. But, as individual training became more important, the onus of discipline shifted to the actors and they continue to be responsible for the schedule and content of daily training. The most obvious aim of this daily discipline, as touched on earlier, is to maintain the actors' performance conditioning. The Odin actors continually exercise their bodies and voices in order to prepare their physical and vocal instruments for performance. Barba maintains that this preparation is not only directed towards expression, because continual training also helps the actor tap the pre-expressive. This pre-expressive mode is based on mastery of the very principles that the actors use in their training. It is based on the use of alteration from one's normal daily balance and centre of gravity, for instance, or on control of opposing tensions in the body. It can also be based on what might best be described as the deconstruction and reconstruction of the body in traditional Eastern performance training; that is, using training to break the normal patterns of behaviour in order to discover a cohesive physical and vocal grammar of performance that engages the body differently from our daily activities and speech (Barba 1986: 115–22).

Training not only develops pre-expressive and expressive skills but also prepares the actors for the rehearsal process. New productions at the Odin usually begin with little more than a theme and/or fragments of texts that are explored in rehearsals. These explorations invariably have their roots in improvisations by individual actors which are then lengthened, shortened, altered, and/or combined in different ways by Barba to develop a single montage of different scenes that constitute the final piece.[3]

For Barba, the use of improvisation in creating new works is connected to its use in training. In training, improvisation is an integral part of the daily work. In dramaturgy, on the other hand, even though the final production montage is set and repeated in each performance, improvisation provides the raw material for the production. The actors rarely develop this material during training, but their studio research builds a lexicon and grammar of improvisation which they draw from during rehearsals to create new pieces. As Carreri put it: 'I keep training in order to be ready to respond, to be able to meet the demands of the new performance' (1985).

Barba regards training as a form of mental conditioning as much as a way of exercising and investigating the means of expression (1985b: 15; 1985c). The ongoing process of developing one's own training (of self-discipline, research and concrete physical and vocal tasks) manifests an attitude towards what is happening. The actors are thus not only exploring their physical and vocal potentials through exercise, but also through a process of mental discipline. Most days at the Odin include a prescribed time when the actors enter the training studio and work for an hour or more. During this time, their minds as well as their bodies are directly concerned with exploring the principles they are working on and indirectly on developing their improvisational skills. Their minds are thus daily focused on the work at hand and on its potential implications for the next production. Barba maintains that this mental focus is as much part of the training process as the physical and vocal exercises because, just as these exercises build a physical routine, the daily mental engagement builds an intellectual discipline. The body and the mind are equally engaged.

Apart from the mental and physical components of Barba's approach to training, there are important personal ramifications involved. One of Barba's aims in making the actors at the Odin responsible for their own training is to make them autonomous, to allow them to create their own training without relying on specific techniques or particular teachers. Through this process, the actor is attempting to discover what Barba refers to as their own 'personal temperature', that is, their own rhythm, their boundaries, their abilities and what is unique about each of them as a performer (Barba 1988a: 298). Thus, when they begin work on a new production, they do not merely apply a set of learned techniques to interpret a text or the director's vision as, say, a Stanislavsky actor might, but rather they use improvisation to explore the relationship between themes suggested by Barba and their own 'personal temperature'.

This 'personal temperature' is also an important factor in the *mise-en-scène* for Barba because of the dichotomous tension between the role and the actor during performance. He maintains that performance is neither entirely the fictional world of the play, nor the actor's experience in portraying it. It is the dialectic between these two, what he calls the anatomical theatre: a theatre in which the relationship between the 'external surface of the actions and their internal parts' (1986: 112) is the central core of any production.

In Barba's theatre, an actor not only portrays the fictional score (that is, the physical actions and vocal delivery decided upon in rehearsal and repeated in each performance), but also their meeting with it. Ryszard Cieslak, Grotowski's leading actor, in talking about this process in an interview with Richard Schechner, used the metaphor of a candle contained inside a glass to explain the difference between the score and his meeting with it during performances of *Akropolis*:

> The score is like the glass inside which a candle is burning. The glass is solid, it is there, you can depend on it. It contains and guides the flame. But it is not the flame. The flame is my inner process each night. The flame is what illuminates the score, what the spectators see through the score.
>
> (Schechner, 1977: 19)

Cieslak goes on to describe how the score remains the same but that the flame varies from performance to performance.

Variations in the flame, in the meeting with the score, are based on several factors in Barba's approach to performance: the audience's reaction to the piece, the actors' psycho-emotional responses to events on stage as well as in the theatre, and the actors' personal associations with particular actions and/or situations in a work they have developed with their colleagues during rehearsal. The tensions between these variables (i.e. the flame) and the score provide the means of realising the anatomical theatre since the score provides a structured resistance ('the external surface of the actions') against which the actor struggles in order to display their inner processes:

> The performance is a tightly woven net, which we must break through in order to liberate, in an unforeseen moment, fragments of our past and our experiences.

> Every evening the actors struggle with this net. Every evening they try to dissolve, to annul the rigid iron structure through which they reveal themselves and which makes them into actors and those who surround them into an audience.

> The resistance that the performance opposes to testimony makes the play into an organism which changes form and turns the rehearsed

gesture of the actor into a gesture which appears to have the force of an improvised reaction.

It is through the convergence of these opposite forces, that our personal experiences can reach others...

(Barba 1986: 181)

This convergence has its beginnings in Barba's individuated training. It is in the studio, where each actor confronts their strengths and limitations daily, that the actor prepares himself /herself for their 'struggle with this net'.

The struggle is, nevertheless, a social act; the actor engages with the dramaturgy during each performance for the spectator. But this engagement must be affective, it must have 'the capacity to stimulate affective reactions' (Barba 1997: 130) in the audience. This effectiveness, like so much in Barba's theatre, lies in the training. It is the individual actor's ability to perform what Barba terms 'real actions' as opposed to simple gestures or movements that generates a change of perception in the spectator (1997: 128). Real actions for Barba are those that produce 'a change in the tensions of your whole body' (1997: 128) because they have their origins in the spine: 'it is not the elbow that moves the hand, not the shoulder that moves the arm, rather, each dynamic impulse is rooted in the torso' (1997: 128). These dynamic impulses are learned actions that have their origins in the principles that form the basis of each actor's training regimen.

Barba's emphasis on an individualised training that draws its inspiration from various cultures as well as different teachers has inevitably led to a diversity of skills and techniques amongst his Odin actors. Should another group of actors choose to embrace his training ideas, the results would no doubt reflect a similar diversity. But one must understand that, for Barba, skills take second place to intention in training. As William Farrimond, a researcher who followed the Odin in the early 1980s, noted about the company, 'It is only in the principles and not in the techniques...that one can trace an element common to the whole group' (1981: 92). Barba's training is concerned with how performance principles, the pre-expressive and individual creativity come together in productions. His emphasis on the research and process orientation of training engenders a continual cycle of growth and renewal in which training, rehearsals and performance are inextricably linked.

Notes

1 Due to the limitations of space, I will only discuss Barba's physical training. For further information on his vocal training techniques see Watson 1995: 63–8.
2 Voice training was somewhat of an exception. Barba taught the basics of Grotowski's resonator voice training in the Odin's early days. Once the actors had grasped the rudiments, however, they developed their own vocal training based on this initial instruction.

3 For a more detailed description and discussion of Barba's rehearsal and dramaturgical methodologies see Watson 1995: 73–103.

Bibliography

Barba, E. (1997) 'An Amulet Made of Memory: The Significance of Exercises in the Actor's Dramaturgy', *The Drama Review* 41, 4 (T156), Winter: 127–32.

—— (1995) *The Paper Canoe*, London and New York: Routledge.

—— (1988a) 'The Way of Refusal: The Theatre's Body in Life', *New Theatre Quarterly* IV, 16 (November): 291–9.

—— (1988b) 'Eurasian Theatre', *The Drama Review* 32, 3 (T119), Fall: 126–30.

—— (1986) *Beyond the Floating Islands*, New York: Performing Arts Journal Publications.

—— (1985a) 'Interview With Gautam Dasgupta', *Performing Arts Journal* (January): 8–18.

—— (1985b) *The Dilated Body*, Rome: Zeami Libre.

—— (1985c) Interview with the author, Nordisk Teaterlaboratorium, Holstebro, 5 September.

—— (1979) *The Floating Islands*, Holstebro, Denmark: Odin Teatret Forlag.

Carreri, R. (1985) Interview with the author, Nordisk Teaterlaboratorium, Holstebro, Denmark, 26 August.

Christoffersen, E.E. (1993) *The Actor's Way*, London and New York: Routledge.

Farrimond, W. (1981) 'Actor Education: An Interdisciplinary Approach – An Analysis of the Training and Performance Principles Applied by Eugenio Barba and the Actors of the Odin Teatret in 1981', Ph.D. Dissertation, University of Copenhagen.

Schechner, R. (1977) *Essays in Performance Theory: 1970–1976*, New York: Drama Book Specialists.

Watson, I. (1995) *Towards a Third Theatre: Eugenio Barba and the Odin Teatret*, London and New York: Routledge.

Wethal, T. (1985) Interview with the author, Nordisk Teaterlaboratorium, Holstebro, Denmark, 2 September.

12 Włodzimierz Staniewski

Gardzienice and the naturalised actor

Alison Hodge

Context

The Centre for Theatre Practices 'Gardzienice' have produced few productions – just five in twenty years[1] – but they have earned the group an international reputation. Richard Schechner recognises Gardzienice as 'one of the world's most important experimental and community-based performance groups'.[2] Almost since their inception in 1977, Gardzienice's reputation has precipitated invitations to tour internationally throughout Europe, North America and in the Far East. In their introduction to Gardzienice's British tour in 1989, Richard Gough and Judy Christie described them as 'one of the most extraordinary theatre companies in the world today; working at odds with any current trend – post modern, autobiographic, dispassionate – pursuing an artistic endeavour that merges with a "Life Project"' (Gough and Christie 1989: 3).

Gardzienice's founder and Artistic Director, Włodzimierz Staniewski,[3] has been the principal architect of this notional 'Life Project' – an intensive artistic programme in which cultural activities, such as expeditions to remote communities, workshops and training interrelate and ultimately function to serve the main purpose, that of theatre making.

The ideological foundation of Staniewski's work is embedded in his notion of a 'new, natural environment of theatre' in which he proposes a rejection of the urban environment in favour of rural surroundings. In a speech made in 1979 Staniewski outlined certain pre-requisites he felt that this demanded of the actor:

- leaving the town, leaving not only the theatre building but also the city street,
- addressing oneself to people – the audience, consumers, who are undefiled by 'routine behaviour', undefiled by...modelled reactions or a stereotypical scale of values, a conventional scale of assessment,
- entering the space that is unknown or that has been abandoned by theatre.

By space, I do not mean yet another 'closed circle', fortified by dry rules, rituals. I do not mean yet another stage. By space I mean an area and the substance of land and the substance of the sky bound by that area. I am not concerned with background or with idle poetic contemplation of nature. My concern is that these substances become the living partici-pants in the event.[4]

In prioritising the theatre's symbiotic relationship with the rural environ-ment (and the indigenous people of these areas) Staniewski acknowledges that the immediate context in which the actor works is important as a primary source and an active partner in theatre making. Staniewski's highly selective choice of place is equally significant; by choosing to live and work alongside fast-disappearing native cultures, he recognises the value of the actor learning from cultural sources which are 'ancient, hidden, forgotten'.[5]

How does this work serve theatre? I believe that it teaches theatre and art, from the contact with their roots, not academically, but [it] teaches:

– to see light
– the truth of gesture
– music
– truth in actions
– ostensible unnaturalness is naturalness, that what seems unmannerly, immoral, is true and profound.[6]

At the same time, through re-integrating the actor with the rhythms and sensibilities of the natural environment, Staniewski is taking into account the pressing eco-political concerns of the late twentieth century: 'It is space that is crucial – finding and creating spatial forms and conditions which are ecologically sound. ... "Ecos" in Greek means home while creativity I understand as a dialogue with the spirit of the space (*genius loci*).'[7] It is Staniewski's deeply held belief that both practitioners and audience can no longer afford to ignore the nature of this sensitive, interactive relationship which demands a re-awakening to the totality of human experience:

to perceive means to be able to absorb with all the senses. This is no longer part of our education, nor is it allowed. The result is that the most fundamental human relationships become aseptic, sport-like, quite banal. ... And what is it that we are afraid of in this reduction, all this castration? Are we afraid to be similar to nature, to animals? ... Why are we afraid that we have senses, that we can be absorbed? ... What does it mean, this desperate will to isolate ourselves from wholeness, from the world?

(Staniewski 1993: 16)

It is this exploration of the actor's reconnection with environment which constitutes Gardzienice's significant contribution to twentieth-century actor training. This search for what Staniewski describes as 'a new natural environment of theatre' has been the guiding principle since Gardzienice's beginnings.

Origins and influences

De-urbanisation is a recognisable process in the history of twentieth-century actor training. Stanislavsky, Vakhtangov, Brook and Copeau have all, at some point, sought rural retreats for their work. In the early 1970s Jerzy Grotowski also moved the focus of his practice from the city, Wrocław, to Brzezinka in rural Poland. It was here that he began a series of paratheatrical projects which moved away from theatre to a more ritualised process of communication and exchange between participants. He sought to abolish the distinction between actor and audience through simple, non-theatrical meetings: 'Examining the nature of theatre...we came to the conclusion that its essence lies in direct contact between people' (Kolankiewicz 1977: 24). The qualitative value of this 'direct contact' could be measured by its ability to remove the debilitating social mask which Grotowski had consistently sought to strip away. The rural environment stimulated this interactive

Figure 12.1   Gardzienice: the chapel
Source: Gardzienice archives

work and as one participant reported: 'Habits brought from the city slowly die out: the defensive attitude (necessary there), the dullness of the senses, and the indifference. ... Gradually we become sensitive to one another, we feel our constant, tangible, warm presence' (Kolankiewicz 1979, quoted in Kumiega 1987: 172–3).

Włodzimierz Staniewski had joined Grotowski in 1971, and was a key collaborator in his paratheatrical work. By 1975 he had left the Laboratory Theatre to form his own group with Tomasz Rodowicz[8] in the eastern village of Gardzienice. They gathered a small group of collaborators,[9] most of whom were university graduates, and work began in a disused sixteenth-century chapel in the eastern village of Gardzienice. Significantly, Staniewski's understanding of the importance of the context in which to work went much deeper than de-urbanisation. The social context, the eastern villages and their inhabitants were a primary concern. The group did not isolate themselves in the rural quiet, rather they went straight to the local people with their performance work. Staniewski's express desire was to make theatre: 'For me it was very important to make something with its own performative architecture, possessing more than changing rituals and ceremonies...' (Staniewski 1987: 159).

Staniewski, Rodowicz and their colleagues began to travel to the villages of eastern and south-eastern Poland where the dominant Catholic church co-exists with more marginal Gypsy, Jewish, Belorussian and Ukrainian cultures. In the late twentieth century, many of these rural communities are on the brink of extinction as the younger people migrate to the towns. Rehearsing and training as they travelled into this unknown territory, Gardzienice performed their first performance, *Spektakl Wierczorny* (*Evening Performance*) – based on Rabelais' *Gargantua and Pantagruel* – to villages *en route*. After performing, the group found that people stayed, and some started singing: 'Singing was the most open channel of communication. We saw that certain stylistic "figures" were emerging. We saw ourselves facing a tradition that had always existed' (Staniewski 1987: 141).

This response inspired the idea of a theatre-gathering between the group and the villages. These gatherings became encounters where songs, myths, dances, rituals and oral histories of the eastern Polish villages could be enacted or retold, and in which Gardzienice also sang and presented frag-ments of their work. Staniewski acknowledges that the gathering is not only a form of communicating, but also a way of 'awakening the cultural under-currents of a given social enclave' (Gough and Christie 1989: 14). The emphasis on communication through song during the gatherings directly translates into Gardzienice's own theatre training where song and incanta-tion provide the initial impulse for all of Gardzienice's practice.

It is worth noting that the Gardzienice project was formulated in the political context of a Poland which had experienced nearly forty years of Communist rule. The government's cultural programme promoted Socialist Realism, encouraging an idealisation of the rural through a sanitised image of folk culture. The authorities celebrated an homogeneous version of peasant life which obscured the underlying diversity (and deprivation) of many rural areas. In direct contrast, Staniewski preferred to use the term 'native' to 'folk' in his reference to traditional culture.

Gardzienice's early expeditions were especially informed by Mikhail Bakhtin and his theories of carnival and grotesque realism[10] which had themselves been developed in the authoritarian climate of Stalinism. Bakhtin's celebration of carnival – the inversion of the social order, the dynamic opposition of high and low culture, and the honesty of physical expression, free of political and social restriction – found echoes in Gardzienice's own political environment, and was directly explored through their use of Rabelais' texts in their first performance, *Spektakl Wierczorny*.

Staniewski's belief in the importance of a reconnection with sensuality in the reception and re-creation of nature and culture is also strongly influenced by the work of Poland's leading Romantic poet and playwright, Adam Mickiewicz. Staniewski's project is imbued with the spirit of Romanticism which has remained a prevalent and dynamic cultural influence in central and eastern Europe well into this century. His own rejection of an aseptic rationalism questions the development of many tenets of Western civilisation, which, in his view, have limited the range of human experience and have led to an increasing pragmatism of social interaction. Mickiewicz's own ethnographic work recognised and celebrated the value of an ancient Slavic folk culture which he regarded as a revitalising source for his country's cultural identity. In many ways, Gardzienice has a similar project, vividly explored in one of their early performances, *Avvakum* (see below).

This rich conflation of influences – environmental and cultural, with echoes of a Romantic sensibility and a subversion of the deadening and repressive political order – has informed the development of Gardzienice's aesthetic. Their stylised performances, driven by song, are modelled on principles of the grotesque body which deal with opposites and contrasts, synthesised within the actor's own physique. The effect is an ambiguity within images which invite the spectator to unravel an enigma, to decipher the body rather than a written text. Halina Filopowicz recognises the depiction of reality in Gardzienice's performance of *Avvakum* as

> entirely problematic, existing in a constant of destruction and reconstruction. This fluid dramatic structure reflects a view of human nature as something infinitely malleable to control and transmutation, and thus succeeds where causal and discursive dramaturgy might fail. The obsessive stream of images is in a process of continuous, kaleidoscopic transformation which divests the work of permanence and closure.
>
> (Filopowicz 1987: 153)

In the forty-minute performance of *Avvakum*, pagan beliefs, rituals and Russian Orthodox songs combine with an extract from the classic Polish

Romantic text, Mickiewicz's *Forefather's Eve*, to tell the story of the Archpriest Avvakum – the charismatic leader of the 'Old Believer' Orthodox movement – in a dramatic structure characterised by juxtapositions and fragmented narratives. Generally regarded as a masterpiece of mediaeval literature, Avvakum's autobiography reflects a world destroyed by passion and commitment. Significantly, the group made *Avvakum* in the Poland of the early 1980s. It was a highly physical and visceral response to the authoritarian conditions imposed by Martial Law.

Facts

Gardzienice's concentration upon the radical, subversive and expressive potential of the body has led to the actors achieving a performance aesthetic more drawn from behavioural, rather than psychological, impulses. The concern is not with what could be imagined or explored within the actor's inner cognitive processes, but what can be achieved through externalised, direct vocal and physical actions in relation to the space and to other actors. Staniewski describes the actor's performance as principally based on *facts*.

> I am concerned with the actor who causes facts. I very much like the word *Causer* instead of actor. ... In Polish *sprawca* is a minor hooligan...someone who did something, who has made something happen that is out of the ordinary and which has consequences. ... The actor should be someone like that,...someone who is looking around in order to cause a fact which has some consequences and not someone who is just speaking lines.
>
> (Staniewski 1993: 25–6)

Staniewski's use of this concept of *facts* reinforces a theatre whose sources of inspiration are acutely pragmatic: 'Our realism is naturalistic. We are working in the given piece of earth, in the given village, in the given geographical territory, at the same time pouring our souls, our imagination, our emotions into this place.'[11]

But through this absolute concentration on the given – the immediate – the training, rehearsals and performance re-create both the intensity of human contact and a sense of our cosmological place. Philip Arnoult describes the company's work as a 'ritualistic, almost religious experience' (Strausbaugh 1986: 30). The Polish academic and critic Leszek Kolankiewicz terms Gardzienice's style as *ethno-oratorio*, and associates their performances with the pageants of the Middle Ages:

> European theatre was born perhaps twice: in the ancient times and in the Middle Ages, both times from the spirit of music. And both times

its true background was folk song. In Gardzienice Theatre, we witness how a Mystery Play is born, yet again, out of the spirit of music.[12]

Staniewski himself sees no contradiction in this combination of mystery and realism: 'I am concerned with this connection between realism and transgression; or transcendence. We would never usually put these things together. They are seen as complete opposites, contradictions. But [within indigenous cultures] I see that they are neighbours.'[13]

By taking the expressive vocal and physical gestures of indigenous people and working on the 'cruciality of the gesture' in actor training and rehearsal, Staniewski seeks to transform it into something which 'breaks this realism'.

As the work has progressed the cultural references have widened, and the actors have encountered indigenous cultures quite different from their own. Staniewski acknowledges the need for the actor to begin with the particularity of their own culture but then to work in a broader field:

> to work in reference to that which is old, ancient, forgotten…somehow universal. So you have to have the ability to transcend your own culture. If somebody is saying, 'I am Swedish and that's me!', I am saying it means that the only thing you can do is contained within the limitations of today. It means nothing else, just a replica of today, a cliché. Ideally, I am going even further, not only demanding that you transcend your own culture, but your own sex. The real acting out is when the man is able to break through the limitation of his male condition and assumptions, to reach the enigma of the female body. But, of course, you cannot find it without identifying with the female soul. And the same the other way round. This is not that big a revelation because it is the old knowledge; of Eastern theatre, of Ancient Greek theatre. But now it is extremely difficult to reach it.[14]

One of the actor's routes to the transcendence of their own culture is through understanding the rhythms and iconography of another, researched through expeditions and gatherings and later studied through iconography and music. In their performance of *Avvakum*, for example, the actors worked both with Russian Orthodox liturgical songs which created specific rhythms, and images taken from Russian icons which led to finding new bends in the spine and oppositions between the upper and lower body. By altering the dynamics of the body this effectively recomposed it. This is a typically practical process which is based on repetitive training.

Avvakum is also constructed from a precise rhythmical base which drives the performance, appearing at times chaotic, even orgiastic, but always underpinned by careful preparation. Albert Hunt describes Staniewski's theatre language as remarkable in its ability to 'celebrate the instinctive, the irrational, the revelatory, whilst remaining, at one and the same time, down-to-earth, practical, disciplined, aware' (Hunt 1993: 5). He describes a performance of *Avvakum*:

> The [theatre] language is extremely difficult to describe in words, precisely because it IS a language of theatre. ... It is a language made up of sounds (including not only the sounds made by musical instruments and the human voice, but the sounds of, for example, huge wooden wheels crashing to the floor, or the stamping of feet striding almost beyond possible limits): and of movements, both individual and collective, which form a counterpoint to the sounds. The movement happens all over the area of the performance space, which is as packed with detailed images as a painting by Hieronymous Bosch or Brueghel – only in a Gardzienice performance this visual richness is extended into movement in time and accompanied by an equally rich and changing texture of sound.
>
> (Hunt 1993: 4)

The rigour of the performances is made possible by the precise demands of the continuous training. The preparation and rehearsal for a new performance will take place over a considerable period of time and it is the training which prepares the actors for the challenges in each new phase of the company's work.

Training[15]

'Training with us is an open matter; there is no method in the sense of an applied normative system' (Staniewski 1987: 153). Staniewski avoids a formulaic approach to training. Each new phase serves to develop a new performance. Staniewski's preliminary ideas; the themes, rhythms, songs and texts – including material gathered on expeditions – are worked on *through* the training: 'Training does not merely serve to prepare an actor for their role. It may be applied – for example, some acrobatic exercises can be transformed to become part of a role, to support the acting' (Taranienko 1997: 131).

Despite the fluidity of Gardzienice's training, two fundamental principles have consistently informed the work: *musicality*, with its complex relationship to the actor's physical and vocal technique; and *mutuality* – a particular way of perceiving.

Musicality

Staniewski defines the term musicality as a specific feeling for music which corresponds with the Pythagorean concept of the *harmonia mundi*: 'I am utterly convinced that the earth is musical, that it has musicality and that every part of nature can be musical' (Staniewski 1993: 11). He regards musicality as the vital source for his theatre: 'everything in our theatre practice comes from musicality and ends in musicality' (Staniewski 1993: 31). Staniewski suggests that musicality has a spiritual significance, that the original power of life and its beginning is sound, and that sound and spirit are very closely connected.

This proposal, with its proximity to the Pythagorean cosmological view (and later that of the Renaissance) of an 'invisible harmony of the spheres', is a concept to which Gardzienice's work has repeatedly returned. Staniewski suggests that if the Gardzienice actors can achieve a sensibility to the musicality of the natural environment, they will find themselves within a language which is the essential sound of the natural world. This will allow them to *re-act*: the method of acting which is integral to Gardzienice's 'naturalised' performance. The actors are not attempting to imitate the sounds of nature but finding their own organic rhythmic sounds and gestures which are rehearsed repetitively with the precise momentum of a musical phrase. The actors are not concerned with their personal ability to express *themselves*, so much as contacting their inner musicality – finding an inner melody which can lead their work. Through this understanding the actors aim to realise a highly sensitised relationship with other performers, which in turn informs the second principle of *mutuality*.

The creative potential of this way of perceiving performance has received further confirmation through Staniewski's discovery of related techniques found in native cultures. Gardzienice have made several expeditions to Lapland where the Sami people are known for their unique vocal technique.

> Yoikers have a very particular way of expressing what they do with the voice. They never say what they are singing. They say that they are Yoiking. ... Usually when we sing, we sing about something. They say rather that they are 'yoiking something'. ... You are sitting in front of me and I can try to Yoik you. This does not mean that I improvise a song about you or that I try to describe you. It means, in my terms, that I am reading you. But it is a particular way of reading you, in which I am not thinking about you, so much as somehow trying to touch the spaces, the shapes of you, your measurements, your softness or hardness, your height, your nerves.
>
> (Staniewski 1993: 14)

These intuitive and instinctive processes of reaction are referred to in all aspects of Gardzienice's activities:

> I believe in instinct and intuition. Soon we will forget them. We will forget that they are parts of our nature. We already find for them sophisticated terms such as para-natural and para-psychical, and by alienating them from our human nature we cut the umbilical cord which holds us

to our origins. But I believe that instinct and intuition are real and I also believe that they cannot exist without musicality.

(Staniewski 1993: 11)

Singing

Songs are learnt orally and through repetition. The actors learn a particular way of singing which engages the whole body – a reflection of their encounters with indigenous people where movement and gesture frequently reinforce the song. Gardzienice have explored harmony, polyphony and dissonance, rhythm and counterpoint. Mariusz Gołaj, a leading actor and the movement director in the company, stresses the importance of partnership: 'When you are singing with somebody all the time, you have to be in correspondence with the voice, with the rhythm, with the colour of the voice you have to be mutual.'[16] Singing forms the basis of the actor's technique; it initiates movement and therefore provides the opportunity for the actors to develop their skills. Gołaj continues: 'You are not controlling yourself by your dreams but by concrete situations; through music, your position in space, your relationship with your partner and with energy.'

More recently, the company has been working with antiphony[17] – a process through which two voices question and answer each other through song. This antiphonal dialogue is concerned with a particular kind of partnership of actors *re-acting* to each other through the stimulus of the voice. The questions may be put in a variety of tones – provocative, compassionate, urgent – but in such a precise way that the partner is forced to respond or 'is obliged to answer'. Staniewski maintains that the deeper and more precise the question, the clearer the response.

Mutuality

This obligation to answer – an unforced, impelling dynamic of musical reaction and interaction – is intimately bound with Gardzienice's second key principle. *Mutuality* is practised in all aspects of Gardzienice's activities. It is simply a way of perceiving, absorbing or dialoguing with a partner and, by extension, with the environment in which the actor works. The reading of the partner is not exclusively psychological but an attempt to absorb the wholeness of the person – to tune into a partner in any given moment. Mutuality disallows Gardzienice's training process to become a system: 'Training as I understand it, is necessarily a mutuality of two live presences. It is sharing energy, warmth. ... How is it possible to make a method or a catalogue out of that?' (Staniewski 1987: 153).

Figure 12.2   Włodzimierz Staniewski and Tomasz Rodowicz
Source: Photo, Zbigniew Bielawka

The spine

Nevertheless, some elements of the training are permanent, and in particular the use of the spine. In colloquial Polish the spine is called 'the cross'. It is regarded as one of the most important parts of the body, as its foundation. Staniewski acknowledges that it is the source of our basic human energy:

> We know that the strength and the power of life are located there. We know that work with the spine releases physical and mental energy. ... The attitude (posture) of the cross when the solar plexus is exposed, is an attitude of questioning, inviting, it's a challenge, readiness, and the beginning and end of action. The importance of the cross for dialogue in partnership, for cooperation of one actor with another, is unquestionable. It evokes a certain state. Without it the work of one actor with another doesn't work; there's no true partnership, only an imitation of it; only token signs of it.
>
> (Taranienko 1997: 149)

Training often begins with a series of exercises which warm up and draw attention to the spine. Twists and turns are explored to facilitate the more acrobatic work that follows. During partnership work the spine becomes the origin of movement for the whole body, and this demands a total physical commitment. The actor is forced to communicate through this often unfamiliar focus, personally challenging and dismantling any preconceived self-image. The flexibility of the spine is maintained through rhythmical and flowing acrobatic exercises and it is this flexibility that enables the Gardzienice actors to fully explore the extreme physicality of their performance imagery. Furthermore, Staniewski is concerned with the spine's cultural connotations:

> We began from the so-called Alexander Principle, but the really interesting things appeared when studying iconography during our work on *Avvakum*. ... In the entire Russian iconography, the human profile is reduced to a drawing of the 'cross'. If we were to 'undress' the figures presented [in the icons] from their clothes, their body mass, a sign of the cross would remain.
>
> (Taranienko 1997: 147)

Acrobatics

For Staniewski, acrobatic training is not only concerned with muscle building, flexibility or stamina; nor solely with the satisfaction of completing specific exercises. It is the energising of a group situation in which the actor can develop a fully articulate body through the mutuality experienced in affirming a physical contact with others. Consequently, the particular exercises are not as important as the mutuality practised through them; and they therefore change or modify within the training process. Acrobatics are practised in many different situations: both indoors and on the meadows of Gardzienice, as a morning wake-up, in the late afternoon or in the late evening rehearsal. The changes in the actor's inner tempo in relation to the time and place alters the character of the exercises.

This is useful information for the actor who is tuning the instinctive and intuitive responses necessary for Staniewski's performances. Each time an exercise is done it is a different experience. The moves may be the same but there is a new relationship, a new spine, body weight, time of day and not least the personal circumstances which an actor brings, all of which inform the quality of the contact made. Exercises are frequently broken down into smaller components. For example, the initial moment of an actor signalling the execution of a handstand to the supporting partner may be practised many times before the move is carried out. It is the quality and intention of the action that is of prime importance – the execution is secondary.

Assistance

Acrobatic moves are assisted by a third or fourth actor who looks for the moments, and areas of the body, which might need additional support. Assistance is a vital element of the training and reinforces the notion of mutuality: that is, the necessity of being alive to the present action, responding instinctively to support others, ensuring safety and at the same time serving the action. Both the actions and intentions stemming from this concern with assistance creates a deep resonance within the performances.

Night running

All the training exercises stem from the symbiotic principles of mutuality and musicality. However, the activity which perhaps embodies the values of Gardzienice's training better than any other is night running, which was introduced by Staniewski in the early stages of Gardzienice's training activities, and which has remained a constant touchstone for the values of the actors' work ever since.

The night run is led by precise rhythms sustained through the stamping feet on the ground. The group bunches in behind the leader, affirming the initial rhythm through those who run behind or in front, sometimes in complete darkness. The ground may be uneven and unseen branches or logs may block a path; in such situations the actors run supporting each other with their arms. As the bodies warm up through the physical exertion, breathing becomes audible. The actors may initiate rhythms through the breath which punctuate or counter those of the feet, working with the energy and the organic rhythms that emerge from the common (and frequently playful) experience of the group. Night running can last for up to an hour or more.

> When you run through the night, when you run together with other people, you search for rhythms, for a common rhythm, for rhythm as dialogue, rhythms in which you look for the relationship with the person who is next to you, on your right side, on your left, ahead or behind of you. When you run, you search for certain dynamics which occur through repetition, through the continuity of the breath, through continuous rhythms, as in *ostinato* in music, and you feel your inner self is growing, extending somehow.
>
> (Staniewski 1993: 24)

As in the acrobatic and assistance exercises, there are elements both of danger and safety within this situation. For some, the initial and unfamiliar experience of the night environment – and the possibility of falling – can create a nervousness which needs to be overcome. This is countered by the care and physical contact maintained by the group, creating a particularly strong and intimate relationship amongst the participants. 'A particular mutuality is one kind of phenomenon which occurs during the running...your relationship to others is very strong; you feel that you are in a very intimate relationship with other people' (Staniewski 1993: 24).

At the same time, running through the forest tracks of the village puts the actors in direct contact with the natural elements, whilst the reduction of visibility greatly enhances the other senses. Gołaj describes the experience:

> You experience nature through the senses. It's dark, you can't see the way. ... You can feel the wind and you can hear the breathing and touch the bodies of partners. It's a very full experience which integrates the group and is also working on many levels. You have the feeling that you are dealing with nature, that you are part of it.

For Staniewski, the practice can also serve as an opportunity for testing material, part of the 'naturalising' process. Initially, pieces of music were introduced into the structure of the run – body gestures and scenes then followed. When it was impossible to incorporate these elements into the run they were done within pauses. Staniewski found this to be a way of rhythmicising work, of discovering how the performance material is directed by the natural stimuli. He believes that actors make discoveries within this form of rehearsal that would not be possible in the closed rehearsal space: 'Suddenly the run creates an incredible pulsation of a given song...you are pumping your diaphragm, you are opening your throat – it happens naturally. You don't have to use artificial methods, you are naturally opening yourself...'

When the night run is done prior to rehearsal, it 'awakens the body', and the breathing provides the concrete and audible link between the two experiences. In the rehearsal that follows the action is achieved through a mutuality of rhythm signalled by the exhalation of breath which supports the move. The mutual action within training is punctuated by the actors' musical and articulate language of breathing. But night running is not exclusively operating as the actor's preparation for rehearsal. In another respect, the activity is regarded as an existential one which embodies the fundamental values of Gardzienice's practice. Staniewski recognises that it provides a concrete and practical way of developing the actor's perception:

> The gate of your perception is open, and in this way you can deal with many things around you. ... Physiologically you could explain this by saying that your senses are reacting more sharply, that your blood is circulating more strongly.
>
> (Staniewski 1993: 25)

This exposes what is perhaps the central project of Staniewski's work: that of accessing the universal, the *harmonia mundi*. He continues:

It is comparable to the way Artaud talked about the multiplied actor, the actor who can transform himself into many existences, the atomised actor who can deal with many realities at one and the same time. I believe this is possible.

(Staniewski 1993: 25)

Artaud's own appreciation of the physiological influence of nature on the artist was nowhere more evident than on his trip to Mexico in the 1930s. During a speech he gave in Mexico City he declared that:

The organism of man functions in harmony with the organism of nature and governs it. And in so far as science and poetry are a single and identical thing, this is much the business of poets and artists as it is the business of scientists.

(Artaud 1976: 373)

Whilst he was there Artaud visited the Tarahumara Indians in the remote Sierra Madre region. Artaud did not witness the running for which the Tarahumara are renown, but his appreciation of an intense harmony between the landscape and its people was confirmed by Staniewski's own visit:[18]

My trip...confirmed for me the truth of Artaud's heritage. It is the experience of a magical reality. The earth of the Tarahumara Indians has such a musical scenario, that everything that Artaud wrote should be considered a precise description.

(Taranienko 1997: 143)

Staniewski was invited to participate in the Tarahumara's traditional *rara-muri* run. Whilst running is part of the Tarahumara's everyday existence, this particular event, where one lap can cover 12 kilometres, lasts for anything up to 16 hours. The main participants are divided into two teams and they run continuously throughout the night, by torch light:

They run with naked feet...down through the valley and up through the rocky paths, quite high. Then they circle round and come back, making a kind of figure of eight...all the time kicking this ball, through the forest, up the mountains. ... It meant, to me, that running could be a way of living:...that during the run, life could be lived to the fullest...

(Staniewski 1993: 23)

For Gardzienice, the goal of harmonising nature and actor, music and action, in performance is never entirely removed from the reality of the interactive meetings between actors and indigenous people that Gardzienice experience in the communal village gatherings. The group offer fragments of new work in these situations. Staniewski acknowledges the value of this process of 'naturalisation' through which the actors can measure their work against the response from those who have often inspired it.

By working with different cultures a distinct training vocabulary has evolved. For example, one early influence was the structure of Gypsy music. The 'avalanche' effect in Gypsy singing (in which the music builds with an overwhelming acceleration, then suddenly cuts off at the climax) has been a reference point in much rhythmical and vocal work. Staniewski describes how specific Gypsy movements have also inspired the group's movement-based pieces: 'I never took entire themes from their dances, but certain electrifying gestures – a bowing of the head, or a hand movement which seemed to me to be a particularly significant expression of the person through their body' (Staniewski 1997: 133).

Gołaj stresses that gestures are not explored for their psychological content, nor are they simply copied:

> I don't believe in copying because you never know exactly what emotions the village people have. Very often they know how to dance the body, how to use the gestures, and very often they are doing this cold. And this is its strength.

From training to performance

Gardzienice's actor training fundamentally serves the performance and is the route to all new productions. The actors play a key role in influencing the character of the work; it is realised by them through the training, but is shaped and moulded by Staniewski in rehearsal. The finely tuned body of actors becomes the image for the new work. Theatrically the group functions as the singer/dancers of the *dithyramb* – the earliest configuration of the Ancient Greek chorus. The precise image of the chorus alters with each production, so, for example, in *Avvakum* the chorus appeared as 'the mob', in *Carmina Burana*, the chorus functions as the choir from which individual characters emerge and are 'sung' by it.

Through Staniewski's personal work with each actor, he slowly integrates the training into the complex layering of images, texts and songs that will constitute the performance. Within this intimate process Staniewski acts as a partner to the actor; challenging, encouraging, berating and questioning. In leading actors towards new territory Staniewski also incorporates use of the *via negativa*: the neoplatonic method of searching for the truth through negations. It is less a question of how to do something, but rather how to discover what not to do in order to find the way forward. This can be an arduous but rewarding process.

In preparation for *Carmina Burana* in 1990, the training for the new work was, as always, part of a number of intensive activities occurring simultane-ously; gatherings, expeditions, the renovation of buildings, workshops and the performance of the existing repertoire all interweave. This means that the performances develop over a long period of time, immersed or 'naturalised' by the processes which surround them. Anna Zubrzycka, who was a long-serving member of Gardzienice, and who played Isolde the Elder in *Carmina Burana*, explains the beginnings of the new process in this production:

> Włodek [Staniewski] has always paved the way slowly by building up the theatrical environment – putting in more and more impulses, visual and literary images and ideas in a very slow fashion. He is not bombarding the actor. For example, we looked at images from Bosch, Brueghel and Memlinc, taking these images as inspiration, not reproducing them. It's not just for the sake of the creation of a movement – these visual references are the source of movement but, at the same time, they are being translated into our experience. Włodek always waited for what it would bring emotionally, as an image, a reaction, whatever. He allowed inspiration to grow within you, worked many times on a particular sequence and suddenly he catches something which is absolutely yours but through the image which you originally took as inspiration. And then he has combined your experience and the source but always through the body.[19]

Although *Carmina Burana* was the first performance in which individual roles were created, the actor's persona was not constructed in reference to psychological realism – the individual role is regarded principally in terms of its function in performance. Mariusz Gołaj outlines his experience in working on his role of Merlin as a *causer*:

> The actor has to find the proper way to communicate. For example, in the case of Merlin he is the one who is evoking things, a lot of things were caused by him, often he was ironically commenting on what happens. So the first question is 'what is your function?' and then, 'how will this happen – theatrically, aesthetically?'

In many ways the process of the Gardzienice actor's stylisation is similar to that of Japanese Noh Theatre, in which the performance is based on two potentially opposing forms: the lyricism of song and dance and the reality of character type. The fluidity of movement complements the articulation of the character. In Gardzienice, the character emerges *through* the repetition of precise rhythms and imagery, and through the 'lines of life' of the songs. Mariusz Gołaj acknowledges that often his initial understanding of a role is through rhythm – a reflection of traditional cultures whose gestures are often intimately connected to music. For him, it is from the precision of movement that the character's emotions evolve, although he never entirely loses himself in feeling: 'We can divide ourselves into different parts, part of

Figure 12.3   Gardzienice's performance of *Carmina Burana*, Berlin, 1995. Left to right: Mariusz Gołaj, Dorota Porowska and Tomasz Rodowicz
Source: Photo, Andreas Lüdtke

me can be embraced by the task to be Merlin, and part can have a distance or control, and ask – "what am I doing now?" '

Ultimately, it is not the music, the multi-layered performance text, nor the actor's interpretation of it which is of primary concern, but the interconnection of all these things. Staniewski stresses that: 'The issue, the subject, the theme is not only that which is spoken or written. It is the way of creating the whole world with the body, with the music, with the spine.' This is reminiscent of Artaud's recognition that the theatre's domain is a physical, rather than psychological, language. In saying this, however, Artaud was careful to insist that the argument should not be based on a straightforward comparison:

> This does not simply mean assessing whether theatre's physical language can attain the same psychological resolutions as words or whether it can not express emotions and feelings as well as words, but whether there are not attitudes in the field of intellect and thought which words cannot assume, which gestures and everything inclusive in this spatial language cannot attain with greater precision than them.
>
> (Artaud 1974: 52)

The articulate language in which Gardzienice's work is expressed is predicated on a particular state of presence which demands that the actor's 'gate of perception is open'. The actor must find a particularly alive, highly tuned state of instinctive response. Staniewski describes the actor's cognitive process as an intelligence 'of the heart'. Within the performance, the Gardzienice actor aims to achieve multiple states of presence, in order to deal with many realities simultaneously. This form of awareness goes beyond the notional duality of the actor's consciousness (identified in Diderot's paradox) to realise a heightened state of performance consciousness which Artaud had reached for as an ideal.

Gardzienice's work is a realisation of a form of theatre which, Staniewski believes, defies the reductive tendencies of late-twentieth-century culture. Commentators have found that it manages to reconnect the actor with instinctive processes and invites the audience to experience the work, not solely intellectually, but through all the senses. Others have recognised Gardzienice's re-connection with everyday life, with actors and their environment and, in performance, reality with transcendence.

The theatre is made possible through a training process in which the actor is 'naturalised' principally through contact with the natural environment and indigenous cultures. The source of the actor's holistic understanding is in the symbiotic principles of *musicality* and *mutuality*. Within the actor's development, the touchstone for this re-connection with an instinctive and subtle awareness begins in the training.

Notes

1 1977 *An Evening Performance* (Spektakl Wiełczorny), 1981 *Sorcery* (Gusła), 1983 *The Life of Archpriest Avvakum*, 1990 *Carmina Burana*, 1997 *Metamorphoses or The Golden Ass (According to Lucius Apuleius)*.
2 See Paul Allain 1997: back cover.
3 Włodzimierz Staniewski was born in Bardo, Poland, in 1950. He graduated in Humanities from Kraków University before becoming an actor in the renowned student theatre group, Teatr STU. From 1970 to 1976 Staniewski collaborated with Jerzy Grotowski in his Laboratory Theatre's paratheatrical projects before leaving to form Gardzienice Theatre Association in 1977.
4 The speech was made at the congress of the International Theatre Institute in Sofia, Bulgaria, 1979.
5 Taken from 'Theatre of the Ruins', a speech Staniewski made in June 1996 at an international training workshop in Gardzienice.
6 A second extract from Staniewski's 1979 speech in Bulgaria.
7 An extract from an unpublished paper, 'Theatre Practices in Relation to Ecology', given by Staniewski at the International Theatre Symposium, September 1991, Gardzienice.
8 Co-founder of Gardzienice Theatre Association, Tomasz Rodowicz has been a leading actor with the group since its inception. He has been Staniewski's close collaborator in the musical research, and in establishing the first group. With Mariusz Gołaj, he also leads the workshop training.

9 The informal ensemble was initially composed of Włodzimierz Staniewski, Tomasz Rodowicz, Jan Tabaka, Wanda Wróbel, Waldemar Sidor, Jan Bernad, Henryk Andruszko.

10 See Mikhail Bakhtin's seminal work: *Rabelais and His World*, 1965, trans. Hélène Iswolsky, Cambridge, MA: MIT Press.

11 Unless otherwise stated, all quotes from Włodzimierz Staniewski are from personal interviews conducted with the author in Ghent, July 1998.

12 This extract is taken from a speech made by Leszek Kolankiewicz 'On Gardzienice' presented at the International Theatre Meetings, Warsaw, 1988.

13 See note 11.

14 Ibid.

15 The training exercises which I describe in this chapter are based on my own experience of working with the company in the period 1989–96.

16 Unless otherwise stated, all quotes from Mariusz Gołaj are taken from a personal interview with the author in Ghent, July 1998.

17 Staniewski further developed the use of antiphony after visiting the Orthodox monastery on Mount Athos, Greece, in 1989. The development of antiphony at the monastery over centuries has brought it to a high degree of refinement.

18 Staniewski visited the Tarahumara Indians in 1987. His participation in the ritual of running is fully discussed in Peter Hulton's interview (Staniewski 1993).

19 Anna Zubrzycka worked with Gardzienice from 1979 to 1994. The quote comes from a personal interview which took place with the author in London, September 1998.

Bibliography

Allain, Paul (1997) *Gardzienice: Polish Theatre in Transition*, London: Harewood Academic Publishers.

Artaud, Antonin (1976) 'Artaud in Mexico', in S. Sontag (ed.), *Selected Writings*, New York: Farrar, Straus and Giroux.

—— (1974) 'Oriental and Western Theatre', in *The Theatre and its Double*, London: Calder and Boyars.

Bakhtin, Mikhail (1965) *Rabelais and His World*, trans. Hélène Iswolsky, Cambridge, MA: MIT Press.

Filipowicz, Halina (1987) 'Gardzienice: A Polish Expedition to Baltimore', in R. Schechner (ed.), *The Drama Review* 113(1): 137–63.

Gough, Richard and Christie, Judy (eds) (1989) *Gardzienice Theatre Association Booklet*, to accompany 1989 UK and Ireland tour, Cardiff: Centre for Performance Research.

Hunt, A. (1993) 'An Introduction' in *Gardzienice, Poland*, Włodzimierz Staniewski, in conversation with Peter Hulton, Dorinda Hulton (ed.), Exeter: Arts Archives, Arts Documentation Unit.

Kolankiewicz, L. (1978) 'On the Road to Active Culture', trans. B. Taborski, unpublished collection of papers. Wrocław.

—— (1977) 'What's up at Grotowski's?' in *The Theatre in Poland* 5–6: 24–5.

Kumiega, J. (1987) *The Theatre of Grotowski*, London and New York: Methuen.

Mickiewicz, Adam (1986) 'Lectures on Slavic Literature Given at the Collège de France', Introduction and trans. by Daniel Gerould in R. Schechner (ed.), *The Drama Review* 111(3): 92–7.

Staniewski, Włodzimierz (1993) *Gardzienice, Poland*, Włodzimierz Staniewski in conversation with Peter Hulton, Dorinda Hulton (ed.), Exeter: Arts Archives, Arts Documentation Unit.

—— (1987) 'Baltimore Interview with Richard Schechner', in R. Schechner (ed.), *The Drama Review* 113(1): 137–63.

Strausbaugh, J. (1986) 'Feast of a Fest', in *The Baltimore City Paper*, 6 June: 30.

Taranienko, Z. (1997) *Gardzienice: Praktyki Teatralne Włodzimierza Staniewskiego*, Lublin: Wydawnictwo Test (unpublished trans. A. Zubryzcka).

Zeami, Motokiyo (1984) *On the Art of the Nō Drama: The Major Treatises of Zeami*, trans. and introduction by J. Thomas Rimer and Yamasaki Masakazu, Princeton, NJ: Princeton University Press.

Index